H+

scs.
Under
Eb
p 540

14

THE PSYCHOLOGY OF
SOCIAL INSTITUTIONS

THE MACMILLAN COMPANY
NEW YORK · BOSTON · CHICAGO · DALLAS
ATLANTA · SAN FRANCISCO

MACMILLAN & CO., Limited
LONDON · BOMBAY · CALCUTTA
MELBOURNE

THE MACMILLAN CO. OF CANADA, Ltd.
TORONTO

THE PSYCHOLOGY OF SOCIAL INSTITUTIONS

BY

CHARLES HUBBARD JUDD

PROFESSOR OF EDUCATION AND DIRECTOR OF THE SCHOOL OF EDUCATION
UNIVERSITY OF CHICAGO

New York

THE MACMILLAN COMPANY

1926

Norwood Press
J. S. Cushing Co. — Berwick & Smith Co.
Norwood, Mass., U.S.A.

PREFACE

Anyone who is concerned with the applications of psychology becomes convinced that the mental life of an individual cannot be understood without taking into account the social environment in which the individual lives. The fashion of one's clothes and the form of one's religion, with all the intermediate social adjustments, such as methods of communication and methods of coöperation in industry, are dictated by the customs and traditions of the group. The author of this book became convinced of the necessity of studying social contributions to mental life when preparing a volume on psychology for teachers in 1903. The foundation for his thinking was undoubtedly laid by the teachings of Wilhelm Wundt, whose lectures and volumes on social psychology constitute the most elaborate contributions which have ever been made in this field.

The chapter on the alphabet in the present book is a reworking of one of the chapters in the book of 1903. The chapter on number is an extension of the corresponding chapter in the earlier work.

In the interval since 1903, the author has canvassed the substance of this volume from time to time in advanced courses on social psychology and has incorporated some portions of the material into articles and discussions in the field of educational psychology. It is his belief that the principles here laid down have broader applications than they can find in a volume on education; he has therefore prepared the general statement which appears in this book both as a foundation for his further writings in educational psychology and as a suggestion of a basic method for other social sciences.

It remains to acknowledge obligations to the publishers and authors who have kindly permitted the use of quotations from their books. Acknowledgments are made in full in footnotes throughout the text. The publishers who have given permission to quote are as follows: D. Appleton & Company; Cambridge University Press; Chapman and Hall; Doubleday, Page & Company; Encyclopædia Britannica; Ginn and Company; Ingersoll Watch Company; Longmans, Green & Company; John W. Luce & Company; The Macmillan Company; Methuen & Company; Oxford University Press; G. P. Putnam's Sons; G. Schirmer, Inc.; Walter Scott Publishing Company; Charles Scribner's Sons; Trübner & Company.

C. H. J.

February, 1926.

TABLE OF CONTENTS

ILLUSTRATIONS

PSYCHOLOGY

OF

SOCIAL INSTITUTIONS

CHAPTER I

INTRODUCTION

The purpose of this book is to concentrate attention on the fact that social influences are of the highest importance in determining the character of human thought and conduct. Respect for property, industry, devotion to systematic daily routine, and all the other virtues which distinguish civilized man from his savage ancestors have been achieved through long generations of community life. These are not traits which belong to untrained human nature. Individuals exhibit, to be sure, even in civilized communities, many characteristics which are due to their personal inheritances, but inherited traits are modified and in some cases wholly transformed by the demands of society.

Emphasis on the social forces which operate to determine the course of human development has not been common in treatises on psychology. The reason is that an individual's organs of sense and an individual's habits are so concrete and readily accessible to the student of mental life that they have pushed the apparently abstract concepts of social consciousness and collective will into the background. Present-day psychology is in the main a psychology of the

1

individual. Even where social tendencies come under consideration it is the custom to attribute them to certain so-called instincts such as gregariousness, communicativeness, and gang spirit. These instincts are described as personal traits which all men bring into the world through inheritance and out of which in some mysterious fashion spring nations and languages and codes of morals.

The attempt will be made in the pages which follow to develop a system of psychology which will show that social consciousness instead of being something vague and intangible is one of the most active and potent facts in the world. Social consciousness expresses itself in certain institutions which are quite as real as the individual's habits and organs of sense. Language, for example, is such an institution. It is the product of long ages of co-operative effort. It is not the expression of an individual's instincts. The individual is indeed equipped by inheritance with vocal and auditory apparatus, but this native equipment is used by the American child in one way and by the Chinese child in a very different way. The particular institutional form which language has assumed in any given country cannot be explained without taking into account the united contributions of a great many intelligences.

It is a striking fact that the scientific study of language has treated this institution as though it were a concrete reality detached from the human minds which gave it birth. Philology has traced the history of words and formulated the laws of syntax and in so doing has very largely omitted all mention of the minds which use words and sentences as means of controlling thought and action.

What is true of language is even more true of such economic institutions as money and credit. The economists write about the various materials which have been used as mediums of exchange, about movements of gold, and about the laws which govern values. In all their writing they make little or no reference to the human desires and interrelations which brought money into being and have directed its evolution. Nor do they carry their science far enough to show the influence of money on human intellectual and emotional life. They ignore the fact that it has become a powerful social force reacting on the individual and determining in large measure his thinking and behavior.

What is needed in order that we may arrive at a more adequate understanding of human beings and of the social and economic world in which they live is a psychology which gives equal consideration to institutions and individuals. The present volume will not undertake to discharge the comprehensive task of expounding such a complete science. A somewhat specialized treatment of a few of the social institutions will be attempted in order to exhibit the methods of this branch of psychology and more especially for the purpose of indicating certain practical applications which grow directly out of the discussion of social institutions.

Throughout this book the term "social institution" will be used in a broad way to cover all those accumulations of social capital which have been produced in the course of community life. For example, the word "institution" covers the fact that by combined effort men have produced tools. The modern world of technical devices is just as truly an exhibition of social intelligence as a blow with the fist is a concrete manifestation of the way in which a human nervous system reacts. The tools which man has invented are powerful influences in determining the course of civilized life. Through the long ages while man has been inventing tools and learning to use them, his mode of individual reaction has been undergoing a change. He is no longer absorbed in direct attack on the prey which furnishes him food. He does not develop more skill in the use of claws and teeth in order that he may cope with his environment. He has adopted an indirect mode of action. He uses instruments which he has devised or borrowed from his forefathers or from his neighbor. Tools have become a part of his world. They are as real and as important as climate and trees and other facts of nature which are produced without the aid of human intelligence.

Other institutions are less material in their character. Government, for example, is the device which social intelligence has evolved to direct and check human behavior so that there shall be harmony within the group. Government is not made of wood and metals, as are tools, but it is a real fact in the world. To think of the strength of individual muscles as a phenomenon important to a science of psychology and to think of the strength of government as something quite abstract and negligible is seriously to invert values. Government is the embodiment of the experience of the race in a system of regulations and practices which have accumulated through centuries and have acquired a kind of independent reality which justifies their recognition as entities distinct from the material world and distinct from individuals, but no less significant than these tangible concrete realities.

Other examples of what is meant by the word "institutions" will be presented in the course of later chapters. For our present purposes it is enough to indicate that the type of psychology which is to be presented in this volume is one which may properly be described as the psychology of social institutions.

CHAPTER II

Tool Consciousness

It has been the practice of historical anthropology to designate the successive steps of civilization by the names of the materials used in making weapons and tools. Thus the earliest ages are called stone ages; later came ages of bronze and of iron; our own age is often spoken of as the age of steel. Another method of classifying epochs in human evolution is by reference to the predominant industry. There was a period when men supplied themselves with food chiefly by hunting. Later came agriculture and herding and finally manufacture.

These methods of classifying different stages of civilization have the virtue of being based on objective facts. One can readily determine by an examination of the remains found in caves and on the sites of ancient villages what materials man was using in the construction of his implements. There is, however, a disadvantage in emphasizing material facts and regarding these as the typical facts in human history. The truth is that man of the stone age was limited to the use of stone because his experience had not yet reached the state where he was acquainted with metals. The physical world contained metal in the stone age even as it does to-day. Metal did not come into human life until man devised methods of securing and using it. The student of anthropology, in noting the transition from stone to bronze, is not dealing merely or chiefly with a physical reality; he is dealing with a change in human experience.

The statement can perhaps be put in its most striking form by pointing out that the animals never make any tools even though they can see stone quite as readily as could primitive man. It is not the objective material which suggests the construction of tools; the invention of tools depends on the inner subjective recognition of the possibility of using stone in a new way. A stone implement is the creation of man's genius, not a material fact.

The same kind of a statement can be made with regard to the evolution of industry. Man was at first a hunter. As such, his experiences and his emotions were little different from those of the animals which live by the capture of prey. He sought as food that which nature offered him. Gradually he evolved the attitude of looking into the future and of seeing the advantages of deliberate domestication of animals and of cultivation of the soil. His foresight transformed his mode of life. He substituted for dependence on wild game the patient coöperative modes of life which have led to the accumulation of that which will support life in greater comfort or that which in the aggregate we call wealth. Wealth has in turn reacted on its possessors until an entirely new world has been set up. This world has its material side — one can see wealth and handle it, but its origin was mental and directly traceable to the inner thought processes of men.

Let us turn from such general considerations to the study of the details of the evolution of tools. The archæologists tell us that long periods of time were consumed in achieving the first successes in mechanical invention. Man did not suddenly break away from the animal method of behavior. When an animal attacks an enemy or removes an obstacle from its path, its behavior is of a simple, direct type; it utilizes its paws or teeth and its direct nervous and muscular energy. Such was also the behavior of primitive man. He used his hands and teeth backed by his personal strength. He did not think, as modern man does, of the possibility of utilizing some object to reinforce his own muscles. The use of levers and sharp weapons came very gradually.

The psychological analysis of what went on in these early stages can be introduced by a description of the pattern of consciousness which appears when a man or an animal deals directly with an object of his desire without the use of any tool. One can draw on personal experience for such a

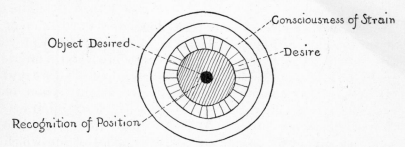

FIG. I. — THE FIELD OF CONSCIOUSNESS WITH A SINGLE CENTER OF ATTENTION

description. Each of us is constantly reaching out with his hands to grasp some object. At the center of attention is the visual experience of the thing desired. Second, there is present in consciousness a recognition of the direction and distance through which the hand must be moved. Third, there is the desire for the object. Surrounding these conspicuous and clearly recognizable elements of consciousness is a background of feelings and sensations which come from the whole organism and constitute the mental stage on which the act is performed. Figure I represents roughly the field of consciousness during one of these direct experiences. At the center is a dark spot representing the visual impression of the object. Around this center are lighter circular areas standing for the recognition of the position of the object and the desire to possess it; and finally beyond these lie a series of circles representing the experiences of strain and effort which make up the total mental situation.

If we try to picture the situation which appears when a simple tool is used, we find it necessary to elaborate the figure by introducing two centers of attention. The actor

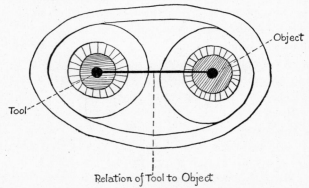

Relation of Tool to Object

FIG. II. — THE FIELD OF CONSCIOUSNESS WITH TWO CENTERS OF ATTENTION

must still give heed to the object of his desire. He must at the same time grasp the tool and consciously direct its movements. Part of his attention will have to turn to this new center of experience. As he grasps the tool, he will have sensations in his hand of a type wholly different from the visual sensations which come from the object of his desire. As he moves the tool toward the object, there will have to be enough attention given to the relation between the two materially to increase the complexity of the pattern of consciousness. Figure II indicates the double character of attention in this case.

Consciousness cannot take on this more complex pattern except in an individual capable of breadth of attention. The reason why animals do not use tools is that they are capable of holding in consciousness only one center of attention. Speaking in terms of their nervous systems, we may say that the paths through the central nervous system of an animal are so direct that there is no possibility of including in a single performance two or more centers of excitation. The animal is wholly occupied in responding to a single impression. If an animal is offered a tool and gives any attention to it, consciousness is temporarily drawn away from the first center of attention and turns for the time being exclusively to the new object.

The following experiment shows how limited is the range of attention even in the higher animals. A monkey was fastened in his cage and a banana was placed just out of his reach. He extended himself in every possible way in the effort to secure the food, but failed. After a time he was shown a stick and given a demonstration of the way in which the stick could be used to lengthen his reach. Monkey-fashion he became interested in the stick. But while this new object of attention was in the focus of consciousness, the banana had no place. The monkey could not deal at the same time with both banana and stick. He never put the two together, that is, he never learned to use the tool; his range of attention could include only a single object.

There are numerous occasions when human consciousness is of the unifocal type. For example, when one tries to catch a companion in play, there is only one all-absorbing center of attention. It is to be noted that such a situation is psychologically very simple and we recognize it as making very little draft on intelligence. The moment play rises to a level which involves the use of some implement, the demands on skill and on consciousness become more exacting and require a wider range of attention.

The mental fact which has been described by the statement that man has a wide range of attention, has its definite anatomical condition in the larger size of the human cerebrum. If we compare the cerebrum of man with that of even his closest relatives in the animal world, we find that man has a much more highly developed organ. The animal kingdom has been gradually evolving this elaborate upper part of the nervous system. The lowest vertebrates, such as the fishes, have nervous centers which control the organs of locomotion and the jaws and provide for the reception of stimulations coming from the organs of sense. These lower animal forms do not, however, have any large number of central nerve cells. Their meager cerebrums do not provide space for complex nervous processes. It is literally true that they have no nervous tissue which can be devoted to attention to involved relations. All their acts are direct and without premeditation. It requires higher nerve centers removed from direct connection with the organs of sense and the organs of reaction to provide for elaborate forms of thought and attention. As we come up the scale of animal life, we find the higher, indirect central nervous structures gradually increasing in size. The process of thus providing for an inner world, where readjustments can be worked out with less and less regard to direct conditions and with more and more regard to complex inner patterns, goes forward until in man the inner world with its many factors and their complex combinations becomes the dominant and characteristic fact.

Man continues to use the lower nervous centers for many of his responses to stimulation. For example, he swallows food when it gets into his mouth just as any animal would. The lower nervous centers take care of this operation. In like manner the fingers close on any object that is grasped in direct response to sensory stimulations, the act requiring no thought or meditation. The important fact about human life, however, is the complete subordination to the higher processes of these direct forms of reaction. It is the higher processes which raise men above the animals and make possible the mode of life which includes the use of tools.

Let us consider how the broader attention of man operated at the time that the first tool was discovered. The term "discovered" rather than the term "invented" is used advisedly; the first club was nothing but a gnarled root picked up in the forest or the bone of some animal used to reinforce the blow of the arm; the first knife was a sharp stone or the talon of some animal. It seems to be a very simple act to pick up one of these tools provided by nature, but it is not. The complexity of the performance lies in the fact that the natural object must be taken out of the setting in which it is presented to experience and must be put into another setting by the active imagination of an intelligent being. Animals have been cut by sharp stones from the beginning of time, but the relation of the animal to the stone has always continued to be the relation set up by nature. The animal has snarled at the stone that cut its foot and has gone on its way. Man had the range of attention and the power of imagination to see the sharp stone in a new setting. If it cut him, he might take it in his hand and make it cut his enemies or serve him in other ways. This power of relating objects in a new way, which we call imagination, has its seat in the higher nervous centers. In these higher centers the stimulus which led the animal to the simple act of growling and passing on was combined with other stimuli and a new and elaborate preparation for behavior was worked out, with the result that human action rose to a new level.

Too much emphasis cannot be laid on the fact that within the human cerebrum a new world is created. Objects are put together in this world in a new way; they are united as ideas in the brains of men and afterwards through human efforts the outer world is correspondingly rearranged. The influence of man in the world is so great that he must be recognized even by the most objective sciences as a factor in transforming reality. Man has gradually cultivated a higher power through the invention of tools. He has ultimately reached the stage where he can redirect the course of rivers. He has brought great masses of rock and metal together into what he calls buildings and has converted the barren plain into a dwelling-place for his tribe. He has tunneled mountains and has made for himself devices for flying in the air. All these achievements he has attained by rearranging the materials which for the animals lie inert and unorganized in the forest and in the rocks. It is man's power of recombining materials which has built up civilization.

The first tool is significant, therefore, both as evidence that the slow process of animal evolution has produced a new species, a species with a big cerebrum, and as the first step in a new method of dealing with the world. As soon as man discovered the advantage which came to him among the animals from the first crude tool, he began his upward ascent toward the mechanical arts and away from the methods of direct physical adaptation which are characteristic of the lower levels of life. No longer is it necessary for man, by the processes of natural selection, to develop powerful muscles and long claws or sharp teeth. His cerebrum puts him absolutely out of the competition where physical prowess and organs of attack are needed.

We must come back, however, to the early stages of human progress during which this new method of adaptation was perfected. After man had picked up the first club and used it to his advantage, he took the next step, which began to change him from a mere discoverer into a manufacturer. He began to improve on nature. He made the handle of his club smooth and small enough so that his hand could readily close over it. He made the striking end as vicious as possible by adding thorns and sharp stones. These changes required the exercise of the same active imagination that was employed in recognizing the usefulness of the weapon, but they required also

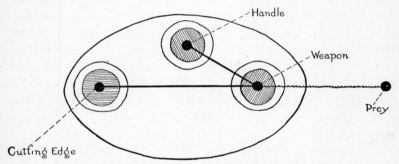

Fig. III. — The Field of Consciousness in the Case of an Artisan

something higher. The improver of a weapon must have foresight enough to be interested in his weapon even when he is not aroused to action by the sight of his prey. He must have in mind motives strong enough to keep him at work during long periods of time and must be patient enough to prepare for action when there is no visible motive for what he is doing.

The artisan stage of human evolution is sketched in Figure III. This shows the prey which is to be attacked as outside the field of direct consciousness and only vaguely connected with it. The weapon itself is one of the centers of attention. Coördinate with this are other centers of attention which are filled with ideas for improvements. Two such are represented in the figure and can be described as ideas of a smoother handle and a more vicious attacking end.

It is significant in this connection to note that primitive man thought of his weapons in very personal terms. The objects on which he had bestowed much effort and which he had used on crucial occasions throughout life came to be parts of his personality in a very intimate sense. When he died, these personal possessions were buried with him. They were not made for use by any hand other than his own.

There are many directions in which the effort to make tools had a profound effect on human evolution. Some members of the tribe, presumably those who took interest in delicate manipulations rather than in the activities of warfare and the chase, began to devote themselves exclusively to the making of weapons. We see in this fact the beginnings of specialization. The figures which have been used to represent the conscious processes involved in the use of tools show a widening of the range of attention. Figure III shows also the converse fact, namely, that there are limits set to this expansion of attention. The human mind will always be too narrow to accommodate with equal hospitality the interests of the hunter and those of the artisan. The hunter is full of interest in the game which he is to follow. Perhaps at times he may be willing to spend a little energy in the care of his weapon, but his patience with this sort of work is small. On the other hand, the type of mind which becomes absorbed in the refinements of tool-making is not the type of mind which finds the activities of the chase congenial. There is in mature human minds a tendency toward particular forms of attention and corresponding forms of behavior. The mind that is full of ideas about handles and cutting edges will tend to drop the idea of prey out of its range of immediate consideration. This is the original basis of the division of labor, which in later epochs has come to be a dominant fact in civilization.

In these facts we see also the reasons why individuals are forced to develop community interests and coöperation as soon as life reaches a level where direct behavior is replaced by indirect, complex forms of action. The simple individual, dependent upon his direct modes of behavior for the maintenance of life, is self-sufficient. The individual who begins to specialize because of his interest in a single complex form of behavior will have to cultivate methods of social coöperation or he will perish.

It is not possible to draw a sharp line and say that on the one side lies animal behavior of the simple direct type and on the other human behavior of the complex social type. There are cases here and there where animals exhibit higher forms of behavior. Animal families have some of the elements of division of labor in their organization and there are animal species which have attained limited skill in rearranging the materials furnished by their environment. The important fact for our study is that animals do not adopt the higher methods of adaptation while man does. However slowly man arrived at the higher level of action, he ultimately substituted tools for natural direct forms of reaction to such an extent that the use of tools became his dominant mode of adjustment to his environment. Somewhere along this line of evolution man stepped out of the world of primitive action into the world of the acquired arts. There may be something natural and spontaneous about picking up a club in the forest and using it to attack one's prey. We might admit that man was still following his instincts in improving his weapon, though the instinct would have to be described as highly complex; but the invention of machinery and the attainment of those higher levels of action which interest us most, are far above mere instinct. Man long since left behind instinctive performances as his chief forms of reaction and ascended into a world of consciously guided and socially organized behavior.

The distinctly social and institutional character of even the earliest stages of human evolution becomes evident when we consider that the human arts show, in contradistinction to anything that we find elsewhere in the animal world, a tendency toward cumulative enrichment. Men evidently watched one another and profited by one another's achievements. Whether this is due to the mastery of that all-important social institution, language, or to other human endowments, the facts of anthropology make it clear that man was very early social in a sense in which no animal has ever been social. Man is social in the sense that each new generation has profited by what was achieved before and has through social inheritance developed tools of ever increasing effectiveness.

An understanding of the method by which this cumulative effect was produced is of the greatest importance for the psychology of institutions. We must digress from our historical narrative, therefore, to discuss the way in which a tool affects the development of human experience and behavior. We have seen how a tool may be thought to have been discovered and improved by some primitive human being. Let us now think of a second person who is unskilled but sees the tool. The experience of seeing the tool is likely to be most impressive if the unskilled person observes the owner of the tool in action and notes the advantages which the owner of the tool achieves because of its use. Seen under such circumstances the tool becomes the external embodiment of a human thought. The maker of the tool has put into material form an idea and the idea works. The unskilled observer cannot look directly into the consciousness of the tool maker, but the tool as an expression of an idea becomes a medium of communication. The receiving mind gets from the tool the idea which was originally in another mind.

The commerce of mind with mind through the medium of external realities is the great achievement which has raised man absolutely above the level of the lower animals. The adaptation of the human race to the physical environment has followed a path that has never been followed by any other animal because the human race has worked out its adaptations through group activities and through long generations. It is this fact that has made human evolution absolutely unique; the accumulation of experience from generation to generation through social institutions has brought into the world a new order of reality. Institutions are crystallized ideas. They make possible the transmission of ideas. They are detached from the minds in which they originated and are capable of affecting other minds.

While we emphasize the enormous importance of institutions as means of transmitting ideas, it is essential to our understanding of human history that we keep clearly in mind the fact that the transmission of ideas was at first very slow and uncertain. Many an invention of human genius has gone to waste because careless observers have failed to get the message which some embodied idea might have conveyed to more alert minds. The effects of institutions such as we have been describing did not begin to accumulate rapidly until men arrived at a recognition of the advantages of imitation as a method of adaptation.

We shall have opportunity later to come back to this discussion of the way in which institutions have reacted on human experience. We return now to a further study of the evolution of tools.

We have seen that division of labor results from the limitations of individual attention and interest. As soon as evolution produced the specialist devoting his efforts to the manufacture of weapons, certain further consequences appear. The specialist is provided, by virtue of his usefulness to the group, with the leisure which makes it possible for him to devise a new kind of improvement. He invented the idea of making his wares out of the most durable materials. Perhaps here again we should say that he discovered the idea or possibly hit upon it through accident. Whatever the process of arriving at this piece of wisdom, the manufacturer of weapons came ultimately to the extensive use of stone. The art of stone construction is a very high product of evolution, though it seems to our modern thinking relatively primitive. Before man could become an artisan in stone, he had to get the idea of stone implements clearly in mind and this he did not do until he reached the level of group life. The spear-head maker, for example, must have belonged to a spear-throwing tribe. He must have invented the device of binding a piece of sharp stone to the attacking end of his spear as a very radical modification of the simpler wooden weapon which his tribe was accustomed to use. Later — probably much later — he thought of shaping the stone; then he began to look for those kinds of stones which were easiest to chip off into sharp and symmetrical forms.

The long ages during which men were perfecting the arts of stone-work give clear evidence that we are dealing with a genuine process of evolution, a process of evolution which is distinctly human and distinctly social. There is no justification for talking about human progress during these vast stretches of time in terms of animal instinct or individual impulses. It means nothing to say that the spear-head maker hunted out obsidian beds in response to a native impulse of acquisitiveness or curiosity. The fact is that an entirely new type of thinking and an entirely new interest were developed, and older and more primitive types of consciousness gave place to the new pattern.

The essentially social character of the evolution which produced the arts can be brought out by calling attention to the fact that the evolution of the artisan's pattern of consciousness could not go forward until human ingenuity created certain institutions with which neither the artisan nor the hunter was concerned as a part of his own trade, but which both found absolutely essential as sustaining activities related to their chief undertakings. These collateral institutions were the primitive forms of exchange. The hunter had food in excess of his personal needs. The spear-head maker had stone points but lacked food. It seems very simple in this day, when the customs of exchange and the means for carrying on trade are fully established and understood, to suggest that the hunter and the artisan enter into a mutually advantageous relation and exchange their products. For primitive man, wholly unsupplied with money, unsupplied with instruments of measurement, and, above all, unacquainted with the idea of exchange, the situation was by no means as readily adjusted as it is to-day.

Exchange is secondary from the point of view of the hunter and artisan but primary from the point of view of the group. Without exchange, specialization would have to be given up. There would be no spear-head maker because everyone would be so absorbed in the mere getting of food that there would be little surplus attention to devote to anything except the direct activities of catching prey. Exchange provides a method of giving to each individual in the group the advantages of combined intelligence and skill. When men unite in social groups, they gain advantages which encourage them to invent new ways of promoting coöperation. Exchange is an institution which promotes specialization and coöperation. Animals steal from one another; they fight for possession of desirable things, but they cannot rise to the high level of comparing commodities and bartering what they have for other things which they need.

In the next chapter we shall take up in some detail the evolution of systems of exchange. At this point we are concerned merely to note the general fact that institutional methods of life beget new institutions.

The materials with which the first artisans worked were of various types. We may think of these early manufacturers as experimenters in materials.

Mason supplies the following description of one of the early arts — that of pottery.

In the last and simplest analysis, sun-dried adobe or bricks are the most primitive things made of clay. They are masses of rude paste worked up by hand, not at first in moulds, and dried in the sun. In all rainless regions of the globe they exist. In Babylon, in Egypt, in Peru, in Mexico, it is the same story. Given the material and the arid climate, and the thing is done, by that universal law, in human affairs as in nature, of following the lines of least resistance. This may not be the oldest treatment of the material since climate is a ruling factor, but it is the least complicated method of handling it.

The next simplest process is to be found in vogue in our day among certain Eskimo tribes on the tundras about the peninsula of Alaska. These cunning people, when most spread out, occupied the northern shores of America from Southern Labrador all the way around to Kadiak Island in Alaska. Almost everywhere they utilized fire only in the lamp-stove. Forests being absent, and even drift-wood being scarce, their only resource has been to burn the blubber or fat of the seal, whale, walrus, and other animals that abounded in that area. There was no lack of fuel. Of the mosses and vegetable fibres that came in their way they fabricated the wicks. For a lamp they took a slab of soapstone about two inches thick, straight along one margin, and curved on the other. This was excavated to form a shallow dish, in which the blubber was put, and the wick. The Eskimo knew both the firesticks and the flint and pyrites method of exciting fire, so it was never difficult to make a blaze. Now, there are in the west, regions where no soapstone exists of which to make lamp-stoves, so the ever quick-witted housewives knead clay with blood and hair, and form it into a thick shallow dish or bowl with the hand, and after drying it only a little, proceed to make thereof a true lamp-stove. The constant use of this simple device hardens it by burning, so that there is no need of firing the ware at all. Nothing save a sun-dried brick could be simpler. The first real potter seems in this way to have been a fabricator of lamps and stoves. Now and then rings are incised around these objects, commencing already in the most simple manner the process of decoration. No rims, nor handles, nor legs, nor bases, nor paint, nor modelled ornaments occur. We are behind the history of the art. [1]

Such accounts as these show man in the long process of learning to master the simplest substances of his environment. They show the gradual evolution of a constructive attitude.

While the men of the tribe were learning to work in stone, the women were developing the art of weaving, which seems always to have been their specialty. For this purpose they used the fibrous parts of plants and afterwards the hair and hides of animals. The clothing and basketry of primitive peoples show that this branch of constructive art is very ancient.

As a part of the constructive activities of the earliest peoples, we find also many forms of wood-working. The shield, as a protective instrument made of wood or of a

[1] MASON, OTIS T. — *Origins of Invention*, pp. 154–155; Charles Scribner's Sons, 1905.

combination of wood and hides, is one of the first human inventions to grow out of the simple unmodified stick which man picked up in the woods and used for both attack and protection. Pitt-Rivers [1] found among the Australians the simplest form of the shield which is nothing but a stick used to parry the darts of the assailant. This stick is afterwards gradually modified after the following manner : "an aperture was then made in the stick for the hand, and the face of it became broader, developing into a shield, the narrow ends, however, being still retained for parrying." [1]

The development of the bow is lost in antiquity. It was in use throughout the stone age, but it certainly represents either one of the most fortunate discoveries of primitive man or one of the most striking examples of his constructive genius.

All of the examples cited are impressive to the psychologist because they show man undergoing a transformation no less radical than that which he produced in the materials with which he worked. Man, the maker of weapons, man, the artisan, is no longer merely an impulsive pursuer of game. He is no longer the nature-man. He is the patient toiler absorbed in perfecting the material in his hand and in making it match the idea which he has worked out in his thought. He is the socialized member of a tribe exchanging ideas and learning the lesson of intelligent coöperation.

Our conclusions can be further supported by following the evolution of tools into its later stages. The artisan, having learned the value of stone and other materials, sometimes turns into a prospector looking for the kinds of raw materials which will best serve his art. Very shortly the prospector forgets all else in his eager quest. A diagram of the prospector's consciousness will illustrate what has happened. Figure IV shows the object of attack pushed

---

[1] MYRES, J. L. (editor) — *The Evolution of Culture and Other Essays by the late Lt.-Gen. A. Lane-Fox Pitt-Rivers*, p. 37 ; The Clarendon Press, 1906.

far out of the prospector's thinking. Not only so, but the weapon also is for the time being thought of not at all or, at most, very vaguely. The quest for flint or obsidian or for the reeds with which to weave a mat or basket is the all-absorbing interest. Landmarks which will guide the quest are matters of attention on the part of the prospector; the desire to find treasures of raw material and the determination to hold them in secret possession are the emotional

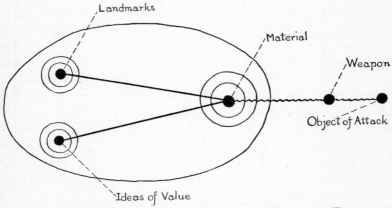

Fig. IV. — The Field of Consciousness in the Case of an Explorer

accompaniments of the search. This is a new form of the hunt. One needs only to read the romances of California and the Klondike to understand how this type of hunting can absorb a human mind. We know that among savages there were tribal secrets which were kept closely locked in the minds of the selected few, and among these secrets the most important were those which related to quarries of stone, to beds of clay, and to sources of the best wood for making bows and arrows. The possessor of these secrets took a place in the tribe hardly less important than that taken by the leader in war.

The psychology of the prospector is the psychology of a man who understands values ; that is, he sees in raw materials the possibilities of power which are not directly revealed. The prospector keeps this abstract idea in mind long enough to devote days to exploration. During these days he is controlled in all of his behavior by a mental incentive which is infinitely higher than the direct concrete desire of the hungry hunter. In order to make the abstractness of the prospector's thinking more evident, we may contrast the human seeker after treasure with the animals. Could the wolf be induced to start on a quest for a stone? Not at all. The wolf must have a direct sensory stimulus ; he must feel hunger and he must catch the scent of prey before he will undertake vigorous action. As the wolf is, so would man be, except that in the world of man's coöperative life and in his world of accumulated experience there are possibilities of appreciation of values, and acquired ideas of value which are just as potent in prompting action as are the pangs of hunger.

There are times even at the highest levels of civilized life when the feelings of hunger become keen and then the higher processes of appreciation of values may be for the time being submerged. We read that this was true of Esau, who exchanged intangible values of large worth for a mess of pottage. The higher processes of mind are at all stages of evolution in jeopardy from the competition of more primitive forms of mental and physical need. It is for this reason that primitive man and his more refined descendants have fortified themselves by all kinds of social institutions which are explicitly devised to prevent relapse into the animal state. Thus when the prospector finds his bed of useful stone, he marks it ; he makes a ceremony of the marking ; he tells a few carefully selected companions and they organize a group within the tribal group. This smaller circle of initiated ones meet and discuss their secret. They make records that prevent their forgetting their secret. In all of these acts they transform themselves from nature-men into men dominated in their thinking and behavior by ideas and abstract values.

The artisan and the prospector with their new interest in materials became aggressive experimenters. Through their experimenting they came in due time upon a special kind of stone. It was a malleable stone and it was a stone which melted in the fire. The way in which this discovery was made can of course be only a matter of surmise, but we can be very sure that, whatever the particular method of this discovery, it was made possible through the gradual accumulation of ideas and practices in the group. Group life had reached a high stage of evolution before man passed out of the stone age.

Pitt-Rivers comments on the discovery of metal as follows:

The fabrication of stone implements would of itself lead by degrees to a knowledge of the metals which are contained in stones. Thus, for example, I have here a specimen of a stone mace-head from Central America composed of a nodule of hæmatite partially coated with micaceous iron ore, the particles of which are distinctly visible on its glittering surface. The weight of this implement, being nearly double that of a mace-head composed of ordinary stone, would at once attract the notice of the savage fabricator, and lead him to investigate the uses of metal.

But, as a general rule, races engaged exclusively in hunting, who rarely turn their attention to the ground except to examine a trail or to search for water, would have little opportunity of profiting by the mineral wealth of the soil over which they roamed. Witness the Australians, who have continued for ages in ignorance of the gold and other mines which are now so attractive to Europeans; or the North and South American Indians, and the Esquimaux, amongst whom the art of smelting metal has never been found associated with those races who are in a purely hunting stage of existence, the wrought metals used by such races to point their weapons being invariably derived from civilized sources.

From hunting wild animals, the savage, in the natural sequence of progress, would turn his attention to their capture and domestication, and thus he creeps gradually into the pastoral life; and as the bones of animals under domestication, through want of exercise and good living, become smoother and of finer texture, the experienced anatomist is thereby afforded the means of distinguishing, amongst the vestiges of antiquity, the remains of domesticated animals from those derived from the chase, and of observing to what extent the domestication of animals was contemporaneous with other changes in the social condition of the people. Still, however, in the pastoral state, the barbarian is not necessarily brought in contact with metals; and hence we should expect in many cases to find the traces of domesticated animals associated with people who are still in the stone age. This was notably the case amongst the ancient inhabitants of the Swiss lakes, where the sheep and horse have been found at Moosseedorf, and other lake habitations which are proved to belong to the stone age, though not in such abundance as in the settlements belonging to the bronze age.

From the pastoral life, the barbarian, hampered by his flocks and herds, and no longer obliged to wander in search of food, settles down to a more stationary life, and by degrees takes to agriculture. Then, for the first time, he digs into the soil, and becomes acquainted with its mineral treasures. It has been proved by the discovery of quantities of carbonized grains of wheat, lumped together, in the Swiss lake-habitations of the stone age, together with the materials for preparing it for food, that a knowledge of agriculture preceded the general employment of bronze in that region, whilst in Britain, and in Denmark also, bronze is almost invariably associated with evidence of domestication and agriculture.

The metals first employed would be those that are most attractive. Copper, in Europe, from the bright colour of its ores, would be noticed more readily than iron, which is often scarcely distinguishable from the soil, and requires greater temperature and more skilled labour to render it available than could be expected of a people emerging out of the savage state. It is not, therefore, surprising that in Europe, copper first, and subsequently its alloy, bronze, should have been employed before iron as a material for weapons. But in those countries where iron is found upon the surface in an attractive form, and in a condition to be easily wrought, we must for the same reason suppose that it would be used instead of copper in the earliest ages of metallurgy.[1]

The discovery of metal has had a most momentous effect on human life and human thought. The arts became increasingly elaborate, demanding on the part of the worker more skill and the cultivation of more ideas than were necessary at lower levels of culture. At the same time the range of possible invention was indefinitely extended. Metals offer no such restrictions to art as do wood and stone, which must be worked on the lines dictated by the material. Metal is difficult to obtain, but once it is secured it is manageable far more readily than are other resistant substances.

The elaborateness of the processes to which primitive man attained in working metal is illustrated by the following statement copied from a lesson on " Iron and Steel " prepared by Professor J. Russell Smith :

Two black men, almost naked, squat on opposite sides of a fire in central Africa. Each of them has a little hand bellows with which he forces the fire. From time to time they lay on the fire lumps of charcoal and lumps of iron ore. All day they work and sweat, blowing and feeding their little fire. At evening, a 10 or 12 pound lump of iron lies in the glowing coals ready to be hammered on the anvil and shaped into spearhead, knife, or kettle.

These men are smelting iron ore, which is a kind of rock with some iron mixed in with several other kinds of mineral. The hot

---

[1] MYRES, J. L. (editor) — *op. cit.*, pp. 155–157.

fire makes the iron melt and run out, so that it can be gathered up and used.

No one knows how long man has smelted iron ore. Iron ore is to be found in almost all countries, and primitive man in many lands knew how to use it many, many centuries ago. Perhaps some primitive man's camp-fire first smelted iron by accident. Legend says that 1,500 years before Christ a forest fire showed the people of the island of Crete how to make iron. Pictures on the walls of Egyptian buildings which date back to 3,500 years before Christ show Egyptians smelting iron with the aid of a goatskin bellows.

Each of many ancient peoples must have found out for itself how to make iron, for it was made by the same method in very ancient times in middle Africa, in China, in India, as well as in the countries around the Mediterranean, and in England where Cæsar found the Britons making it very much as the explorer may still find it made in remote parts of Africa and Asia.

The Romans were unable to make much improvement on this process of making iron. It produced all the metal with which Cæsar armed his victorious legions. The iron which bolted the oak of the little ships of Columbus was made in a simple fireplace like a blacksmith's forge. The iron for Washington's cannon and muskets was made in forges or tall furnaces not unlike big stone chimneys. The fire was fed by the forced draft commonly produced by a water wheel.[1]

It is evident from this description that the art of handling metal requires a high type of mental ingenuity and a high degree of patience. The metal worker, even more than the prospector, is laboring toward a goal which is far away. He must have enough imagination to look into the remoter possibilities of his labor and he must guide his action toward satisfactions which are far removed from his immediate expenditure of energy. He must be backed in the devel-

[1] *Lessons in Community and National Life*, Series C, p. 81; United States Government Printing Office, 1918.

opment of these personal attitudes by a social desire for the products of his labor which will assure him of the largest satisfactions as rewards of his industry.

The discovery of metal and the influence of one worker on another opened up gradually certain final stages in the evolution of the technical arts. For our purposes it will be enough to condense the many steps in this later evolution into a very brief statement. Metal is manageable enough and permanent enough so that with it man can try a great variety of experiments. The result of these experiments is the discovery of principles. As the prospector learned to think of values, so the experimenter is able to see that various implements are in fact embodiments of the same principle. The lever, for example, turns up in many different forms. One works with this lever and with that and finally learns how to think of the principle of leverage which is back of all of the concrete cases.

It required long generations of experience with one mechanical contrivance after another before man arrived at the point where he could look beyond the particular implement and see the principle. He had to provide himself with certain favorable conditions before the processes of discovering principles could be consummated. First, he had to provide himself with leisure to think. He had to have a highly evolved language in order to record the stages of his thought.

When once a single mechanical principle was segregated from its concrete manifestations, the course of human thinking was for all time thereafter determined by that fact. If we may use a trivial example to make clear a stupendous happening, we may refer to a person solving a puzzle. For a long time the puzzle seems baffling. One combination after another is attempted. Patience is required for this succession of trials and failures. The person who is trying to find the solution has plenty of experience, but it is of a primitive type. Suddenly, by some stroke of good fortune or through some insight of intelligence, the mystery is solved. From that time on the puzzle has a wholly new appearance. Not only so, but puzzles in general will be attacked in a new way because the experimenter has discovered that there is a method of looking into puzzle situations.

As it is in solving a puzzle, so it has been with man in his mastery of nature. Endowed with instincts, man, like the animals, attacked the world about him and attempted to wrest from it what he needed in the way of food and comfort. The instincts carried him successfully through many situations. Then he began to use his higher powers to reconstruct nature. Instinct began to give way to constructive effort. Slowly the puzzle began to be solved. Finally, construction passed over into deliberate scientific study and man learned to think of principles. Tools thus served a double purpose. They helped man to secure a fuller and better living and they reacted on man to make him more reliant on ideas and less reliant on brute force. Man the artisan, man the thinking being is no longer merely a creature of instincts. There is no instinct in the world which will lead an individual to smelt iron or make a wheel. Anyone who describes machine civilization as a result of instinctive adjustments shuts his eyes to the most significant fact which we know in the universe, namely, the evolution of intelligent methods of thought and action.

One final comment may be added to this outline of the evolution of tool-consciousness. The modern man is able, by the aid of language and through social coöperation, to secure by a short method all the advantages which the race has secured through its age-long efforts ; he is brought even in his early and helpless youth into the presence of the most elaborate mechanical devices and principles. Instead of leaving instinctive adjustments behind after long periods of gradual induction into the simple arts, modern man finds himself in possession at once of the ripest products of co-operative thinking. He need not discover iron; it is here at his hand in every possible form. He need not invent the pulley; it is here with a careful explanation of its uses and can be had for less than the asking. If instincts were dominant in the primitive world, they are most certainly not in the modern world of mechanical appliances. The man who lives in modern society has to develop modes of thought and modes of action which are appropriate to a world where tools have attained an importance so superior to bodily organs that no one thinks of using his unaided strength even in satisfying the most urgent of his physical needs.

CHAPTER III

Systems of Exchange

This chapter will be devoted to the discussion of exchange, money, and the more elaborate instruments of credit which civilization has devised as means of facilitating commercial coöperation. The purpose of this discussion is to reinforce the conclusion reached in the foregoing chapter, that life in the present era is a highly organized system of intelligent adaptations.

The primitive struggle on the part of animals to secure the things desired for subsistence and comfort consists in sharp trials of strength between individuals. The stronger individual or the more cunning takes advantage of the less able and as a result secures superior enjoyment of the good things of life.

There are frequent occasions in civilized life when individuals engage in ruthless competition, but the methods of this competition are different from those which appear in animal life. Human struggles are very seldom hand-to-hand encounters; they are struggles carried on by social methods and have as their stake the possession of the symbols of wealth rather than the objects desired. Whenever men resort to brute force in competing for that which they desire, society sets its machinery in operation to defeat them. Their strength sinks into a position of little importance as contrasted with the intelligence which directs the behavior of commercial and economic antagonists.

Not only so, but society has devised certain rules of conduct which are intended to foster virtues that are appropriate to a system of coöperative life as distinguished from the cruder traits that lead to success in animal competitions and in savage combat. These rules of conduct favor industry and conservation of property; they are enforced by the group and are ultimately accepted by all of its members.

To be sure the most civilized of men enjoy from time to time what may be called a theoretical lapse into primitive unregulated conduct. One reads the romances of pirate adventure and bandit robberies and derives from these something of the pleasure which must have attached to the human struggles which are now for the most part superseded by the well-ordered activities of trade.

The robber stage of human existence resembles in its mental pattern the hunting stage. There was much the same kind of fierce pleasure in wresting a piece of food from a fellow man that there was in capturing wild prey. Just when and how men came to a more peaceful method of sharing the goods that contribute comfort to life can be, of course, only a matter of speculation. The appearance of an abundant supply of food undoubtedly reduced competition and made it easy to pass out of the robber stage into one of social coöperation. The invention of tools made men so efficient in supplying abundance of food and at the same time so interdependent that barter was substituted for violence.

Whatever the circumstances under which barter first came into the world, it was destined to replace robbery. Step by step barter has in turn been replaced by higher forms of exchange. Not only so, but in the course of this evolution there have been invented certain devices which are utterly unintelligible to beings who have not learned

methods of institutional life. Offer an animal a coin or a
jewel of great value as a reward and the abstract character
of human exchange and its dependence on inventions will
instantly be apparent.

We may draw from one of Kipling's stories the lesson
that civilization is wholly different from the lower stage at
which the animals live. In the story of "The King's Ankus,"
Mowgli, the wild boy, it will be remembered, found the
glittering bejeweled thing in the ruined city where the
monkeys had carried him. He played with it until he lost
interest in it and threw it away. A man found it and was
enriched by it beyond the dreams of avarice. Soon the
finder was killed by another who desired the ankus. Surprise after surprise came to Mowgli, the child of nature, as
he observed the struggles that men will undertake for possession of the thing. To his natural and instinctive mind
there was nothing about the ankus to satisfy the immediate
desires which a human being or an animal has for food or
drink or for the ordinary comforts of life. The remote and
highly abstract devotion to jewels was utterly unintelligible
to him.

Another illustration of the highly artificial character of
money exchange can be seen in the behavior of children.
Little children have no regard for the value of coins. They
like a silver dollar because it is flat and hard, because it can
be rolled and otherwise used as a plaything. They have no
interest at all in its purchasing value. Little children have
to go through a long series of civilizing experiences before
they come to have anything of the feeling which the ordinary
adult cherishes for currency.

The formulas which were used in the chapter on tools
may properly be repeated in the effort to explain how the
first stages of exchange arose. The robber animal has no
consideration for its victim because it is intent upon one

object, namely, the piece of food which will satisfy hunger. Furthermore, for the animal the object which can hold attention must be something which will yield direct satisfaction. Nothing that involves long thought processes or abstract knowledge can appeal to the animal because it is unequipped with the powers necessary for these higher forms of experience.

When primitive man evolved to the level where he practiced barter, which is one step above anything of which the animal is capable, the range of attention was infinitely wider than it was at the stage of robbery. Each of the parties to a transaction of barter has a strong disposition, as does the animal, to hold his own possessions, but the barterer is able to give some attention to the commodities in the possession of the man with whom he is about to arrange an exchange. The mind of the barterer has more than one focus of attention. Indeed, if we think of the watchful observation of the person with whom the barterer is trying to drive the bargain, we may say that there are three centers of attention.

While barter is thus seen to be far above the range of animal attention, it is psychologically simple in that it depends primarily on the appeal to direct sensory desires. The Indian trading with the sophisticated European was always worsted because the Indian lived and moved in a world of immediate sensory satisfactions. Bright beads caught his eye. He did not understand the value of land deeds and other like inventions of a higher civilization. He was no match for the civilized man in exchange. He was satisfied to part with values and accept colors, because barter is a form of direct perceptual exchange.

Early barter must have exhibited the wildest fluctuations. The hunter who found game plentiful was willing to part with his possessions for slight returns. When game was

scarce the hunter made hard terms. The strong undoubtedly bullied the weak and purchased at their own rates
whatever they desired. Barter was unsystematized and
unregulated ; it often included a large element of robbery.

With all its defects, barter served to establish certain new
ideas in the world, the ideas of comparative value. The
individual who bartered his wares began to form some
notion of relative desirability and to realize that his goods
had potentialities of exchange even before he began to
barter them. Not only so, but gradually the idea of desirability became especially prominent in connection with some
one or more objects because these objects were equally and
universally acceptable to all persons. The objects which
were in this way selected as readily exchangeable were the
first examples of what we call "money."

How various have been the objects which have served as
money is related by Bastable. He says :

On a review of existing savage tribes and ancient races of more
or less civilization, we are surprised at the great variety of objects
which have been used to supply the need of a circulating medium.
Skins, for instance, seem to be one of the earliest forms of money.
They have been found among the Indians of Alaska performing
this service, while accounts of leather money seem to show that
their use was formerly more general. As the hunting stage gives
place to the pastoral, and animals become domesticated, the
animal itself, instead of its skin, becomes the principal form of
currency. There is a great mass of evidence to show that, in the
most distant regions and at very different times, cattle formed
a currency for pastoral and early agricultural nations. Alike
among existing barbarous tribes, and in the survivals discovered
among classical nations, sheep and oxen both appear as units of
value. Thus we find that at Rome, and through the Italian
tribes generally "oxen and sheep formed the oldest medium of
exchange, ten sheep being reckoned equivalent to one ox." . . .
The Icelandic law bears witness to a similar state of things;

while the various fines in the different Teutonic codes are estimated in cattle.

* * * * * * * *

On passing to the agricultural stage a greater number of objects are found capable of being applied to currency purposes. Among these are corn — used even at present in Norway — maize, olive oil, coconuts and tea. The most remarkable instance of an agricultural product being used as currency is to be found in the case of tobacco, which was adopted as legal tender by the English colonists in North America. Another class of articles used for money consists of ornaments, which among all uncivilized tribes serve this purpose. The haique-shells . . . are an instance, cowries in India, whales' teeth among the Fijians, red feathers among some South Sea Island tribes, and finally, any attractive kinds of stone which can be easily worked. Mineral products so far as they do not come under the preceding head, furnish another class. Thus salt was used in Abyssinia and Mexico.[1]

A study of this list of commodities which were used in standardizing and stabilizing trade reveals clearly what must have been going on in men's minds. Confronted with the fluctuating desires of their fellows and with the varying conditions in regard to supply, men found it necessary to discover some relatively stable and permanent center to which they could always refer when they arranged to make a trade. They needed this stable center of thought and desire in order to guide their thinking. As soon as they found a satisfactory commodity to which they could attach their thinking they elevated it to a position of unique importance. The commodity became something more than a material thing. It became a social instrument, a symbol of coöperation, a device for guiding later thought because it had been selected as satisfying a mental need for stability in comparisons.

[1] BASTABLE, CHARLES F. — " Money," *Encyclopædia Britannica* (Eleventh Edition), XVIII, p. 697; Cambridge University Press.

As soon as money of the type described began to appear, the need of further systematization of thought and human relations began to make itself manifest. Barter was not possible without some notion of quantity. At first quantity must have been roughly estimated by mere inspection, but soon the demand for a more highly refined method of measurement began to be recognized. This is not the proper place for a discussion of the evolution of weights and measures ; a later chapter will be devoted to that topic. It is in place, however, to emphasize the fact that progressive systematization of thought is the essential condition of economic evolution. Money is not a collection of objects ; it is a system of symbols used in guiding thought and conduct. The use of money stimulates minds to new levels of thought entirely removed from the sphere of animal instincts and animal combat.

The progress of money standardization can be traced to show how men gradually raised themselves from the level of interest in perceptual enjoyment to more abstract modes of thought. The Indians carried on much of their trade by the use of wampum. Wampum is made of shells strung on a thong. The string of shells was used as an ornament very much as beads are used by modern women. Sometimes the shells were polished and matched in size and coloring as a modern string of pearls is matched. The ornamental value of the string of wampum was thus due in part to the appeal made directly by the shells to the eye, but far beyond this was the secondary meaning which every beholder came to attach to the wampum. The shells were counters, and back of them was the value which they represented. The shells meant that the rich possessor could match each shell with some other goods. When the purchaser handed over a string of wampum to the seller, it became a promissory note to be redeemed later by an agreed-upon number of pelts or quantity of food. Wampum was at once an object of display and a counter or abstract symbol of value.

Economists have frequently pointed out the close relation between ornament and money. When one thinks of ornament in psychological terms, there is no mystery about this close relationship. Human love for that which is permanent is not a mere physical desire ; it is an ideal. Gold is that with which kings have surrounded themselves and with which men have embellished their tombs. Gold comes very near to the human ideal of the immortal. Not only so, but it is also capable of infinite variety in its molding. It attracts the eye with color which does not tarnish with age. Tribes which do not possess gold have used other materials that approach it in qualities as their standard of exchange and at the same time as their means of personal decoration. Wampum and precious stones are the striking examples of the human choices of permanent materials other than gold to be used as means of expressing the ideal of permanent value.

At the close of a chapter on ornament and money, Carlile writes as follows :

At the dawn of mediæval history, the connection between ornament and money is found to be so intimate as to merge into virtual identity. The gold armlets with which the Anglo-Saxon noble delighted to bedeck himself were, like the earrings that Abraham sent to Rebekah, made on a definite scale of weight and standard of purity, and apparently were also so made as to be readily divisible into portions of a definite weight. The *scillingas,* from which our word shilling is derived, were originally pieces cut or broken off from these armlets, and were eventually at any rate equated with the weight of the Roman solidus. A "ring-breaker," both in the Anglo-Saxon and Norse languages, came to be used in the sense of "a distributor of treasures, an attribute especially given to princes." In "The Traveller's Song" a prince, whom Mr. Hodgkin identifies with Alboin, is described as being " the man who, of all mankind, had the lightest hand to win love, the most generous heart in the distribution of rings and bracelets." [1]

The psychological forces which are at work in evolving money have been recognized in some measure by economists. The following passage may be quoted from Carlile:

Let us glance, in the first instance, at the current explanation of the origin of money, as put into shape by Adam Smith. It runs, it will be remembered, somewhat as follows. The division of labour having been established, the power of exchanging commodities must frequently have been embarrassed by the difficulty which a would-be exchanger would often feel in finding any one who happened to possess a superfluity of the commodity that he wanted, and who at the same time would take what he had to dispose of. To avoid the inconveniency of such situations the prudent man would naturally endeavor to have by him a certain quantity of some one commodity or other *such as he imagined few people would be likely to refuse in exchange for the product of their industry.* . . . "Many different commodities it is probable were successively both thought of and employed for the purpose." In the end, however, "irresistible reasons" led all civilized nations to give the preference to the metals, and eventually to the precious metals. The "irresistible reasons" were of course the high value in small compass, the homogeneity, fusibility, divisibility, and so on, of these metals. On this explanation, the criticism at once suggests itself that, if the prudent man could find any commodity that few would refuse in exchange for their products, then money was already virtually established. The very thing that we want to know is, how did first one commodity, then another, and finally gold and silver, attain such a degree of universal acceptability as ensured their being refused by none in exchange for their products? Professor Walker, whose discussion of the subject in his *Money, Trade, and Industry* (page 6) is, within limits, most lucid and

[1] CARLILE, WILLIAM W. — *Evolution of Modern Money*, pp. 248–249; Macmillan and Co., 1901.

enlightening, after defining money as that which every one receives without the slightest reference either to his own need for consumption or to the credit of the person who offers it, remarks, " When an article reaches this degree of acceptability, it becomes money, no matter what it is made of, and no matter why people want it." This conception of an article as "becoming money" spontaneously as soon as it has reached a certain required degree of "acceptability" is certainly much nearer the truth than Adam Smith's conception, which seems to assume that the prehistoric communities first decided that the establishment of money would be desirable, then experimented with a variety of commodities as money, and finally, for irresistible reasons, fixed on the precious metals.[1]

In such a discussion we see acceptability used as a vague general term to cover a whole group of psychological facts. Acceptability, as we have shown, is not a mere matter of appeal to the senses and the animal desires for food and comfort, or even the æsthetic tastes of men. Acceptability results only when the higher demands of systematic thought are satisfied by the commodity adopted as money. Money could not exist at all without a sufficient development of intelligence to make it possible for those who have commodities to look beyond the present fact, to think in terms of permanent values, to see the advantages of social coöperation and the desirability of regulating this coöperation so that it shall be equitable to all concerned.

What the psychologist objects to in the statement of the economist is the idea that things become money because of their own qualities. Money is invented to support human thought processes. It is created in response to a demand which is strictly psychological. To be sure, gold is homogeneous, but it requires a discriminating mind to recognize this. It is true that gold is divisible into small units, but

[1] CARLILE, WILLIAM W. — *op. cit.*, pp. 226–228.

this virtue must first appeal to a mind which seeks to divide. To talk about money as explained by the inherent qualities of the precious metals is like trying to explain a work of art by reference to the qualities of paint and canvas.

The economist's statement can be recast. First came individual foraging for food and the other good things of life. Then came robbery. Then came barter. But barter was clumsy and full of unsatisfactory hazards and so men gradually systematized their exchange. They recognized certain permanent qualities in things and became discriminating. They began to pile up property against a day of need. All this came very slowly, but it contributed to the evolution of an idea — the idea of comparative value. This idea is an abstraction. One cannot see comparative value or taste it, but it is a quality resulting from the relation of objects to human comfort. Under the idea of value, objects are brought together which in the world of things do not belong together at all. The skins that make the wigwam, the flint that makes the arrowhead, the flesh that is to be used as food, all stand in the same relation to human life in that they make it pleasanter ; and because of this common relation to man, all of these objects are classified as valuable. Furthermore, there soon arises in the mind which has classified all these things under the general term "value" a need for some kind of a device by which the place of each object under the general idea can be determined and marked. The products of the hunt have a value, but their value is less permanent than that attaching to the product of the prospector's endeavor. The arrowhead is of high value because it can serve again and again in the quest for food. Man thus gradually trained himself to look beyond mere obvious qualities and to see a quality which, as indicated before, is abstract.

Once the idea of comparative value is apprehended by men,

they begin to act under its guidance. They seek some method of giving it expression. Economists have seen clearly that it is permanent objects which are chosen for money, but they have been slow to recognize that permanency is discovered by the mind rather than supplied by nature. Money is the instrument by which men help themselves to understand and express their subjective needs. Substances having permanency are selected because they correspond to the idea of value. The reason why we esteem the precious stones and the precious metals so highly is not that they satisfy our hunger directly or give us bodily comfort, but that experience has shown them to be unaffected by time and erosion. There is a feeling of confidence which attaches to a piece of gold that cannot be aroused by any fragile object, however useful it may be at the moment. Gold did not select itself as the medium of exchange; it was selected by human beings who were striving to secure a tangible expression of the idea of permanent value.

What has been said regarding the permanence of money can be said also of those other qualities of the precious metals so often emphasized by the economists, namely, divisibility and fusibility. The recognition of the comparative values is immediately followed by a desire that such values when exchanged shall be justly equated with each other. There is in objects as they exist in the outer world no reaching out in the direction of comparison with other objects. One animal furnishes much food and another furnishes little, and each is unaware of its great or little value to man. Man, on the other hand, recognizes that the small animal has small value in relation to his own needs and the large animal a greater value. In order to adjust matters he must invent a device for expressing the difference. This device he finds in some third or neutral substance to which he refers both the small and the large animal. This neutral substance must be readily divisible so that it can be matched to the commodities which are to be compared.

As a matter of fact, man has encountered in the metals a great deal of resistance to this demand for divisibility. He has therefore superimposed on the metals another system, the system of theoretical division or calculation. If he cannot actually divide a bar of gold, he will divide it in his thought and will say that the bar is made up of so and so many grains. This theoretical division of the bar will in many cases serve the purposes of exchange and make unnecessary any actual division.

It may be well to digress for a moment and comment on the ingenuity which man had to exercise in order to make possible the theoretical division of his gold into small units. The use of the word "grain" shows the device to which man resorted. Of all the small objects of nature, the grains of the field were most nearly uniform. Just as permanency had been found in the metals, so uniformity was found in grains. The word "carat," which is used in modern times to express the fineness of gold, is derived, like the unit of weight called a grain, from the name of a seed. In Abyssinia there is a coral-tree which has small uniform seeds. This tree furnished the weights with which small quantities of gold were originally compared. Long ages ago this natural aid to subdivision was given up in favor of an authorized and socially sanctioned unit of comparison, but the name of the original seed-unit still remains to bear testimony to the fact that the active human mind used the material things about it for its own purposes. Seeds were not merely seeds to the discerning mind; they were counters of exceptional value because of their uniformity. The idea of uniformity was needed in order to control human relations. It would be a wholly inverted statement to say that nature imposed uniformity on the human mind through seeds and grains. The human mind picked out seeds and grains because they correspond to its own ideas.

If the argument up to this point has failed to convince any reader of the strictly psychological character of money, the study of coinage will certainly show him that it is mental rather than material forces which have operated to produce the economic system of civilization.

Let us go back in imagination to the conditions of trade when there were no coins. Semicivilized man was somewhat skilled in the methods of barter and of partially standardized money exchange. He had discovered gold and silver and was using them as the standards of value. He had a system of weights by which he could actually or theoretically divide his bars of metal. We are thinking of such a period as that recorded in early Hebrew history when gold was measured by the talent, which is a unit of weight.

In such a stage of dawning civilization as this, the uncertainties of trade were, of course, very great. Suppose that the gold bar were diluted with copper; the purchaser who received full weight would not receive full value. There came, therefore, to be a distinction between gold and fine gold. Also there came in human relations the first remote beginnings of that which in modern life has come to play so large a part in exchange — confidence, built on reliability. The merchant whose gold bars were always pure, the country from which gold of a pure grade came, were held in superior esteem. Was not the gold of Ophir better than the gold from unknown lands? The value of a designation thus began to appear as supplementing and guaranteeing the value of the metal itself.

It should be noted that society in this early day was not compact enough to guarantee protection to the trader. Each merchant was obliged to be his own guarantor. The contrast with present-day society is mentioned at this point in order to keep as vividly as possible in the reader's mind the idea that social institutions evolve only after ideas emerge through accumulated experience. That gold from Ophir is pure must first become a matter of common knowledge; then human intelligence will recognize the importance of letting it be known that the gold in hand came from that particular and highly creditable source. It was not until long ages after the ideas of quality and reliability had been developed that human experience reached the stage where it could suggest the modern device of giving it an appropriate stamp. It was a still later step when methods of artificial purification made it possible to bring all gold to a designated level.

Let us go back to the days when a name began to have significance. It soon came to pass that the authority of the ruler was appealed to in exchange and the metal standards of exchange were looked upon as most satisfactory when they bore the name of the ruler. His name on a bit of metal meant that the force of organized society was back of the guarantee. At first the stamp was crude; the coin was irregular in shape; there was no milled edge to protect the coin against reduction in value by abrasion; there was no clear designation of the value — merely a guarantee that the ruler recognized the metal as a part of the social machinery which his people must use in securing the goods necessary for life and comfort.

This is not the place to attempt to trace in any detail the history of coinage, but reference to one historical episode will throw a flood of light on the psychology of coins. During the reigns of Henry VIII and Edward VI in England, it was believed by the sovereigns and their advisers that it was the sovereign's authority which determined the value of currency. This theory of wealth as related to government was accepted as the basis for the further contention that the sovereign had the right to take advantage of his authority as though it were equivalent in importance to the purity and weight of metal. Such a view led finally to the issuance of coins which were inferior in quality and weight. It was very soon found, however, that the underweight coins were not received freely by tradespeople, and, of course, they could not be used for trade in countries beyond the range of the influence of the ruler who issued them. The monarchs tried by edicts to force the depreciated currency on their subjects. They tried to set the price of corn and other necessities of life at a point which would maintain the prestige of their coins; but the royal edicts did not avail. It was thus discovered that the sovereign's guarantee must be a genuine guarantee. It is only on the basis of a guarantee corresponding to the facts that confidence can be maintained.

In the light of this illustration we may seek the answer to two questions. The first may be stated in these terms: How could a king and his advisers make so radical a mistake in their definition of the sovereign's relations to coinage? The second question is: How far does the ordinary man understand the value of a coin?

Both questions are answered by the statement that a coin is one of the most abstract objects in the world. It carries in its official sanction and in the actual metal which it contains an epitome of racial evolution. Its value can therefore be readily misinterpreted by anyone who becomes confused in the system of ideas which he attaches to the coin. The king's advisers selected from the complex of ideas which attach to the coin the one notion of sovereign authority and overemphasized this. They did not carry popular thinking with them and consequently the scheme which they framed in their councils failed. The common man was more affected by such ideas as came to him when he found that foreign exchange did not recognize the authority of his sovereign than he was by any judgments of the king's advisers. Once the common man began to have his attention called to grounds of suspicion regarding the completeness of his sovereign's powers, the coins became distasteful and unacceptable. The common man's system of thinking is very easily disturbed by the slightest suspicion as to the reliability of the authority which put its stamp on the coin.

We see from the facts cited not only that a coin is dependent on ideas for its acceptability, but also that the system of ideas in question is peculiarly social in character, involving a recognition of such matters as governmental and sovereign authority. In short, the psychology of the coin is something other than the psychology of individual perception or individual thinking. The possessor of a coin is at the end of a long series of evolutionary stages and although his present apprehension of the meaning of the coin does not by any means depend on an explicit knowledge of all the history that has gone into the making of the coin, it epitomizes this history in a feeling of dependence on the group. The coin is subject to laws of social relationship which the individual from his limited contact with it cannot fully comprehend, but emphatically feels. The coin was built up by human coöperation and depends for its continued use on mutual human confidences. The individual recognizes himself as a part of a scheme of social interdependence.

Perhaps the most striking way of putting the matter is to come back to the fact mentioned earlier, that children have the greatest difficulty in understanding coins. The child finds in the world into which he comes this hard round thing which seems to command a kind of respect that is altogether unique. On a certain eventful day he finds that if he takes the coin in his hand and goes to the store he can acquire as his own certain very desirable objects, but he will have to give up the coin. Just why he gets so many things and no more is not clear, but the possibility of purchasing things with coins is a fact of experience and an important fact.

It is not necessary to do more than suggest such a line of thought. Each member of modern civilized society has had his introduction to coins and understands something of the character of a coin and the endless network of relationships into which the coin brings him.

These discussions show that the coin is not explicable by any of the devices known to individual psychology; nor is its explanation the duty of the student of physics or chemistry or zoölogy. A coin is not a matter of sensations or percepts or instincts; nor is it a mere piece of metal. Coins are symbols of a series of social interrelationships and as such can be fully understood only after a study of the way in which men live together and control their coöperative activities through symbols. Coins are symbols of a system of ideas and of a system of mutual confidences and suspicions.

There will be occasions in later chapters when the discussion will return to social symbols. Coins are by no means the only symbolic devices which have been created by social coöperation. Our present task, however, is to place before the reader one clear concrete example of a human invention based on an abstract idea. We turn, therefore, to certain final stages in the evolution of money exchange.

After metal coinage comes the use of paper, first as a substitute for coins and afterwards in various other forms, some of which have proved to be legitimate and useful, others of which have proved to be ill conceived and disastrous.

Obviously, paper money could not be used until a long series of developments had taken place in society, making the number system and the art of reading common possessions of the majority of the members of the community. In a large sense of the word, the use of paper money is as much a result of learning to read and write as it is an outcome of economic development. If we set aside, however, for the moment considerations of this type which we shall take up later in connection with the study of language, it may be pointed out that the use of paper money calls for a type of mental process which is higher and more abstract than that which is required for the use of metal coins. When a person sees paper money he must have confidence that there is a sufficient organization of society back of this substitute for tangible metal values to assure him that he can secure for his paper a substance much nearer his ideal of permanence. As soon as confidence in society is at all shaken, the value of paper money, which is a doubly abstract social medium, is entirely lost. Confidence in paper money is, therefore, less stable than confidence in metal coinage; and we have seen that confidence in metal coinage is dependent on the integrity of the coins.

An interesting psychological problem of the type suggested in an earlier paragraph arises at this point; it is the problem of determining what form confidence in the social organization back of paper money takes on in the individual's mental life. Every time one looks at a dollar bill one has confidence in society, and yet this confidence does not come to the surface in the form of a full conscious picture of the social organization which is back of the currency system of the country. To be sure, if a person pauses to define clearly to himself the attitude which he assumes toward the paper money, he may be able to call up more or less vividly a picture of the central government and of its power to enforce his rights in connection with paper money. But this elaborate mental process which may on occasion be brought out and inspected has an adequate substitute in ordinary life. This adequate substitute we may describe by saying that it is an attitude of confidence in the familiar paper itself. This attitude of confidence in turn is the outgrowth of repeated experiences in which we have seen the paper accepted without hesitation by tradespeople. We come to have, as a result of what we have observed, complete faith that the paper money will pass. We handle it, therefore, with assurance and offer it at the store without ever stopping to go back to the remoter grounds of our faith. Assurance is in this case a feeling directly connected with a certain series of behaviors; it is the mental accompaniment of a habit of action.

Passing the feeling of confidence, we may go on to consider another of the psychological processes which arise in the individual's mind when he deals with paper money. The paper money is substituted for coins because it is convenient; it is easily handled; it can be made in uniform size, whatever the denomination. In all these respects society has been working out a practical problem of ease of manipulation. Society has deliberately invented a device which is economical of its own energy.

In order to satisfy its desire for convenience, society has found it necessary to expend a great deal of energy in developing and safeguarding the system itself. In other words, in order to save energy, society has expended time and energy in developing an artificial system. Some of the steps which are required in the elaboration of this artificial system become apparent when it is considered that society has to make a special form of paper on which to stamp its paper money. Society has to produce for the printing of its money elaborate plates which it will be difficult for unauthorized people to duplicate. Society has to employ a group of men whose business it is to protect the community against forgeries. Society has to develop agencies for the distribution and for the ultimate collection and re-issue of paper money.

History shows that paper money, like coins, is subject to the laws of its own origin. Society cannot ignore the relations which give paper money its acceptability without suffering evil consequences. This generation has witnessed the collapse of European paper money. The experience of modern Europe is very like that which, on a much smaller scale, came to the United States after issuing so-called fiat money during the Civil War. In the early years of the eighteenth century we find a striking example in France which shows the impossibility of supporting national finance on mere paper money. France allowed herself, under the leadership of the Scotch financier, John Law, to imagine that she could develop to her own great financial advantage the unexplored territory of Louisiana. On the basis of the most extravagant hopes, a feverish period of economic activity was ushered in. Paris bought shares in the company which Law formed and the national bank issued nearly three billion livres of paper money. Shortly, public confidence began to waver and a run on the bank led to a complete collapse of the whole scheme. The government found it necessary to cancel most of the paper which was in circulation.

All these examples show that paper money is a social institution which must be safeguarded and must be supported by real values or it will not contribute to exchange. What happens when confidence in paper disappears can be described by saying that men assume toward the paper an attitude of dissatisfaction and this is aroused every time it is put into their hands. Their coöperation is interrupted rather than promoted by offering them paper money. The social scheme which the paper is intended to promote thus fails to establish itself.

Sometimes confidence breaks down on wholly inadequate grounds. An unjustified run on a bank is a blind mob act.

Because one man loses confidence, a whole group follows his example. There is a high emotional tension on such occasions and the excitement sweeps away the earlier attitude of trust. Introspectively, the lack of confidence which develops in such a case is not a clear-cut matter of ideation and yet the effect of the falling away of confidence is such as to bring men to the point where they begin to assert vigorously individual demands for recognition and for protection against what they feel to be an unsafe social power.

Conversely, if under conditions of doubt everyone who is doubtful succeeds in getting coin for the paper money and in turn gets commodities for his coin, confidence will be restored. If confidence is thus supported by various trials, it will come to be so thoroughly reëstablished that the number of questions raised about the system will be fewer and fewer and the grounds of skepticism will have to be very much stronger before anyone will again raise any question.

What has been said with regard to paper money could be repeated with regard to the more elaborate instruments of credit and exchange. When one gives a bill of exchange or a note that looks into the future and is a substitute for all forms of currency, one is exhibiting a type of imagination which is incomparably broader in scope than anything which is required to establish confidence in a system of paper money or coinage. Here convenience is still further emphasized. Not only is a note of credit a simple way of expressing elaborate transactions, but it is also convenient because it makes possible long periods of readjustment.

The psychology of credit is worthy of a great deal of study and comment in order to warn against certain very common fallacies. We find municipalities very ready to make public improvements on a credit basis. The selling of public bonds for the erection of public buildings in this generation will undoubtedly impose serious problems on the next generation. Most of the recklessness exhibited in the use of credit is due to a lack of sufficiently broad imagination to see the consequences of indulging in this particular type of expansion. The history of business concerns is full of examples of lack of clear vision of the future and lack of comprehension of the difficulties which lie in the path of the consummation of arrangements which have been projected in the form of credit loans. In spite of hazards such as these, society finds this form of business adjustment so necessary for the large transactions now common that the system has been developed on a huge scale and is one of the most characteristic features of our modern industrial organization.

Up to this point, this chapter has been concerned chiefly with the processes by which the modern commercial system has been produced. There is a wholly different side of the matter which was referred to briefly in an earlier paragraph and is part of the general psychology of civilization. Money when once it has been brought into being reacts upon human life and very powerfully influences behavior and thought.

A striking individual example of the influence of money as an agency in determining conduct can be seen if one thinks of the life and occupation of a banker. During his working hours the banker devotes himself entirely to recording and distributing credits and handling the tangible symbols of credit. For this service, society is willing to pay, and it thinks of the banker's calling as thoroughly commendable and as no less necessary to the life of the social group than are the callings of those who produce food and shelter. The banker is one of a number of persons whom the monetary system of society has taken away from what may be called direct methods of earning a living and has assigned to a purely abstract occupation.

Besides specializing individuals in their occupations, money affects the lives of every member of civilized society.

We think in terms of this standard of comparison. We estimate success and failure in quantitative terms by referring a man's achievements to this system of measurement. When we find that we cannot secure enough money to satisfy our expectations, we suffer depression. In short, we, who live under a system of civilized society, think more often about money than we do about food and the articles which contribute directly to comfort. We live in a world where ideas and symbols of ideas are more important centers of attention than are objects.

It is very proper to say, in the light of these statements, that man has created for himself a new environment. He has subjected himself to new and powerful influences which were first the creatures of his own efforts but have now become the guides of his behavior. Especially is it true of the individual that he is dominated by the social system. The individual is so inferior in his power to the social institution that he usually thinks of money and credit as something wholly impersonal and even unpsychological in character.

It is the purpose of this book to correct the popular view about social institutions and to point out that the environment which man has made for himself in civilization is a psychological product. It is also the purpose of these chapters to show that the psychological products of social coöperation make men into superior beings by their reflex effect upon thought and conduct. The adaptations of civilization are not instinctive reactions but higher forms of conduct which transcend animal behavior to such an extent that the use of biological terms in the description of human evolution is likely to mislead rather than clarify thinking regarding the methods of this evolution. It is only through an understanding of the way in which human ideas have been recorded in institutions that one can arrive at a true conception of the method and character of human life.

CHAPTER IV

SOCIAL INSTITUTIONS AND THE INDIVIDUAL

Before going further with the study of particular illustrations of the way in which men have used their intelligence to reconstruct the environment, it will be well to consider the psychological effects produced in the individual by social institutions. A member of civilized society ordinarily finds himself so much in accord with the institutions which surround him that he does not see that there is any need of an explanation of the agreement between his modes of behavior and the demands of the social group of which he is a part. Thus, in terms of the discussion of the last chapter, the ordinary man sees nothing to explain in his desire for money. To him this is quite as insistent a personal trait as the desire for food and comfort. In his present consciousness the ambition for wealth seems natural and immediate. To the student of human nature, who notes the gradual evolution of the economic system and observes that animals and even primitive man are destitute of the idea of standardized commerce, it is evident that the present attitude of a civilized human being toward money demands an explanation.

The same conclusion is arrived at if one studies the development of the child. The infant begins life wholly innocent of any disposition to carry on financial transactions. It is not until much experience has been accumulated under the careful guidance of his elders that the developing individual arrives at the point where he assumes the common attitude toward money.

Such considerations as the foregoing ought to convince anyone that he cannot rely upon introspection for an explanation of his traits. What seems natural and spontaneous in mature consciousness may be the product of influences which are not at all native to the individual. We must be prepared here, as in the natural sciences, to set aside observed facts and accept explanations which seem at first to contradict the testimony of our senses. To the observer the earth looks flat ; it required long generations of experience to set aside this observation in favor of the truth. In like fashion, introspection seems to prove that language and money and tools are natural outgrowths of individual endowments. It is the duty of science to go beyond introspection and to set up a system of explanations which will make clear the true nature of institutional control over men's minds and lives.

By way of further support of the general contention that many habits are not the products of traits born in the individual, let us consider one of the ordinary customs of social life, that of conventional salutation. The roots of our present custom are to be found in animal behavior. The dog which encounters a friend of its own race or of the human kind gives expression in obvious and well-known ways to the satisfaction which it experiences. In like fashion an enemy is greeted with unmistakable signs of resentment. Animal salutations of the kind here under consideration may be described as the spontaneous natural responses of an individual to whatever he encounters. The explanation of these natural responses is to be found in a study of the animal and its organism. The dog wags its tail or growls because its nervous system is such that various types of stimulation issue naturally in the one or the other of these forms of reaction.

When we come to human life, we find at the outset the

same types of natural reaction which were exhibited by
the animal. The savage wandering through the forest
hears someone approaching; instantly his excited nervous
system responds with the reaction of defensive preparation.
If the experience which comes to the excited observer when he
secures a complete view of the approaching figure is such as
to intensify the defensive reaction, the savage may attack
his enemy, or he may run away. We are still dealing with
forms of behavior which are natural. If, on the other hand,
it turns out that a friend rather than an enemy approaches,
the initial attitude of caution will give way to a relaxation
of the defensive tension and to a more or less vigorous
expression of the gratification which is felt in finding an
acceptable companion.

The natural form of this second attitude, or attitude of
friendly salutation, is by no means as clearly dictated by the
individual's nature as is the attitude of defense. How
does one express satisfaction? Let us return for a moment
to our example of the dog. The dog, pleased to find someone
whom it likes, may jump on its friend and bark vociferously,
or it may crouch down on the ground, showing an utter
collapse of the strained attitude of attack which was exhibited during the preceding period of preparation for
defense. Friendliness is thus a kind of general and undefined excitement. Not only so, but it may be at times
wholly inconvenient to the recipient. One does not need to
go to animal life for illustrations of this fact.

Because of the undefined character of the attitude of
friendliness, the social group begins to impose its conveniences
and preferences on all of its members. At first the convenience of the most powerful member of the group was the
determining factor. Obeisance is the form of salutation
demanded in primitive tribes by the dominant members.
Obeisance on the part of the less powerful members of the

group has a variety of justifications. It shows that the bowing or prostrate figure is not intending to make an unfriendly attack. It opens a safe path for the strong. At the same time it cultivates in the saluting individual a fixed attitude of nonresistance and thus makes for a permanent recognition of the superior rank of the individual saluted.

Obeisance is natural in its origins but not in its ultimate forms. It passes very early into a social requirement. Let an inferior presume to express his delight at seeing his master in a way which is overeffusive, and the group will exercise its power to put the offender back in his place or to eliminate him summarily from further possibility of breach of group convention. On the other hand, let an inferior refuse to accord to a superior the kind of salutation which has become common, and there results a new kind of enmity, the enmity which comes from disappointed expectation.

The fact which is described by the term "expectation" is at once a product of group life and a dominant fact within the individual. Once an expectation has been created it becomes a guide to conduct. The breach of an expectation gives just as acute distress as a physical pain. In this sense expectation is a new form of reality capable of being described and demanding respect on the part of all members of the group.

Expectations of various types appear in human consciousness as a result of experiences. William James, in an article written after he had experienced an earthquake, describes vividly the terror which comes into the human mind when the solid earth, the earth which has always been the most substantial and immovable fact in one's experience, begins to break down all expectations and quake under one's feet. The resulting fear is not mere anxiety lest harm shall come to one; it is a fundamental terror which comes from a disturbance of one of the most completely established expectations in life.

Expectation may be described as the conscious counterpart of a habit. Putting the matter in terms of the neural conditions of mental life, we may say that when the nervous system of a human being has acted several times in a certain way the tendency to repeat the same kind of action becomes established. The established tendency may be due to a purely individual act or to a response which was set up through social coöperation. The final result will not show whether the cause of the expectation was the one or the other.

It is to be noted that there is no requirement in the establishment of a social expectation that the persons who participate in creating it be aware of what they are doing. They do not start out with the idea that the weak ought to be taught to bow down to the strong. They merely go forward along the lines dictated by their individual natures and group convenience. As soon as they have arrived at a settled mode of behavior, they have evolved a new fact, an expectation. The strong expect to receive obeisance and the weak expect to give it. A form of psychological compulsion is thus set up. If for any reason a single individual in the group exhibits a lapse of behavior and does not meet the expectation of those about him, the group will be so insistent that on the next occasion the recalcitrant or neglectful individual will be stimulated not only by the expectation which arises in his own mind but by a very pointed recollection of the punishment which his fellows inflicted when he did not conform to the general expectation.

The psychology of civilization not only has to interest itself in such initial stages of social convention as have been sketched but also has to concern itself with the later evolution of conventions. Thus the customs of salutation have been differentiated in the course of human evolution. There is one type of salutation which is appropriate for members of the same family, another for members of the same social class, another for those whom one knows only casually, another for highly ceremonial occasions. This differentiation of salutations results ultimately in a very complex code of expectations. The code differs with nationalities. The newcomer, especially if he wishes to conciliate the group to which he comes, must be careful to adopt and follow the code which obtains among those to whom he is to be introduced. A modern diplomat, for example, who goes from the United States to some country where modes of salutation are different from those which he has learned in our somewhat informal social order, has to be carefully instructed lest he should shock the expectations of the nation which he seeks to influence.

The code of salutation ultimately becomes complicated with social conventions which on the surface are very far removed from personal greetings. Note the different ways in which we greet, even in a highly democratic society like that of the United States, persons of different appearances. One speaks to a man dressed in working clothes with a degree of freedom and informality which would not be regarded as permissible in the presence of a man dressed for an afternoon reception. One speaks to a child when one would not venture to speak to the parents. The position of woman is very different from that of man in the matter of priority in salutation and all that it implies. In each of these cases we see that salutation is not a separate convention; it is part of the general social scheme.

The illustration has perhaps been carried far enough to make the point. Social groups produce by their interaction modifications of individual behavior. These we call conventions. The convention is recorded in the individual as an expectation and as a habit of personal conduct. It should not be overlooked that expectation while it is related to behavior is not synonymous with individual habit. The superior expects a certain type of salutation from the inferior, but the superior does not himself cultivate as a personal habit the mode of salutation which he expects. Habit and expectation issue in highly elaborated systems of behavior and in complex codes of conduct to which the group not only gives its sanction, but on which it is prepared to insist with adequate power to enforce its demands.

The example which has been discussed up to this point may be reënforced by another which will more fully illustrate the extent to which the social group is prepared to enforce its expectations. At the present stage of social development, a citizen of the United States must pass on the right anyone whom he meets on the highway. This is written in the ordinances of cities and in the laws of states and is upheld by the courts. An offender against this law will be made to suffer material and personal penalties and will have heaped on him violent reproof. Of course it is evident at once that there is nothing natural about turning to the right. In some parts of the world, society defends with equal vigor the rule that one shall pass on the left. Also it is evident that the present practice is the outgrowth of a long evolution and not one which arose spontaneously in the minds of all men and commanded at once their approval and their willingness to bring to its defense the power of the group. The enactment of ordinances and laws with regard to passing must be thought of as a very late act of the group, following after a long period the establishment of the habit which is formally sanctioned by the legal enactment.

Here, as in the case of salutations, convention grew out of social contacts. Two men who met on a narrow path such as a mountain trail had to devise some way of sharing the road. The man of superior rank, which at first meant the man of superior strength, pushed the weaker man aside.

When two men of equal rank met, they sometimes decided who should have the path by trial of strength. In either case, the tendency was ultimately developed for the weak to defer to the strong. The psychology of the situation is obvious. Indeed, all that we describe by such terms as "prestige" and "rank" is in the making when men meet on a narrow path, not because the path in itself conveys the idea of prestige but because the social situation creates a certain type of expectation and a consequent effort to meet this expectation.

As roads multiplied and social situations of the kind under discussion became increasingly frequent, the necessity of arriving at a form of expectation that could be more readily and safely acted upon led to the device of passing regularly in a fixed way. The growth of democratic ideas operated also to equalize the demands on all who use the road. The tendency to defer to rank has not entirely given way even under modern conditions; the city street is closed to ordinary traffic to make way for a procession or for some highly honored individual. In the main, however, social convenience has reached the point where it dictates that an equal and clearly defined share of the road shall be given to each traveler.

If one notes one's own reactions in such a situation as that under discussion, one finds that the social drill results in a tendency to turn to the right even when no immediate social necessity is present. If a driver of an automobile finds that he must turn out of the road to avoid some physical obstacle, he will turn to the right by preference, because his training has fixed in him that one of the two equally easy directions of action. The tendency to carry out this acquired habit is so strong that if by any chance one is prevented from doing what one has been trained to do, one is often aroused to anger and gives vent to vigorous demands that convention be respected. An individual drilled to obey a convention thus becomes one of the strongest possible agencies for the enforcement of the convention. Society enforces its decisions by first compelling the individual to conform and afterwards supporting the individual in demanding that others also shall conform.

Besides being recorded in individual habits, social conventions are in some cases made matters of explicit formulation. Such is the case where laws grow out of conventions. We shall pass over for the present the fact that society has found it necessary to set up lawmaking bodies as special agencies for the formulation of its pronouncements. It is enough for our present purpose to point out that a law is an explicit demand that individual habits shall be developed in compliance with the expectations of the members of the group. All goes well when the law and the habits of individuals can be made to move in the same direction. Even where disagreements between individual habits and law are sporadic, society gets on fairly well. Sometimes it requires time to translate law into individual modes of behavior. This is especially true when an immature individual is suddenly injected into a highly organized social group. There then arises a necessity with which we are all familiar, the necessity of an initiation of the individual into the practices of society.

The word "expectation," which our examples have emphasized, designates a trait in the individual which is not instinctive or natural but derived as a result of contact with social institutions. Take, for example, the young member of a semicivilized tribe who observes his elders making a weapon or using the weapon in the capture of food. The observation does not leave the youthful mind unmodified. Still more is it true that the consciousness of the learner is changed if a tool comes into his hands. However clumsy he may have been the first time he used the tool, he will never forget the experience which filled his vision and gave him a new sense of power.   The use of a tool is a transforming experience; it creates a desire to use the tool again.   It makes the user into a being with a new kind of expectation.

Every social institution becomes in this way not merely the embodiment of an idea or tendency which brought it into being, but a force influencing the consciousness and behavior of all who come into contact with it.

The individual must have the capacity for developing expectations and modifications of his own conduct, but the particular modes of behavior which he takes on are not determined by his natural tendencies; they are determined by the demands and example of society.

Perhaps this doctrine can be more impressively expounded by referring to the neural facts which are involved.   It is a well-known fact that the nervous systems of the lower animals are from the beginning of individual life largely mapped out in paths and combinations of paths which express the adaptations of the ancestors of the individual.   There is very little of the tissue of an animal's nervous system which is left to be mapped out in the course of individual experience.

In contrast with the animals, man possesses a vast area in the cerebrum which is not determined by inheritance. The cerebrum has evolved in the course of animal history as a center for new adaptations.   It may be called the organ of individual variation, the organ of acquired responses.

Given an organism such as the human being is, with a major part of its reacting mechanism undetermined by inheritance — the importance of those influences which determine education at once becomes obvious.   It is the compelling demands of social life which are largely responsible for human education.   The instruments which society employs in expressing and enforcing these demands are

institutions. Institutions become through long ages of
evolution so influential in controlling the conduct of groups
and individuals that they have been termed social inheritances. They are traceable to the experiences and efforts of
past generations, but the way in which they influence individual life is wholly different from the way in which
animal adaptations have been transmitted through structural inheritance.

The psychology of social institutions thus arrives at a
formula of evolution which is wholly different from that
which biology supplies in its explanation of animal instincts.
An instinct is a mode of behavior which is transmitted
through structural inheritance. For example, all of the
higher animals are supplied with muscles which are active
in the swallowing of food. The muscles of the swallowing
mechanism are inherited. In like fashion the nerve fibers
and nerve centers necessary to set these muscles in action
are inherited. Swallowing is an instinct.

If one contrasts with the description given of this instinct
the account which was given of the slow and elaborate
evolution of tools and the monetary system, one realizes
instantly that human commerce and the technical arts are
not instincts. They are institutions achieved by coöperative effort and influential in determining the thinking and
conduct of every child who is brought into contact with
them, but the manner of their control is wholly different
from that which is provided in inherited instincts.

The formula of evolution which is supplied by the psychology of social institutions clears up much of the ambiguity
which has dominated social psychology up to this time.
Writers on social psychology who have not introduced into
their systems of thought the link which social institutions
supply have often felt somewhat vaguely the necessity of
something other than that which biology or purely individual

psychology can supply. For example, Professor Ross,[1] one of the pioneers in the field of social psychology, used the concept of "suggestion" to explain the special mode of human evolution which results from social coöperation. "Suggestion" is a term used by hypnotists to describe the control which they exercise over their subjects who are in an abnormal trance. Professor Ross holds that we, as social beings, accept suggestions regarding modes of dress, that we accept suggestions when we adopt religious beliefs, that we are dominated in our political attitudes by suggestion. Everywhere the individual is guided by a kind of mysterious force which is at once the master of individual action and the least understood psychological influence in the world. Professor Ross draws all of the examples in the first half of his book from behavior which is half abnormal or wholly so. The Children's Crusade, the stigma put by the élite on common toil, the dancing mania of religious fanatics, American dollarocracy, the fatalistic attitude of common people, are typical examples for Professor Ross of the kind of control over the individual which is exercised through social suggestion.

The French sociologists have written in the same general vein. The mob is for Le Bon[2] the typical social group. Tarde[3] uses the term "imitation" in much the same way that Ross uses his favorite concept of suggestion.

The result of the adoption of these mysterious and half-explained forces as the fundamentals of social theory is that writers on these subjects are likely to be impressed by pathological rather than normal manifestations of human mental life. Much current writing in sociology revels in sex psychology and explains governments as aggregations

[1] Ross, Edward Alsworth — *Social Psychology;* Macmillan Co., 1908.
[2] Le Bon, Gustave — *The Crowd;* London, 1903.
[3] Tarde, G. — *The Laws of Imitation.* Translated by Parsons. Henry Holt & Co., 1903.

of intrigue and family life as of the same type as life in an ant hill. Primitive nations are exhibited as the purest expressions of uncomplicated and undiluted group solidarity.

It is not difficult to understand the reason why theorists have been overwhelmed by the mysterious when we note that the psychology which has been supplied as a basis of all the social sciences is individual psychology. When a person views the world of social influences from his personal point of view, there is something dominating and overwhelming and utterly inexplicable in social control. The individual finds himself conforming to customs and practices which he does not seem to have originated. In the circle of his introspective experience, social demands break in with a force that he cannot resist. The result of all this is that the individual, finding no fact in his own mind which corresponds directly to group will and group feeling, begins to compare social forces to those disrupting psychological forces which in cases of abnormality break down the continuity of mental life and seem to baffle explanation.

If we would genuinely understand group consciousness and its relation to individual experience, we must have something broader than this individual psychology. We must get outside of our personal introspective experiences and look for realities which are just as concrete as our own visual impressions and muscular expressions, but so different in character from these facts of individual life that we must construct a wholly new type of psychology in order to give them adequate treatment.

The point of view which is necessary in order to supply a psychology of the group has been illustrated in the two chapters immediately preceding this. It was shown in the chapter on tool consciousness that the group has by a succession of steps gradually invented tools and in this way brought into the world certain technological creations which in turn have reacted on men's minds so as to change human modes of life and modes of thought in the most radical fashion. It was shown in the chapter immediately preceding this that the social group has built up in its system of exchange a new world of interaction between individuals. In this latter case the group has gone so far as to devise in money an instrument for the facilitation and standardization of commercial intercourse, which instrument is one of the most elaborate and abstract creations of human coöperation.

The effects produced on the individual by his social contacts are not superficial or trivial. They are genuine transformations of his thinking and conduct. In an interesting article in the *Psychological Review* of 1896, Professor Dewey has described what he calls the patterns of consciousness which arise from various industrial specialties. What he has to say is worth quoting at length as reënforcement of the argument which has been presented in this chapter and in the earlier discussions of the industrial and commercial systems.

He writes as follows:

We must recognize that mind has a pattern, a scheme of arrangement in its constituent elements, and that it is the business of a serious comparative psychology to exhibit these patterns, forms, or types in detail. . . . . If we search in any social group for the special functions to which mind is thus relative, occupations at once suggest themselves. Occupations determine the fundamental modes of activity, and hence control the formation and use of habits. These habits, in turn, are something more than practical and overt. "Apperceptive masses" and associational tracts of necessity conform to the dominant activities. The occupations determine the chief modes of satisfaction, the standards of success and failure. Hence they furnish the working classifications and definitions of value; they control the desire processes. Moreover, they decide the sets of objects and relations that are important, and thereby provide the content or material of attention, and the qualities that are interestingly significant. The directions given to mental life thereby extend to emotional and intellectual characteristics. So fundamental and pervasive is the group of occupational activities that it affords the scheme or pattern of the structural organization of mental traits. Occupations integrate special elements into a functioning whole.

Because the hunting life differs from, say, the agricultural, in the sort of satisfactions and ends it furnishes, in the objects to which it requires attention, in the problems it sets for reflection and deliberation, as well as in the psychophysic coördinations it stimulates and selects, we may well speak, and without metaphor, of the hunting psychosis or mental type. And so of the pastoral, the military, the trading, the manually productive (or manufacturing) occupations, and so on. As a specific illustration of the standpoint and method, I shall take the hunting vocation, and that as carried on by the Australian aborigines. I shall try first to describe its chief distinguishing marks; and then to show how the mental pattern developed is carried over into various activities, customs and products, which on their face have nothing to do with the hunting life. If a controlling influence of this sort can be made out — if it can be shown that art, war, marriage, etc., tend to be psychologically assimilated to the pattern developed in the hunting vocation, we shall thereby get an important method for the interpretation of social institutions and cultural resources — a psychological method for sociology.[1]

Another line of argument which reënforces the position taken throughout this chapter is supplied by Herbert Spencer. He points out that primitive man had a very limited range of experience in space and time, while civilized man has been able to extend his contacts and his ideas so as to cover vast stretches of space and time and to measure these with precision. Referring to the extension of space experience, he says:

[1] DEWEY, JOHN — "Interpretation of Savage Mind," *Psychological Review*, IX (1896), 217–230.

From early races acquainted only with neighbouring localities, up to modern geographers who specify the latitude and longitude of every place on the globe — from the ancient builders and metallurgists, knowing but surface-deposits, up to the geologists of our day whose data in some cases enable them to describe the material existing at a depth never yet reached by the miner — from the savage barely able to say in how many days a full moon will return, up to the astronomer who ascertains the period of revolution of a double star — there has been a gradual widening of the surrounding region throughout which the adjustment of inner to outer relations extends.[1]

The significance for our discussion of a series of facts such as these is that the individual has been changed in his breadth of interest and in his modes of thinking by the evolutions which have gone forward in the course of human history. It is not true that the modern astronomer is merely an animal or even an isolated human individual gazing into celestial space. The scientist has in his possession facts and insights and methods of thinking which the race has discovered and invented and he can extend and organize his experience in a way which is wholly impossible at the lower levels of life. Especially is there a sharp contrast between human interests and the interests and modes of consciousness of animals. Spencer, in pointing out this contrast with respect to the recognition of time, writes as follows:

Save in respect to rapid mechanical changes, no correspondences of this order are shown by the lower classes of creatures; and, lacking as they do the ability to estimate time, even the higher mammals supply but few and imperfect examples of it. The lion that goes to the river-side at dusk to lie in wait for creatures coming to drink, and the house-dog standing outside the door in expectation that some one will presently open it, may be cited as ap-

[1] SPENCER, HERBERT — *Principles of Psychology*, pp. 318–319; London, Williams and Norgate, 1890.

proximative instances. But only when we come to the human race are correspondences of this degree of specialty exhibited with distinctness and frequency. In preparing his weapons against the approaching immigration of certain birds, in putting aside to dry the skins which he preserves for clothing, in making the fire by which to cook his food, the savage adapts his conduct to the special changes undergone by special bodies during definite intervals.[1]

There is in all this extension and systematization of personal experience nothing that needs to be hidden behind such vague words as "suggestion" or "imitation." The fact is that civilization has not merely accumulated inventions and new modes of adaptation to the world; it has also spent much of its energy in devising methods of giving individuals a broader experience and a broader view. The social system, by its methods of transportation, by its science of geography, and by its incentives for exploration, has supplied the individual with experiences which he could never have collected through his own restricted efforts. Through social coöperation the individual has become part of a social whole; he has become in a very important sense of the term, society in miniature. Not only so, but because the individual becomes an embodiment of social modes of behavior and an exponent of social institutions, he serves as a powerful agency for the preservation and propagation of society's practices. The socialized individual is intolerant of provincialism and narrowness because the enlargement of his experiences of time and space leads him to seek the same extension of view for all with whom he is brought into contact.

The transformation which is wrought in individual human nature by the institutions of society is largely overlooked by those who attempt to find in instincts the sources of

<hr>

[1] SPENCER, HERBERT — *op. cit.*, pp. 338–339.

civilized modes of life. McDougall was the originator of a tendency in social psychology to derive society from individual instincts.[1] The degree of his absorption in instincts is shown by reference to the index of his *Introduction to Social Psychology* where one finds fourteen lines devoted to instincts and absolutely no mention of tools or money or those more elaborate institutions such as language and the fine arts to which we shall come in later chapters.

A social psychology which is absorbed in a description of instincts is nothing but a transformed biology, oblivious of the fact that the human group has acquired a new mode of adaptation as much higher than instinct as instinct is higher than mechanical friction. Even from the point of view of a strictly individual psychology it is futile to attempt to catalogue human traits in terms of instinct. Language is not an instinct. The skill exhibited in using a bow and arrow is not instinctive. The natural instinctive adjustments have to be greatly transcended when one rides a bicycle or drives an automobile. There is no instinct which explains the professional behavior of a banker.

Individual life has become a series of acquired adaptations to social realities. Human conduct in civilized society cannot be explained by physical inheritance or biological adjustments because it has taken on the forms dictated by coöperative intelligence. Social demands are new facts in the world; before their appearance the world was wholly different from that which confronts the individual living in modern civilization. Psychology will never give an adequate account of mental processes until it gives full regard to these facts.

Perhaps it will be well to give these comments point by direct reference to McDougall's position in his recent book.

[1] McDougall, William — *An Introduction to Social Psychology;* Methuen & Co., 1909.

He devotes a chapter in this book to the discussion of the views of various writers, and ends by subscribing to the following passage from Mr. E. Barker's book, *Political Thought in England from Herbert Spencer to the Present Day*, as the most satisfactory definition of group mind:

" All the institutions of a country, so far as they are effective, are not only products of thought and creations of mind: they *are* thought, and they *are* mind.   Otherwise we have a building without a tenant, and a body without a mind.   An Oxford college is not a group of buildings, though common speech gives that name to such a group: it is a group of men.   But it is not a group of men in the sense of a group of bodies in propinquity: it is a group of men in the sense of a group of minds.   That group of minds, in virtue of the common substance of an uniting idea, is itself a group-mind.   There is no group-mind existing apart from the minds of the members of the group; the group-mind only exists in the minds of its members.   But nevertheless, it exists.   There is a college mind, just as there is a Trade Union mind, or even a 'public mind' of the whole community; and we are all conscious of such a mind as something that exists in and along with the separate minds of the members, and over and above any sum of those minds created by mere addition." [1]

McDougall then goes on in a series of chapters to illustrate the lower and higher forms of group mind.   The mob is a lower form, the army is a higher and consciously organized group, and the nation is one of the highest forms of organized society — especially such a nation as England.

The difficulty with such discussions is that they leave the reader grasping at a vague abstraction.   The group mind is something, somewhere.   It gives out something to the individual from time to time, and it has a kind of permanence which makes it respectable if it is English in its traits

[1] McDOUGALL, WILLIAM — *The Group Mind*, pp. 25-26;   G. P. Putnam's Sons, 1920.

and hardly so respectable if it inherits its characteristics from a less noble stock.

The purpose of this critique and of the inductions of the earlier chapters in this book is to substitute the concept of social institutions for the vague ideas of a group mind. Civilization is a collection of realities; it has parts and aspects. It is dynamic and controlling. It is something to which the individual mind adapts itself and against which the individual mind can react.

The advantage of such a view is that one may be entirely complacent in leaving to the metaphysician the invention of some kind of group mind and group will. The student of science is interested in this metaphysical abstraction only when it gets into action. Group action always results in some kind of institution. The institution is not the group but it is the product of cumulative group action and the source of group influence. The psychology of civilization may therefore take as its point of departure in every discussion some concrete institution. Money is an institution. It is not enough for scientific purposes to know that human minds, working on the problem of exchanging commodities, have devised this instrument. It is highly important that we note that money, when once devised, commands the attention of every newcomer in the group. Money dominates individual behavior and in so far as it does, we are justified in saying that the group, through its institutions, exercises control over the individual. Machine industry is an institution. It has made it possible for the group to produce vast stores of goods. It holds a great majority of individuals under its power. Daily these individuals toil and sometimes they rebel under the domination of machines which are at once the products of human genius and the masters of human lives. Social institutions are real and powerful influences in the world. There is no need of any remote abstraction in explaining the effect of the group on the individual if we consider the nature and influence of these institutions.

If one is in need of a definition of a social group, one may think of it as that collection of human individuals which is capable of setting up an institution. The group has a consciousness or will just in the degree in which it can effectively launch its institutions. The institutions are as manifold as the needs of group coöperation. The only general definition that can be given of an institution is that it is a device for promoting human coöperation ; it takes material form in certain aids and instruments which have been evolved in the process of its establishment and in the process of its transmission.

These definitions are nothing but abbreviated restatements of what has been said in concrete terms in the foregoing chapters of this book. The psychology needed as a basis of all social science is the study of human institutions.

CHAPTER V

THE PSYCHOLOGY OF NUMBER

The institutions which were described in the foregoing chapters were selected for early discussion because they deal with concrete tangible objects which make it easy to see that human intelligence has produced by its coöperative effort something new in the world. We turn now to an institution which is not material and tangible, but is of the greatest influence in guiding human thought, namely, the number system. This institution with language and certain of the fine arts exhibits perhaps more fully than any other factor of civilization the way in which the mind of the group has reconstructed the world in which man lives.

In the earliest stages of human life there was no number system. There was at those stages no exact quantitative thinking. A vague general idea of quantity, such as could be gained from direct perception, was all that men possessed. The character of this original experience of quantity can be judged from the common perceptual discriminations of which we are all capable in the presence of large or small objects and complex or simple groups. We recognize at once the difference between a crowd of people and a small company made up of four or five persons.

There was little or no motive in primitive life for going beyond the direct perceptual evaluation of the objects of experience. The hunter, especially if he is alone, has no reason for defining the objects of his interest with greater exactness than his perceptions make possible. The family group is not in need of any elaborate system in order to make sure that its members are present.

The demand for something higher than perceptual discrimination comes with the development of complex experiences. As soon as man acquired many possessions or as soon as the tribe took the place of the small compact family, it became necessary to invent some method of thinking clearly about numerous objects. Man resorted to a number of experiments in his efforts to satisfy his needs. These experiments are recorded in the history of number systems.

The contrast between perception and the type of experience which is made possible by the use of number may perhaps be rendered more emphatic by reference to some of the laboratory experiments which have been performed with a view to determining the limits of perceptual discrimination. Let an observer look at a group of fifteen dots scattered in irregular order over a square inch of paper and ask him to form so clear a picture of the group in his mind that he will know the next time he sees the group whether it is changed in any way. The observer looks fixedly at the dots in the effort to carry away a detailed image. He will at once recognize the fact that he is limited in the number of dots which he can master. He will try to help his limited power of perception by arranging the dots in various patterns. Usually he adopts in this effort to arrange the dots the device of counting which he has learned from the race. He has, thanks to his training in an advanced civilization, a method of dealing with the situation. The complex series of dots would baffle him if he were obliged to depend altogether on his powers of direct recognition. We see by the tendency of the observer to resort to his ability to count what it is that makes him superior to his savage ancestors.

As men emerged from the lower stages of savagery and hunting to the higher levels of orderly tribal life they were

increasingly confronted with complex situations in which
some device had to be adopted in order to supplement direct
sense-perception. They were led, as was the subject in the
laboratory experiment, to seek some method of arranging
and systematizing experience. The nomadic herdsman,
for example, had to keep track of his flock of sheep. In
order to do this he used a simpler method than counting;
he gave heed to the individual characteristics of each member
of the flock and gave to each member a name.

We shall have occasion later when we take up the study of
language to note that a name is a device for aiding thinking
and for giving stability to discriminating consciousness.
Names are, however, particular devices. They do not fall
into a general scheme of arrangement such as the number
system supplies. Names can be used, to be sure, in helping
an observer to think of several different members of a group,
but names have to be remembered and associated with a
more or less complete recall of all the characteristics of the
individual to whom the name has been applied. Naming
is a clumsy device for keeping account of property.

The invention of a series of number names and the transition from particular designation of objects to abstract counting were long and laborious processes. This is shown by the
fact that the earliest number words are names of objects.

The Chinese name for " two " is *ny* or *eul*, both of which
mean *ears*. The early user of these words evidently had in
mind some such analogy as would be expressed by the sentence
"I have as many of these as a man has ears." The mental
comparison is between two mental pictures, both of which
are concrete and both of which have in them much detail.

Other examples of the same type are supplied by Gow in
the following paragraph :

Two is in Thibet *paksha* "wing" : in Hottentot *t'Koam* "hand" :
and so also among the Javanese, Samoyeds, Sioux and other

peoples. So again with the Abipones, " four " is *geyenknate*, " os-trich-toes " : " five " is *neenhalek*, " a hide spotted with five colors " : with the Marquesans " four " is *pona*, " a bunch of four fruits," etc.[1]

The intimate relation between direct perception and the earliest names of numbers is further attested by the fact that primitive peoples have a very limited number vocabulary. They can carry enumeration only so far as their perceptual powers make it possible for them to make direct, concrete comparisons between the sizes of groups. The limitations of early number systems are clearly set forth in the following quotation :

In certain parts of the world, notably among the native races of South America, Australia, and many of the islands of Polynesia and Melanesia, a surprising paucity of numeral words has been observed. The Encabellada of the Rio Napo have but two dis-tinct numerals ; *tey*, 1, and *cayapa*, 2. The Chaco languages of the Guaycuru stock are also notably poor in this respect. In the Mbocobi dialect of this language, the only native numerals are : *yña tvak*, 1, and *yñoaca*, 2. The Puris count *omi*, 1, *curiri*, 2, *prica*, many ; and the Botocudos, *mokenam*, 1, *uruhu*, many. The Fuegans, supposed to have been able at one time to count to 10, have but three numerals — *kaoueli*, 1, *compaipi*, 2, *maten*, 3. The Campas of Peru possess only three separate words for the expression of number, — *patrio*, 1, *pitteni*, 2, *mahuani*, 3. Above 3 they proceed by combinations, as 1 and 3 for 4, 1 and 1 and 3 for 5. Counting above 10 is, however, entirely inconceivable to them, and any number beyond that limit they indicate by *tohaine*, many. The Conibos, of the same region, had, before their contact with the Spanish, only *atchoupre*, 1, and *rrabui*, 2 ; though they made some slight progress above 2 by means of reduplication. The Orejones, one of the low, degraded tribes of the Upper Amazon, have no names for number except *nayhay*, 1, *necacome*, 2, *feni-nichacome*, 3, *ononocomere*, 4.   In the extensive vocabularies

[1] Gow, JAMES — *A Short History of Greek Mathematics*, pp. 6–7 ; The Cambridge University Press, 1884.

given by Von Martins, many similar examples are found. For the Bororos he gives only *couai*, 1, *macouai*, 2, *ouai*, 3. The last word, with the proper finger pantomime, serves also for any higher number which falls within the grasp of their comprehension. The Guachi manage to reach 5, but their numeration is of the rudest kind, as the following scale shows: *tamak*, 1, *eu-echo*, 2, *eu-echo-kailau*, 3, *eu-echo-way*, 4, *localau*, 5. The Carajas counted by a scale equally rude, and their conception of number seemed equally vague, until contact with the neighboring tribes furnished them with the means of going beyond their original limit. Their scale shows clearly the uncertain, feeble number sense which is so marked in the interior of South America. It contains *wadewo*, 1, *wadebothoa*, 2, *wadeboaheado*, 3, *wadebojeodo*, 4, *wadewajouclay*, 5, *wadewasori*, 6, or many.[1]

Several investigators have pointed out that the presence or absence of number names is not always safe ground on which to judge the extent to which savages have developed number ideas. Some tribes use gestures as substitutes for words and by this means are able to indicate numbers far above the point reached by their spoken vocabularies. However, even after full weight is given to such considerations, it remains quite certain that the range of number ideas is very limited among all savage tribes.

The superficial inference which is sometimes drawn from such facts as the foregoing is that the savage mind is in some sense of less fine a quality than is the civilized mind. The general evidence does not support this conclusion. The savage turns his attention to matters other than those which commonly attract the civilized man. What the savage lacks is an instrument for carrying on quantitative thinking. The savage has a sufficiently good mind, but he is not equipped with a number system and as an individual he is not able to

[1] CONANT, LEVI LEONARD — *The Number Concept*, pp. 22–23; The Macmillan Company, 1896.

invent such a system. If someone brought him such a
system he would adopt it as indeed he has done again and
again in the history of the world. His relation to number is
exactly the same as his relation to technical tool-making and
exchange. He has not yet discovered them. He lives at
the level of immediate action and direct adaptation to his
environment. Little by little men living in coöperative
groups will invent and discover indirect modes of dealing
with their environment, and as a result of the invention of a
new method of dealing with objects every individual's mode
of thinking and mode of living will be transformed. What is
necessary is coöperative effort and time for the accumulation of the institutional capital in the form of a number
system.

The laboriousness of the process by which man has evolved
his number systems is described by Conant in the following
paragraphs :

By the slow, and often painful, process incident to the extension
and development of any mental conception in a mind wholly unused
to abstractions, the savage gropes his way onward in his counting
from 1, or more probably from 2, to the various higher numbers required to form his scale. The perception of unity offers no difficulty
to his mind, though he is conscious at first of the object itself rather
than of any idea of number associated with it. The concept of
duality, also, is grasped with perfect readiness. This concept is,
in its simplest form, presented to the mind as soon as the individual distinguishes himself from another person, though the idea
is still essentially concrete. Perhaps the first glimmering of any
real number thought in connection with 2 comes when the savage
contrasts one single object with another — or, in other words,
when he first recognizes the *pair*. At first the individuals com-
posing the pair are simply " this one " and " that one," or " this and
that " ; and his number system now halts for a time at the stage
when he can, rudely enough it may be, count 1, 2, many. There
are certain cases where the forms of 1 and 2 are so similar that one

may readily imagine that these numbers really were "this" and "that" in the savage's original conception of them; and the same likeness occurs in the words for 3 and 4, which may readily enough have been a second "this" and a second "that." In Lushu tongue the words for 1 and 2 are *tizi* and *tazi* respectively. In Koriak we find *ngroka*, 3, and *ngraka*, 4; in Kolyma, *niyokh*, 3, and *niyakh*, 4; and in Kamtschatkan, *tsuk*, 3, and *tsaak*, 4. Sometimes, as in the case of the Australian races, the entire extent of the count is carried through by means of pairs. But the natural theory one would form is, that 2 is the halting place for a very long time; that up to this point the fingers may or may not have been used — probably not; and that when the next start is made, and 3, 4, 5, and so on are counted, the fingers first come into requisition. If the grammatical structure of the earlier languages of the world's history is examined, the student is struck with the prevalence of the dual number in them — something which tends to disappear as language undergoes extended development. The dual number points unequivocally to the time when 1 and 2 were *the* numbers at mankind's disposal; to the time when his three numeral concepts, 1, 2, many, each demanded distinct expression. With increasing knowledge the necessity for this differentiation would pass away, and but two numbers, singular and plural, would remain. Incidentally it is to be noticed that the Indo-European words for 3 — *three, trois, drei, tres, tri,* etc., have the same root as the Latin *trans,* beyond, and give us a hint of the time when our Aryan ancestors counted in the manner I have just described.

The first real difficulty which the savage experiences in counting, the difficulty which comes when he attempts to pass beyond 2, and to count 3, 4, and 5, is of course but slight; and these numbers are commonly used and readily understood by almost all tribes, no matter how deeply sunk in barbarism we find them. But the instances that have already been cited must not be forgotten. The Chiquitos do not, in their primitive state, properly count at all; the Andamans, the Veddas, and many of the Australian tribes have no numerals higher than 2; others of the Australians and many of the South Americans stop with 3 or 4; and tribes which make 5 their limit are still more numerous.

Hence it is safe to assert that even this insignificant number is not always reached with perfect ease. Beyond 5 primitive man often proceeds with the greatest difficulty.[1]

The invention of a number system of wide range and universal applicability was accomplished through the use of the fingers. The fingers were concrete objects readily under the control of the person who was in need of a tally system. They are sufficiently numerous to rescue the mind from the limitations which are imposed so long as the names of small groups of perceptual objects furnished the only means of counting. They are always present and equally applicable to all kinds of situations. That the fingers were early used for purposes of counting is amply proved by the researches of the anthropologists.

Cushing gives an account of the number system of the Zuñi Indians. Their number words are as follows:

1	topinte	taken to start with.
2	kwilli	put down together with.
3	hai	the equally dividing finger.
4	awite	all the fingers all but done with.
5	opte	the notched off.[2]

This finishes the list of original simple numerals. Compounding now begins:

6	topalikya	another brought to add to the done with.
7	kwillilikya	two brought to and held up with the rest.
8	hailikye	three brought to and held up with the rest.
9	tenalikya	all but all are held up with the rest.
10	astemthila	all the fingers.
11	astem'thla	
	topayathl'tona	all the fingers and another over above held.[3]

---

[1] CONANT, LEVI LEONARD — op. cit., pp. 74–76.

[2] CUSHING, F. H. — "Manual Concepts," American Anthropologist, V (1892), 289.   [3] Ibid.

The method of compounding indicated in designating 11 is used in the succeeding numerals up to 19. Then follow such compound expressions as the following:

20	kwillik'yenastem'thlan	two times all the fingers.
100	assiastem'thlak'ya	the fingers all the fingers.
1000	assiastem'thlanak'yenastem'thla	the fingers all the fingers times all the fingers.[1]

The fact that modern number systems have 10 as their base shows that the use of the fingers came to be fairly universal in building up number series. The discovery of the possibility of clarifying thought by using the fingers was one of the great discoveries of primitive man. Gow commenting on the historical facts uncovered by a study of language writes as follows:

It has been already pointed out that in Aryan languages there is a difference in kind between the first three or four numerals and the last seven or six. The former are adjectives and are so inflected: the latter are nouns neuter in form and uninflected; interjections, as it were, thrust into the sentence in brackets, like the dates in a history-book. This difference in kind seems to point to a difference in etymology and also in antiquity. The higher numerals, being nouns, are names of things, and, being uninflected, are names of things which are not really connected with, and subject to, the same relations as the other things mentioned in the same sentence. Secondly, the general abruptness of the transition from low inflected numerals to higher uninflected forms points to some sudden stride in the art of counting. All the facts are readily explained if we conceive that among the Aryans, as among many other races, the counting of low numbers was learned before the use of the fingers suggested itself, and that so soon as the fingers were seen to be the natural *abacus*, a great advance in arithmetic was immediately made. The higher unit-numerals would then be the names of the gestures made in finger-counting, or, as among

[1] *Ibid.*

the Algonquins, etc., the actual names of the fingers in the order in which they were exhibited in counting.[1]

The use of the fingers with the accompanying word series as a means of expressing number led to the evolution of the abstract idea of a series. This idea was not present at first, the fingers being used in the beginning without reference to their full serial possibility. Thus Schmidl cites a number of instances in which the fingers are used by African tribes in counting but not in such a fashion as to indicate the presence of the full serial idea.[2] For example, when the Kinga and Nyaturn tribes want to express 5, they close the fist and place the thumb between the middle finger and the ring finger, in this way making a combination of $2 + 1 + 2$. They evidently can carry in mind the collection of small units represented by the five fingers, but it does not occur to them to spread out the hand and note all five fingers at once. Schmidl reports also an observation made by Dennet on the natives of the French Kongo. When they count up to 5, they do so by tracing on the ground a series of tallies; the first is made by the index finger, the second by the middle finger. When the middle finger is making its stroke, the index finger repeats the first tally by tracing it again. The third and fourth tallies are traced by the index finger or by a repetition of the method employed in tallying 1 and 2. The fifth stroke is a cross stroke binding together the two groups of 2.

These examples show that the idea of a full series of 5 does not arise from the mere existence of five fingers on one hand. The notion of a series of 5 has to be evolved by much practice with shorter series.

[1] Gow, James — op. cit., pp. 9–10.
[2] Schmidl, Marianne — Zahl und Zählen in Afrika, pp. 163–209; Mittheilungen der Anthroplogischen Gesellschaft in Wien, 1915.

As soon as the notion of a series emerges there are opened up endless possibilities of expression. The evolution then turns in the direction of a refinement of the series idea. Here early races added to the manual series more or less elaborate systems of tallykeeping. Several examples may be borrowed from the history of mathematics.

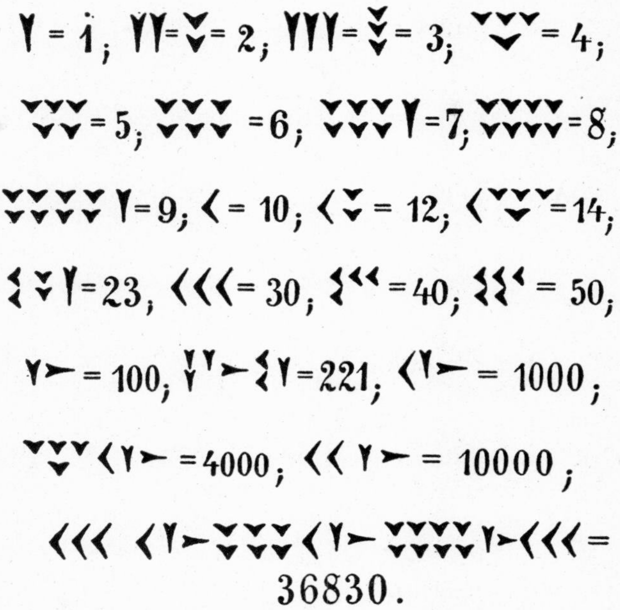

FIG. V. — CHALDEAN CUNEIFORM NUMBERS. (After Sterner.)

The first example, taken from Sterner and reproduced in Figure V, is the Chaldean system as found in the cuneiform writings.[1] It will be noted that the numbers beyond 3 in this system are composite, indicating that the span of attention then, as now, is approached by three objects unless the

[1] STERNER, MATTHÄUS — *Geschichte der Rechenkunst*, p. 26; München und Leipzig; Oldenbourg, 1891.

series is grouped so that each subdivision of the group may be seen as a new kind of unit.

One of the methods used by the Egyptians in recording the number series is given by Sterner as shown in Figure VI.

The Roman system of notation is sufficiently familiar to render unnecessary its reproduction here.   One peculiarity

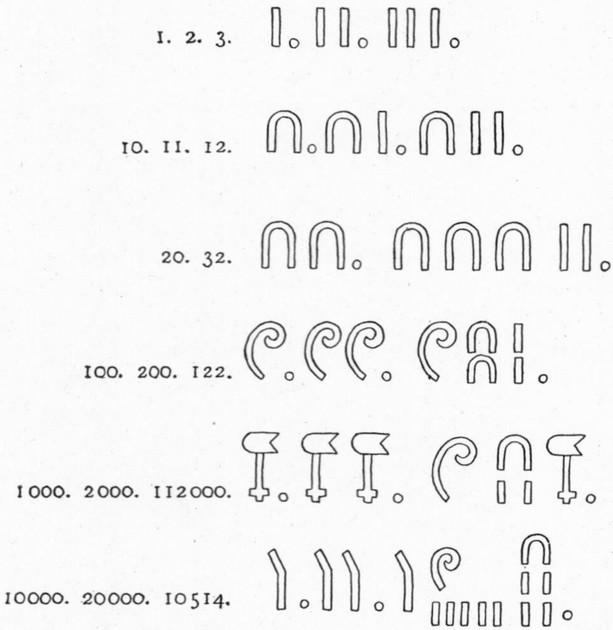

1. 2. 3.

10. 11. 12.

20. 32.

100. 200. 122.

1000. 2000. 112000.

10000. 20000. 10514.

Fig. VI. — A System of Egyptian Numbers.   (After Sterner.)

of this system of notation is so distinctly psychological in its character that it calls for comment.   There are several points in the Roman system where a number is expressed by subtracting from a number which is of nodal importance. Thus nine is one less than ten.   The mental process here involved is one of concentration on the complete number 10, and a recognition of the fact that this number is approximated but not fully attained. There are other examples of this type which can be found in other systems.

Conant enumerates among others the following cases :

The origin of numerals of this class is to be found in the idea of reference, not necessarily to the last, but to the nearest, halting-point in the scale. Many tribes seem to regard 9 as "almost 10," and to give it a name which conveys this thought. In the Mississaga, one of the numerous Algonquin languages, we have, for example, the word *cangaswi*, "incomplete 10" for 9. In the Kwakiutl of British Columbia, 8 as well as 9 is formed in this way; these two numbers being *matlguanatl*, $10 - 2$, and *nanema*, $10 - 1$, respectively. In many of the languages of British Columbia we find a similar formation for 8 and 9, or for 9 alone. The same formation occurs in Malay, resulting in the numerals *delapan*, $10-2$, and *sambilan*, $10 - 1$. In Green Island, one of the New Ireland group, these become simply *andra-lua*, "less 2," and *andra-si*, "less 1." In the Admiralty Islands this formation is carried back one step further, and not only gives us *shua-luea*, "less 2," and *shu-ri*, "less 1," but also makes 7 appear as *sua-tolu*, "less 3." Surprising as this numeral is, it is more than matched by the Ainu scale, which carries subtraction back still another step, and calls 6, $10 - 4$. The four numerals from 6 to 9 in this scale are respectively, *iwa*, $10 - 4$, *arawa*, $10 - 3$, *tupe-san*, $10 - 2$, and *sinepe-san*, $10 - 1$. Numerous examples of this kind of formation will be found in later chapters of this work; but they will usually be found to occur in one or both of the numerals, 8 and 9. Occasionally they appear among the higher numbers ; as in the Maya languages, where, for example, 99 years is " one single year lacking from five score years," and in the Arikara dialects, where 98 and 99 are " 5 men minus " and " 5 men 1 not." The Welsh, Danish, and other languages less easily accessible than these to the general student, also furnish interesting examples of a similar character.

More rarely yet are instances met with of languages which make use of subtraction almost as freely as addition, in the composition of numerals. Within the past few years such an instance has been noticed in the case of the Bellacoola language of British Columbia.

In their numeral scale 15, " one foot," is followed by 16, " one man less 4 " ; 17, " one man less 3 " ; 18, " one man less 2 " ; 19, " one man less 1" ; and 20, " one man." Twenty-five is " one man and one hand " ; 26, " one man and two hands less 4 " ; 36, " two men less 4 " ; and so on. This method of formation prevails throughout the entire numeral scale.[1]

By the time number series were as fully established as the foregoing paragraphs indicate, it became possible for men to perform some of the simpler operations of addition and subtraction, and even to use certain devices which anticipate in fundamental character the process of multiplication. The number series which have been described show abundant evidence of the mastery of simple addition. The prominence of 3 in the Chaldean system and the special character of 5 and 10 in many other systems show the beginnings of multiplication. Beyond these evidences, it is noted by anthropologists that savage tribes often use notches cut in sticks or knots tied in strings or pebbles or shells to mark the completion of some minor unit in the series of enumerations. Thus in certain cases each time 5 is reached in a count on the fingers, a stick is laid aside as a counter. The counters thus become units of a higher order.

As soon as men learned to manipulate tallies and combine them through processes of addition, they began to have ideas which are pure ideas of number rather than comparisons of groups of objects with one another. The number system began to take on an independent character as a system of thought. The mind of man had created a device which nature had not provided, but which has proved to be of major importance in its influence on human history.

One cannot contemplate the growth of science without realizing that most of its achievements would be absolutely

[1] Conant, Levi Leonard — *op. cit.*, pp. 44–46.

impossible without the use of numbers. Even the common relations of modern life are dependent for their precision on number and the related devices of measurement which have been made possible through the applications of number to weights and measures.

It is not too much to say that the attitude of civilized man is one of demanding quantitative exactness and numerical equity in all the transactions of life. If one tries to imagine what the world would be with number taken out of it, one begins to understand what is meant by the statement so often repeated in this book that man has made his environment through his invention of institutions.

In the case of number the institution is so nearly a purely mental affair that it serves perhaps better than do tools or money to emphasize the extent to which modern civilization is made up of intellectual contributions.

The statement that number is purely mental must be qualified. Even at the highest levels of civilized thought we think of numbers by picturing in our minds the written symbols or by sounding to ourselves the number names. There is thus a sensory or imagery basis for even our most abstract thinking. The sensory elements of the number system are, however, not the dominant elements. The ideas of comparison and definition are the important factors in the experience of number.

The highly abstract and immaterial character of the number system may be emphasized by calling attention to the fact that the ideas which arise in consciousness in the presence of a number are in many cases wholly unrelated to the quantitative meanings which these symbols were devised to express. Schmidl states that in Semitic and Indo-Germanic traditions there is a taboo against counting living beings such as men or animals, and also against counting valuables, lest the envy of evil spirits should be aroused. It is also related on the authority of Jurrod that when a native of the Thonga tribe was asked how many people there were in a certain company, he replied, "What! Do you want to count us? Who is here that you want to destroy?" The taboo here described arises evidently out of the purely subjective association between the number system and a fear on the part of the thinker. The mind has within itself both kinds of experience, the number idea and fear. There is a possibility in the subjective world of these two experiences arising together. They become associated when they occur simultaneously and the result is a wholly unmathematical and wholly intangible, but very real, connection.

Let us consider another series of purely subjective associations. Many such were set up by the Pythagoreans, a group of Greeks, disciples of Pythagoras, who flourished in the sixth century before Christ. Aristotle reports that Pythagoras taught that 5 is the cause of color, 6 of cold, 7 of mind and health and light, 8 of love and friendship and invention. In commenting on the vagaries of this early Greek thinking, Gow remarks:

Primitive men, on seeing a new thing, look out especially for some resemblance in it to a known thing, so that they may call both by the same name. This develops a habit of pressing small and partial analogies. It also causes many meanings to be attached to the same word. Hasty and confused theories are the inevitable result.[1]

Associations of the type described in the foregoing paragraph are not unknown in modern times. Prejudice and fear are coupled with the number 13. Whatever the historical sources of these unfavorable associations, the fact remains that they are purely subjective. They are psycho-

[1] Gow, James — op. cit., p. 67.

logically possible because the number system is abstract and capable of attaching to itself any accidental association which is not warded off by critical thinking.

While the abstract number system is capable of taking on arbitrary and wholly accidental associations, it is also capable of refinement through the careful study of its own logical implications. Given the idea that 2 and 2 make 4 and that 1 and 1 make 2, it is readily possible to show that 2 and 1 and 1 must make 4. Any refusal on the part of a rational being to accept this series of propositions shows that he has not refined his thought processes by critical analysis. This simple illustration shows what is meant by the statement that the mind following its own laws can evolve a series of propositions all of which must be true if one is true.

Furthermore, it is a highly important fact that, when the logical necessities of number thinking have once been revealed through critical reasoning, the mind can retain the conclusion and can attach the conclusion to the numbers concerned without fully repeating the original train of thought. Thus if one has determined that 4 and 3 make 7, and is satisfied that the conclusion is valid, it is not thereafter necessary to go through the whole process of critical thought by which the conclusion was reached. All that is necessary is that 3 and 4 and 7 be united by a fixed association, and memory will operate as a substitute for the critical process which justifies this association.

Mathematical thinking may thus become a mixture of rational trains of logical thought and purely mechanical memories. As a result of its abstract character the number series is at once open, as the foregoing illustrations show, to all kinds of fallacious associations and also to the most useful reductions to simple and readily available formulas.

An illustration of a mixture of logic and memory with an element of pure superstition is found in the so-called "magic squares":

4	9	2
3	5	7
8	1	6

The numbers in these squares total 15 in whatever direction they are added. So much have men in many ages and countries been impressed by this series of combinations, that in Europe in the Middle Ages it was used as a charm to drive away disease and to bring good fortune, and in China and elsewhere in the Orient it serves to-day the same superstitious purpose.

The last stages in the perfection of the number system are of special interest because they are recent enough so that we can describe them on the basis of a large body of accessible evidence and because they show with perfect clearness that an intellectual institution can be passed on by one generation or one people to another very much as a material object can be taken from place to place. The number system which is used to-day everywhere in the civilized world is not a native product of European thought; it was borrowed at a comparatively recent date from the Orient. The very name "Arabic numerals" makes it clear that Europe took its number system from a source wholly different from that which supplied modern occidental states with language or government or social customs. Once the Arabic system came into Europe it superseded for all practical purposes the clumsy Roman system which preceded it.

In order to understand the fundamental virtues of the Arabic system it is necessary to go back to the history of the

mechanical devices which men invented to aid themselves in
making calculations.

One of the earliest devices for using numbers and testing
the logic of number combinations was a mechanical contrivance, the abacus. A common form of this device, employed even to-day in many parts of the world to aid the mind
and record the results of its operations with numbers, is
shown in Figure VII. Beads are strung on a number of
vertical wires and the wires are fastened in a frame. The
frame is divided by a horizontal bar into an upper and a
lower compartment. Each wire
carries in the lower compartment
five beads and in the upper compartment two. The person who
uses the abacus tallies off on the
extreme right-hand wire in the
lower compartment each unit
which he wishes to record until he
has pushed five beads to the top
of this right-hand lower wire. He
then records the fact that he has
exhausted the possibilities of the
first row of unit beads by drawing
down one of the two beads in the
upper compartment on the extreme right wire. He repeats
the operation until he has drawn down the two upper right-
hand beads. He now substitutes for these, one bead on the
second right-hand wire in the lower compartment. Each
bead on this second wire in the lower part of the frame thus
stands for ten objects. In like fashion each bead on the
third wire in the lower part of the frame stands for one hundred objects, and so on.

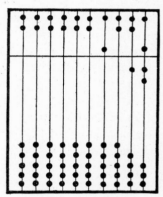

Fig. VII. — The Abacus.

The psychological value of the abacus is that it relieves
the mind of the necessity of carrying an immense amount of

detail. It records each step of the number thinking performed by the mind in such a way that the next step can be taken with the full advantage of what has been thought out before. The inventive mind of man has thus provided itself with a recording device which is a reflection of its own operations and at the same time an invaluable support to further and more elaborate thinking.

A unique virtue of the abacus record is that it takes advantage of position to enlarge the range of the number series. A bead on one wire means a higher number than the bead on another wire. This positional method of recording number reduces to a minimum the demand for distinctive symbols to express numbers of higher denominations. While the Roman system was obliged to resort to the letters L, C, D, and M, the abacus made it possible to represent each of these higher numbers with the same kind of a bead as that used to represent a number of lower order. Position thus came to have a major significance in the number system.

The abacus is not the product of individual endeavor. For long centuries before the form described in a foregoing paragraph was perfected, the principle underlying its construction was recognized and employed in various crude forms. Instead of wires for the different denominations of numbers, lines in sand were used. Instead of beads, pebbles or shells were employed. From such crude beginnings the later perfected instrument was derived.

The development of the abacus required the expenditure of a great deal of attention and the exercise of much ingenuity. The abacus is like any other tool in this respect. The discussion of an earlier chapter should be kept in mind as one considers the relations of the number system to mechanical devices. A tool is a device to which men find it advantageous to give thought and energy because of the ultimate saving in energy which it accomplishes. At the time of its invention and throughout the process of its improvement, it distracts the mind from the ends which it is intended to serve. Thus the arrow maker is taken away from the hunt in order to manufacture arrow points. The abacus maker is not at the time of his devotion to the instrument which he is making, using the number system for any practical purpose. The abacus operator also finds it necessary to devote much time and energy to a mastery of his instrument. It is said that an expert can add figures with the Chinese *suan pan* as fast as they can be dictated to him. Such skill can come only through long practice. We express the facts by saying that the operator must learn to use the abacus. Such learning will be facilitated by an understanding of the principles of number combination, but learning the abacus and learning the use of numbers are two different kinds of mental activity. Both require time and effort; they are therefore in a sense in competition with each other. It is only when both types of learning are complete that they unite and produce a kind of proficiency which would be impossible if only one kind of learning were undertaken by the individual.

From what has been said, it is easy to formulate a statement which is of great significance for the psychology of intellectual institutions. The mind has developed in its various institutions modes of behavior and modes of thinking which are not present in the early stages of individual thinking and which enormously extend experience. This invention of institutions and the mastery of them absorb very legitimately a great deal of the mental energy of the race.

While the abacus extended the usefulness of the number system and made possible elaborate calculations, it had the distinct disadvantage of being a thing quite apart from the mind that used it. The training of the mind which uses an abacus is not complete because the processes of combination which such a mind uses are mechanical and external.   The abacus served a useful purpose in that stage of civilization when the mind of man had not attained to a number system which is detached from all mechanical devices and yet possessed of all of the virtues that the mechanical device contributes.   The abacus gave way to a perfected number system as soon as that appeared.

The Arabic numeral system has the virtues of positional range and simplicity of expression and other virtues which no earlier system possessed.   The Arabic numbers are human inventions.   They are the products of long ages of coöperative thinking.   They were first used in India and after traveling across Arabia and possibly across Africa and Spain, they came to the consciousness of Europe.   Until they arrived, Europe had been using the Roman system.   This system is a decided improvement over the limited systems of primitive peoples, but it suffers from serious defects. Conspicuous among these is the impossibility of any of the more elaborate arithmetical operations.   Let anyone try to set down a problem in multiplication in Roman numbers and he becomes instantly aware of the clumsiness of that system as contrasted with the Arabic system.   Even addition is a cumbersome operation.   Europe was, however, so thoroughly committed to this system that it did not occur to her native thinkers to abandon it.

The arrival of the Arabic numerals in Europe and their adoption as the means of all exact quantitative thinking are described by Smith and Karpinski in the following passages :

As a matter of fact, it was not until the ninth or tenth century that there is any tangible evidence of their presence in Christendom. They were probably known to merchants here and there, but in their incomplete state they were not of sufficient importance to attract any considerable attention.

As a result of this brief survey of the evidence several con-

clusions seem reasonable : (1) commerce, and travel for travel's
sake, never died out between the East and the West ; (2) merchants had every opportunity of knowing, and would have been
unreasonably stupid if they had not known, the elementary
number systems of the peoples with whom they were trading,
but they would not have put this knowledge in permanent written
form ; (3) wandering scholars would have known many and
strange things about the peoples they met, but they too were not,
as a class, writers ; (4) there is every reason a priori for believing
that the gobar numerals would have been known to merchants,
and probably to some of the wandering scholars, long before the
Arabs conquered northern Africa ; (5) the wonder is not that the
Hindu-Arabic numerals were known about 1000 A.D., and that
they were the subject of an elaborate work in 1202 by Fibonacci,
but rather that more extended manuscript evidence of their
appearance before that time has not been found. That they
were more or less known early in the Middle Ages, certainly to
many merchants of Christian Europe, and probably to several
scholars, but without the zero, is hardly to be doubted. The
lack of documentary evidence is not at all strange, in view of all
of the circumstances.[1]

The opposition to the adoption of the new numerals and
the gradual spread of their use are sketched in the following
paragraphs :

The period from the time of Gerbert until after the appearance
of Leonardo's monumental work may be called the period of the
abacists. Even for many years after the appearance early in the
twelfth century of the books explaining the Hindu art of reckoning, there was strife between the abacists, the advocates of the
abacus, and the algorists, those who favored the new numerals.
The words *cifra* and *algorismus zifra* were used with a somewhat
derisive significance, indicative of absolute uselessness, as indeed
the zero is useless on an abacus in which the value of any unit is

[1] SMITH, DAVID EUGENE, and KARPINSKI, LOUIS CHARLES — *The Hindu-
Arabic Numerals*, p. 90 ; Ginn & Co., 1911.

given by the column which it occupies. So Gautier de Coincy
(1177–1236) in a work on the miracles of Mary says:

> A horned beast, a sheep,
> An algorismus-cipher,
> Is a priest, who on such a feast day
> Does not celebrate the holy Mother.

So the abacus held the field for a long time, even against the new
algorism employing the new numerals.

Of the medieval writers, probably the one most influential in
introducing the new numerals to the scholars of Europe was
Leonardo Fibonacci, of Pisa. This remarkable man, the most
noteworthy mathematical genius of the Middle Ages, was born
at Pisa about 1175.

Leonardo's father was a commercial agent at Bugia, the modern
Bougie, the ancient Saldæ on the coast of Barbary, a royal capital
under the Vandals and again, a century before Leonardo, under the
Beni Hammad. It had one of the best harbors on the coast,
sheltered as it is by Mt. Lalla Guraia, and at the close of the
twelfth century it was a center of African commerce. It was
here that Leonardo was taken as a child, and here he went to
school to a Moorish master. When he reached the years of young
manhood he started on a tour of the Mediterranean Sea, and vis-
ited Egypt, Syria, Greece, Sicily, and Provence, meeting with
scholars as well as with merchants, and imbibing a knowledge of
the various systems of numbers in use in the centers of trade.
All these systems, however, he says he counted almost as errors
compared with that of the Hindus. Returning to Pisa, he wrote
his Liber Abaci in 1202, rewriting it in 1228. In this work the
numerals are explained and are used in the usual computations
of business. Such a treatise was not destined to be popular,
however, because it was too advanced for the mercantile class,
and too novel for the conservative university circles. Indeed, at
this time mathematics had only slight place in the newly established universities, as witness the oldest known statute of
the Sorbonne at Paris, dated 1215, where the subject is referred
to only in an incidental way. The period was one of great com-

mercial activity, and on this very account such a book would attract even less attention than usual.

It would now be thought that the western world would at once adopt the new numerals which Leonardo had made known, and which were so much superior to anything that had been in use in Christian Europe. The antagonism of the universities would avail but little, it would seem, against such an improvement. It must be remembered, however, that there was great difficulty in spreading knowledge at this time, some two hundred and fifty years before printing was invented. "Popes and princes and even great religious institutions possessed far fewer books than many farmers of the present age. The library belonging to the Cathedral Church of San Martino at Lucca in the ninth century contained only nineteen volumes of abridgments from ecclesiastical commentaries." Indeed, it was not until the early part of the fifteenth century that Palla degli Strozzi took steps to carry out the project that had been in the mind of Petrarch, the founding of a public library. It was largely by word of mouth, therefore, that this early knowledge had to be transmitted. Fortunately the presence of foreign students in Italy at this time made this transmission feasible. (If human nature was the same then as now, it is not impossible that the very opposition of the faculties to the works of Leonardo led the students to investigate them the more zealously.) At Vicenza in 1209, for example, there were Bohemians, Poles, Frenchmen, Burgundians, Germans, and Spaniards, not to speak of representatives of divers towns of Italy; and what was true there was also true of other intellectual centers. The knowledge could not fail to spread, therefore, and as a matter of fact we find numerous bits of evidence that this was the case. Although the bankers of Florence were forbidden to use these numerals in 1299, and the statutes of the university of Padua required stationers to keep the price lists of books "non per cifras, sed per literas claros," the numerals really made much headway from about 1275 on.

It was, however, rather exceptional for the common people of Germany to use the Arabic numerals before the sixteenth century, a good witness to this fact being the popular almanacs.

Calendars of 1457–1496 have generally the Roman numerals, while Kobel's calendar of 1518 gives the Arabic forms as subordinate to the Roman. In the register of the Kreuzschule at Dresden the Roman forms were used even until 1538.[1]

The discussion of the Arabic numerals will not be complete for our purposes without special comment on the importance of the character zero. This single character is essential to the system as a place marker. It serves in the numeral system much the same purpose as do the fixed wires in the abacus. Without it the digits could not express units, tens, hundreds and higher denominations. The zero seems to be a relatively late addition to the system of characters and certainly its importation into Europe is later than that of the other numerals. Its presence in the system shows the extent to which abstraction had attained, for nothing can be more abstract than a symbol the sole function of which is to hold a place.

The complete realization of the value of the Arabic system did not come with the adoption of the characters for the simple purposes of counting and addition. The centuries which have followed the adoption of this system in Europe are filled with inventive efforts to use the numerals for such processes as multiplication and division. Device after device, table after table have been invented to facilitate elaborate arithmetical processes. The modern child in the schools and the banker who uses a table prepared to facilitate the calculation of interest, are inheriting not only from Leonardo but also from a host of mathematicians and practical men who have spent time and mental effort in devising methods of combining the numerals in new and useful ways.

For the purposes of our discussion, the history of the number system has been followed far enough. It remains to

_____
[1] SMITH, D. E., and KARPINSKI, L. C. — op. cit., pp. 128–133.

point out explicitly some of the psychological lessons that our survey yields.

First, it is evident that number thinking cannot be explained by describing human instincts. There is no instinct which will lead a child to calculate with the abacus or to acquire the Arabic numerals through laborious attention to their intricate forms. Addition, multiplication, division, and subtraction require the mastery by the child of symbols, forms of behavior, and types of interest which are far removed from those with which he was born.

Second, the existence of a perfected scheme of number thinking has so expanded human experience in the direction of exact number calculations that modern minds are capable of types of thinking which must have been altogether impossible in primitive life. We are prone to think of primitive man in negative terms; he did not have tools or money or Arabic numerals. If we could make an intimate comparison of our experiences with his, we should doubtless find that our absorption in modern modes of thinking has withdrawn us from many of the observations which fill the mental horizon of the savage. He would say to us, "How empty your eyes are, you did not see that rustling leaf which gave evidence of the escaping squirrel. You are deaf, you did not hear that faint call which means that we are detected by the herd of wild sheep. You do not smell, you did not notice the odor of woods which means the coming of the storm." Above all, primitive man would be utterly unable to comprehend the absorption of the mathematician in the pursuit of his abstract solutions of number problems. Modern devices of thinking have brought into being a world of new ideas and new interests. There has been set up through this transfer of mental energy a new series of goals for ambition and a new series of recognized social values. Men are proud of their ability to add rapidly to-day, while primitive man was proud of his skill in the hunt, in war, and in the practical arts which he practiced.

Third, the evolution of a number system has gone so far that the individual mind finds itself dominated by the system. We are all compelled by the very perfection of the number system which society possesses to submit our thinking to rigid training which leads to conformity to the system. Society very often does not even take the trouble to explain to the individual why he should thus follow its practices. Society insists that its scheme is so much better than any other which can be devised that it imposes its methods of operation on all comers. It is literally true in modern life that an individual cannot maintain himself socially or physically unless he can share in the general social use of number.

CHAPTER VI

The Psychology of Punctuality

There is no device more useful in promoting civilized coöperation on a large scale than a universally accepted plan for reckoning time. When we consider the fact that the industrial system, including the scale of wages, is regulated by time; when we think of the impossibility of a safe and convenient system of transportation without time tables and all that they imply; when we think of social engagements and their dependence on the ability to name days and hours; when we recall that religious festivals have been one of the chief centers of interest in the making of the calendar, we begin to realize what time measurement means to civilization.

The savage supplied with only the crudest methods of observing the grosser natural indications of the passage of time, and without names with which to designate successive periods, is controlled by a great variety of motives which in the case of civilized man have been superseded by what we call routine. The savage typically works only when he is in need of food or comfort. The motive for effort with him is direct and immediate. He responds vigorously to hunger, to light and darkness, to heat and cold, that is, he accommodates himself at any given moment to the facts in his environment which are most impressive. Contrast with him the modern workingman who goes to his task at the same hour in the morning winter and summer, or think of the regularity with which the modern family gathers about the dinner

table at a perfectly well-understood hour toward which all
the domestic machinery has been converging.

The impressive fact about the modern method of life is
that it finally takes so firm a hold on the individual that
he becomes a living embodiment of the social demand that
everyone guide his conduct by the clock. The impatience of
the man who finds a train thirty minutes behind the sched-
ule and, still more, the petulance of the man who finds his
dinner belated by that span of time, are familiar illustrations
of the fact that an institution accepted as a part of civilization ultimately becomes the source of definite expectations
and forms of behavior in the individual. The demand for
punctuality is a fact which reaches into the individual
nervous system and dominates the behavior and thinking
of each and every member of civilized society. Routine
has become the controlling fact in our lives and once we have
adopted the regular program which our watches dictate, we
are forever lost to that life of response to accidental motives
which characterizes the savage.

Civilization did not tame the savage and make him a
routinist in a day. There were long ages when the authority
of religion had to be invoked and the call to prayer had to
be enforced on a reluctant group. The strict discipline of
military organization must even now impress itself on the
recruit through many long days of training and campaigning
before the soldier learns that coöperation is effective only
when it is well timed. The modern child has to be punished,
sometimes severely, for the wholly artificial offense of being
late. In order to make these different types of training
possible, human ingenuity had to expend itself lavishly in
devising ways of dividing the day into precise subdivisions
and the year into namable months and days.

Here, as in a number of other cases which have been
canvassed in earlier chapters, the objective facts very often

have attracted so much attention that the related psychological facts have been overlooked. Time has been a subject of a great deal of scientific study. The physicist and the astronomer have devoted much energy to its measurement and to its definition. These scientists have, however, thought of time as a fact of nature, not as a system of organized human experience.

How is the psychologist to make clear his relation to this matter? He can study and has studied the accuracy with which the individual can estimate short intervals of time. He can write on the apparent differences between the duration of periods which are filled with interesting experiences and the duration of periods which are empty. The psychology of time is, however, of infinitely greater scope than is revealed by these studies of individual recognition of time and intervals. The whole mechanism of recording time is man's contribution to the world. Hours and minutes and seconds are human inventions. Nature furnished objective time, but man subdivided it into units by which he can control his own conduct and that of his fellows. He has come to see that all of his thinking even about objective time is made more precise through the subdivisions which he has worked out. What he often does not see is that his own nature has been regulated as a result of his exact measurement of time.

An outline of the steps which man has taken in passing from the savage attitude toward time to the attitude of the modern civilized individual will make more convincing the statements in the foregoing paragraphs.

In common with the animals, man has always been governed in his behavior by the presence or absence of light. The period of sunlight is, therefore, always a period of interest to him. In this connection it may be noted that the earliest ideas of a day coincide not with our present idea of a twenty-four hour period, but with the period of day-light. The early Hebrew records say, as rendered in the English translation, that the morning and the evening were the first day. Nilsson, commenting on this matter, writes as follows :

For primitive man the day is the simplest and most obvious unit of time. The variations of day and night, light and dark-ness, sleeping and waking penetrate at least as deeply into life as the changes following upon the course of the year, such as heat and cold, drought and rainy seasons, periods of famine and plenty. But for the primitive intellect the year is a very long period, and it is only with difficulty and at a later stage that it can be con-ceived and surveyed as a whole. Day and night, on the other hand, are short units which immediately become obvious. Their fusion into a single unit, the day of 24 hours, did not take place until later, for this unit as we employ it is abstract and numer-ical : the primitive intellect proceeds upon immediate perceptions and regards day and night separately.[1]

Within the daylight period there were early recognized by primitive man the larger subdivisions which he distinguished even as we do in modern life by the names "morning," "noon," and "evening." These subdivisions were, of course, closely related to his observations of the sun and its movements ; hence the practice which is common among all primitive peoples of referring to the position of the sun when they want to indicate subdivisions of the day.

Here again we may borrow from Nilsson :

For the indication of a point of time within the day the reference to the course of the sun is the means that lies nearest to hand, and the indication can indeed be given quite concretely by means of a gesture in the direction of the heavens. This language of signs is especially common in Africa. The Cross River natives of

[1] NILSSON, MARTIN P. — *Primitive Time-Reckoning*, pp. 5-6; Oxford University Press, 1920.

Southern Nigeria indicate the time by pointing to the position in the heavens which the sun occupies at that time of the day. When someone asked a Swahili what time it was, he answered, "Look at the sun," although this tribe knew other ways of indicating time. The Wagogo in order to show the time of day indicate with the hand the position of the sun in the heavens. In Loango the people indicate the time satisfactorily enough from the motion of the sun, in divisions of two hours, by dividing the vault of the sky with outstretched arm, often using both arms as indicators. Moreover, most peoples have descriptive expressions for parts of the day, as for instance, the inhabitants of the Lower Congo, the Masia of East Africa, who estimate the time of day from the position of the sun, and the Hottentots, who express with certainty and clearness both points and duration of time by referring to the position of the sun. In Dahomey the natives tell the hours by means of the sun; they say that the sun is here or there, in order to give the time of day. The Caffres are able to give the exact time of day by pointing with outstretched arm to the spot at which the sun appears at the time they wish to indicate. So, for example, when the Caffre wishes to show that he will come at two o'clock in the afternoon of the next day, he will say, " I will be here tomorrow when the sun is there," — pointing to the position occupied by the sun at 2 P.M.[1]

Primitive man noticed also, as soon as his attention was drawn to parts of the day, various facts which were concrete enough to appeal to his senses and at the same time so regular in their recurrence as to serve gradually as substitutes for direct observations of the position of the sun. He noticed especially the movements of animals.

Nilsson's examples are of interest in this connection. He says :

The phenomena of Nature afford little basis for the naming of the times of day, since there is hardly one of them which recurs regularly every day at a definite time, with the exception of cock-

[1] NILSSON, MARTIN P. — op. cit., pp. 17–18.

crow, which is in great favor as an indication of the time before su rise. Other exceptional cases are such names as that mentioned for the Society Islands, " the stirring of the flies " ; one given for the Mahakam Kayan of Borneo, *tiling* (a cricket which is only to be heard at sunset) *duan* (to sing) ; a couple of expressions of the Wadschagga, " the cry of the partridge " in the evening, " the turning of the smoke down the mountain " ; and one of the Nandi, " the elephants have gone to water." But a people which devotes itself to cattle-rearing or to agriculture may borrow from its regular daily occupations expressions for the times of day. Thus the Mahakam Kayan, besides the above-mentioned name for late afternoon and the term for noon (*beluwa dow*, " half-day "), have an expression for about 4 P.M. — *dow uli*, *i.e.*, " the time of the home-coming from work in the fields." The Javanese are strongly influenced by civilization and have, especially for astronological purposes, a fully developed chronological system ; not seldom, however, the times of day are given in relation to the rural labour. So they say, " when the buffalo is sent to the pastures," " when the buffalo is brought back from the pastures," or is " housed," etc. ; but for the time of the occurrence of any event the position of the sun is usually indicated.[1]

The subdivisions of the day must have been paralleled very early by subdivisions of the night. The earliest records which we have of civilizations in Egypt, Mesopotamia, and China show that man had advanced far in his observations of the night sky. He had mapped out the constellations, fitting them to the weird conjectures of his imagination and naming them from the animal forms which were familiar to him. He had noticed the wandering stars which by one name or another he designated as planets. He had become well acquainted with the movements of the moon and with its waxings and wanings.

How intimately these observations of the heavenly bodies were coupled with men's thinking about themselves is

[1] NILSSON, MARTIN P. — *op. cit.*, pp. 30–31.

indicated by the body of superstition which accompanied all these early beginnings of astronomical science. The relation of the stars to human life was not thought of as a matter of vague chronological coincidence but as a real and causal fact. The planets were raised to the level of deities and we still record the religion of our ancestors in our seven-day week and in the designations which we employ when we name the days. Saturn's day and the Sun's day and the Moon's day are readily recognizable from the modern English forms of their names. The other four days of the week bear the names of Teutonic deities. Tuesday as the day of Mars is difficult to recognize because the name of Tuv, the German God of War, has been substituted for the name of Mars. In like fashion the other days of the week belonged to Jupiter, Mercury, and Venus, and have come down to us bearing the names of Woden, Thor, and Fria.

The week, which marks off a period less directly observable than the day, is a purely conventional span of time. It was adopted by man because he wanted to do equal honor to each of his seven major deities. To each of these he gave a day set apart for special worship. To each god he attributed control over a certain group of human relations. What could be more natural than that he should relate the success or failure of the enterprises upon which he entered to the favor or displeasure of the particular deity having control over this relation. Should one go to war on the day assigned to the goddess of beauty and love? Certainly not. The result of such reasoning is that even civilized men who have long outgrown astrology prefer not to begin any large enterprises on Friday.

There are parts of the world quite untouched by the ancient mythology which accounts for our week of seven days. One can find in the Congo region of Africa to-day tribes which determine their short cycles of days on grounds wholly different from those which governed the Babylonians from whom we derive our week of seven days. For these tribes the market days are significant and the market privileges are shared by neighboring villages. The market day for a given village comes in regular rotation every fourth day. The week is therefore four days long.

The market week appears in other parts of the world as a period of greater or less length but always coupled with the idea that dominates our week, namely, a recurring day of rest. Nilsson makes the following statement about one case of this type :

In ancient Mexico a market was held every fifth day at every important place, just as in Africa on different days in neighboring districts ; the day was a rest-day, and with the market, games and amusements were associated. This five-day market-week appears also in other parts of Central America. The Muysca of Bogota in Columbia, on the other hand, held markets every third, and the Inca peoples every tenth, day, when the country-folk ceased from labour, assembled in the towns, and engaged in traffic and games. These three- and ten-day periods are said to be brought into connection with the month; if this statement be correct, they are not continuous periods, and the market-day must sometimes have been pushed out of place in order to secure the agreement with the moon; but the certainty cannot be ascertained.[1]

The natural units for periods of time longer than the day or week are the month and year. At first primitive man made no effort to combine these two ideas. His attitude can be understood when one thinks of our common practice of neglecting altogether the relation of the week to either the month or year. The considerations which have determined the length of the month are wholly different from the religious considerations which gave us the seven-day week. So it was with primitive man's treatment of the month and

[1] NILSSON, MARTIN P. — op. cit., pp. 328–329.

year. For him the year was at first the cycle of the seasons
and the month was the cycle of the moon. When he wanted
to refer with exactness to a relatively short span of time, he
said it was one or two or more moons ago. When he wanted
to cover longer periods, he spoke of it as two winters or two
rainy seasons ago. Either form of expression was precise
enough for his purposes and both were used freely and without thought of conflict.

It is a fact of human experience, however, that sooner or
later two modes of thinking which originate separately but
touch the same phases of life and conduct will begin to come
together through the purely subjective relations into which
they are brought. The year as a unit of time and the
month as a unit of time will sooner or later be thought of in
relation to each other. When that association is set up, the
making of a calendar will follow in response to a human
demand.

The calendar is not an objective fact, but a device for controlling conduct and thinking. The history of the calendar
is a history of successive efforts to bring human experience
into a form which will include in a single self-consistent
statement the complex observations which have been made
on the recurrence of the seasons and on the movements of the
moon.

The earliest efforts to make the calendar were dominated
by attention to the moon. Indeed, there are savage peoples
to-day with whom the year is a somewhat indefinite unit,
while the moon and its phases are so evident and impressive
that the calendar is for these tribes an enumeration of moons.

For the Babylonian priests, who had gained very detailed
information of the heavenly bodies, the adjustment between
the year and the month was simplified by the assumptions
that the year contains 360 days and that the cycle of the
moon is exactly 30 days. The priests must have known that

these figures were not exact, but they adopted them as close approximations. A correction was introduced, as it is to-day in the Jewish calendar, by interpolating an additional month at such intervals as were necessary to correct the error. The psychological motive for assuming that the days of the year and month could be expressed in round numbers was the same as the modern motive for substituting round numbers for irregular numbers, which are difficult to manipulate in calculations.

The method of approximating the year in 360 days and of subdividing the 360 into twelve equal parts has been handed down to us in a number of very important institutions. Our method of dealing with circles is to divide them into 360 degrees. This is the result of a Babylonian subdivision of the circle which was first drawn to represent the yearly path of the sun. Another practice which has come to us from Mesopotamia is that of dividing not only our year but also our clock face into twelve subdivisions.

In contrast with the Babylonians, the Egyptians, who were also well advanced in astronomical knowledge, held more nearly to the observed facts and gave their year 365 days. The months were evidently less significant for them, for they made an annual correction, keeping the year nearly right and allowing the moons to fit into the observed year as best they could.

The Jewish calendar consists of months which are made up alternately of 29 and 30 days with additional months inserted from time to time so that in a cycle of 19 years there are 7 additional months inserted. The year varies in the extreme from 353 to 385 days. We see in this practice, which closely approximates that adopted by the Greeks in the time of Solon, an effort to hold to the lunar unit as closely as possible. Since this unit is approximately $29\frac{1}{2}$ days, the plan of alternating from 29 to 30 days in succeeding months makes an immediate correction for the moon and leaves the longer unit, the year, to adjust itself with less exactness and over long periods of time.

The confusion in seasons which results from any calendar which centers attention on the moon has led in the long run to the adoption of the Egyptian method of neglecting the moons and holding to the unit of a year. The Julian calendar and the Gregorian calendar are year calendars rather than month calendars.

One fact of large significance for the student of civilization is the fact that the calendar is the work of kings and popes. There is no need of a pope to mark off the day; that is a natural fact so direct in its sensory impressiveness that it requires no authority to bring it to the attention of men. The moon's phases, too, are obvious and constitute the basis for a natural grouping of days into larger units of time. The year is less obvious because it requires a long span of memory, and the number of days requires a high development of the power to enumerate. The year will, therefore, at first be less likely to receive attention than the month. In the calendars based on the moon's phases we see, therefore, the natural tendency to follow the obvious. As society becomes more complex and its relations take on larger range, the immediate and easily seen facts become less and less dominant. It is then that some authoritative sponsor of the larger interests of the group steps in and decides by edict how the group shall think. The Greek calendar was adjusted by the wisdom of Solon; the Roman calendar was adjusted by the civil power of Julius Cæsar, and later by the ecclesiastical power of Pope Gregory. In each of these cases we see the social group expressing itself and determining the way in which the individual is to think and act.

To be sure the individual may continue to harbor individual notions even after the group has spoken. The phases of the moon look important to modern civilized man. Even if they are not to determine his calendar, he may consider privately whether it is better to see the new moon over his right or left shoulder. He may try to decide whether there is to be much or little rain during the days following a new moon by the apparent position of the opening of the bowl. He may do his planting according to the phases of the moon as his remote ancestors did and in spite of the demands of the seasons. All these private modes of thought and action are permitted to anyone; but when a man meets his neighbor and agrees to complete a contract or pay a debt on the first day of March, he will have to give up thinking about the moon and adopt the device of Pope Gregory. The best that he can do to escape the rules of group thinking in such a case is to secure a few days of grace according to another social convention.

Turning from the fact that man devised a system for defining large units of time, we may consider how man improved the means which nature provided him of subdividing the day into lesser parts.

Here again we find an admixture of nature and sheer convention. Let us ask how many parts the day has and we find no answer in nature. The day is continuous. As was pointed out in an introductory paragraph, primitive man began with a gross division, but that did not suffice, especially when the demands for social coöperation began to require great precision. Suppose that my neighbor asks me to meet him somewhere and says he will be there to-morrow morning. That is not exact enough to satisfy me; I shall grow impatient waiting.

How primitive man approached the problem of a more detailed subdivision of the day, we know. He noted the length of shadows. He set up a staff and marked the movement of the shadow with a semicircle of stones. He soon discovered the disconcerting fact that the shadow varied in length and direction of movement with the changing seasons. Nevertheless, he held to his shadow because it made it possible for him to subdivide his day.

By the time we come to Babylonian history, we find that men had decided to divide the day, which meant the period of daylight during which their sundials could be observed, into twelve hours. The subdivision of circles into twelve parts was a familiar practice with the Babylonian priests, but a similar subdivision is not at all natural so far as the day is concerned. There might have been ten hours in the day. Indeed, during the French Revolution the edict was given that the day be divided into ten hours. So fixed had become the habit, however, of thinking in terms of twelve hours, that watchmakers and clockmakers had to put two dials on their timepieces, one with the ten-hour division to conform to the edict and another inside of this marked with the conventional twelve divisions which people had learned and understood. Twelve hours seem to us natural now because of our training, but the convention might have been otherwise if the Babylonian priests had been of the mind of the French revolutionists.

Sundials have a great many shortcomings. The projection of a shadow on a flat surface does not give equal spacing for equal lengths of time. The effort was made to meet this difficulty by casting the shadow on the inner concave surface of a hemispherical bowl which was the small counterpart of the larger hemisphere through which the sun travels. Also the effort was made to meet the difficulty by making the dial on which the shadow was cast very large. But when everything possible had been done, the sundial served only under highly restricted conditions.

Man found it necessary, therefore, to resort ultimately to certain mechanical means, and in so doing he gave up entirely dependence on shadows and astronomical observations and imposed on the natural day a series of subdivisions which he could control at will. The first of the mechanical devices which he employed was the water clock.

A series of descriptions of water clocks employed by various peoples is given by F. A. Seely of the United States Patent Office in the following paragraphs :

If, taking our lives in our hands, we could step on board a Malay proa, we should see floating in a bucket of water a cocoanut shell having a small perforation, through which the water by slow degrees finds its way into the interior. This orifice is so proportioned that the shell will fill and sink in an hour, when the man on watch calls the time and sets it afloat again. This device of a barbarous, unprogressive people, so thoroughly rude in itself, I conceive to be the rudest that search of any length can bring to light. It is in all aspects rudimentary. One can scarcely conceive of anything back of it but the play of children, and, as a starting point for this history, it is much more satisfactory than what is disclosed in the polished ages of Greece. There is nothing in its structure, if we were to consider that only, to prevent it from being a survival of an age long antecedent to the use of metal. The protolithic age might have originated it if we can conceive that protolithic man could have had use for it.

Leaving our piratical friends, to whom we are so much indebted, and passing to their not remote neighbors in Northern India, we find the rude cocoanut shell developed into a copper bowl. Its operation is the same, but the attendant, who stands by and watches the moment of its sinking, now strikes the hour on the resonant metal. It is easy to see — in fact it would be difficult to doubt — that this has been an improvement on an apparatus like that of the Malay and the natural result of improvements in other arts, eminently that of metal-working. It is more enduring, more perfectly accomplishes its purpose, and is in the precise direction that improvement on the ruder appliance might be expected to pursue.

Passing from Southern Asia to a people geographically remote,

I next observe the water clock in use up to this day in China. We find the metal vessel with its minute perforation as before, but it has undergone a radical change in respect to its manner of use. It is now filled and the water flows from it in drops. Obviously enough the flight of time might be indicated by merely observing when the vessel has emptied itself, and then re-filling it, which, as will presently appear, was exactly the simplest Greek and Roman clepsydra and differs in no mechanical respect from the ordinary sand-glass.

But in the days when the Chinese were a progressive people and developed inventions for which Europe had many centuries to wait, this water clock advanced far beyond the crude thing we have been considering. It would seem that the problem was to increase its usefulness by subdividing the unreasonably long intervals required for the complete emptying of the vessel. If this was done by marking graduations on the inside of the vessel and so noting the decline of the level, the difference in its rate could not fail quickly to make itself manifest. The solution of this problem, not obvious at first, was found in so arranging the vessel that it should discharge into another, where the indication would be read in the rise of the surface, and contriving to hold the water in the upper vessel at a constant level. This was done by employing a third source, from which there was a constant flow into the first equal to its discharge. As the head in the middle vessel is thus maintained constant, the rise in the lowest is made uniform. Another radical improvement enhancing the practical utility of the device was the arrangement of a float on the surface of the water in the lowest vessel. Upon this was an indicator or hand which, in its rise, traveled over an adjacent scale, and so gave a time indication visible at a distance.[1]

Water clocks served many social purposes in the Greek and Roman civilizations, some of which are recorded for us in the literature of those peoples. Again we may quote from Seely :

[1] SEELY, F. A. — "The Development of Time-keeping in Greece and Rome," *American Anthropologist*, I (1888), pp. 25–50.

If the increasing burden and tediousness of litigation led to the enactment of a statute restricting and apportioning the time of speakers in the courts, and providing this means for its regulation, it is easy to see that the use of such means must become at once familiar. I have found no trace of such enactments, but that strict ordinances existed there is no doubt. We know that the time of speakers was carefully proportioned to the importance of the case; and trials of importance enough to have the time apportioned were known as πρὸς ὕδωρ while those of trifling importance, in which perhaps no lawyer appeared, were known as ἄνευ ὕδατος, two terms which may be freely rendered *wet* and *dry*, the dry case being as it happens most quickly disposed of. In a case of great moment to the state, involving a charge of faithlessness in an embassy, each party was allowed 10 amphoræ, or about 50 gallons of water. Nothing, however, seems to be known of the actual length of time indicated by this quantity of water. A passage in Aristotle gives some idea of the form of the clepsydra as commonly used; it was a spherical bottle with its minute opening at the bottom and a short neck at the top into which the water was poured. The running out of the water at the bottom could be stopped by closing this neck. In using the word bottle, I do not mean to imply that this clepsydra was of glass. Glass vessels of a suitable size could not be made at that period. We find Demosthenes charging his opponent with talking . . . . "*in my water*"; and on another occasion he shows the value he attached to the time allotted to him by turning to the officer, when interrupted, with a peremptory . . . . "You there! Stop the water!"[1]

A final quotation from Seely shows how Plautus satirized the water clocks which had become common in Rome.

> When I was young, no time-piece Rome supplied,
> But every fellow had his own — inside;
> A trusty horologe, that — rain or shine —
> Ne'er failed to warn him of the hour — to dine.

[1] SEELY, F. A. — *op. cit.*, pp. 37–38.

Then sturdy Romans sauntered through the Forum,
Fat, hale, content; for trouble ne'er came o'er them.
But *now* these cursed dials show their faces
All over Rome, in streets and public places;
And men, to know the hour, the cold stone question,
That has no heart, no stomach, no digestion.
They watch the creeping shadows — daily thinner —
Shadows themselves, impatient for their dinner.
Give me the good old time-piece, if you please,
Confound the villain that invented these! [1]

The water clock was paralleled in its later history by another mechanical device which is said to have been invented in Alexandria about the middle of the third century before Christ, the hourglass. This instrument is sufficiently familiar to require no description here.

Still other timing devices have been used. The Chinese and Japanese use slow-burning ropes knotted at regular intervals or cylinders of glue and sawdust. The Eskimos watch the burning oil in their lamps, and the taper at many an altar records the vigil of the worshiper.

The era of strictly mechanical time measurement came with the inventions of the medieval monks. How the monks happened to be factors in this history is told by a popular writer from whom the following paragraphs may be quoted:

"It is quite possible," writes M. Gubelin Breitschmidt, the younger, an eminent horologist of Lucerne, Switzerland, "that a large number of the technical inventions of antiquity were lost during the migrations of the barbarians and under the chaotic conditions prevailing during the first thousand years of Christianity, but the most perfect surviving instrument for measuring time was the water clock, known as the clepsydra, which was able to maintain its supremacy long after the appearance of the

[1] SEELY, F. A. — *op. cit.*, p. 42.

wholly mechanical clock, just as the beautiful manuscripts of the artist monks and laymen were favored by the cultured classes long after the invention of the movable types for printing.

"The spread of Christianity throughout Europe caused the foundation of many religious communities, and the severe rules by which they were governed — fixing the hours of prayer, labor, and refreshment — forced their members to seek instruments by which to measure time. In the year 605, a bull of Pope Sabinianus decreed that all bells be rung seven times in the twenty-four hours, at fixed moments and regularly, and these fixed times became known as the seven canonical hours. The sound of the bells penetrated and came to regulate not only the life of the religious bodies but also that of the secular people who lived outside the walls of the monasteries. Oil-lamps, candles, hour-glasses, prayers and — for those who had the means of buying them — clepsydræ served as chronometers for the brotherhoods; so that one can easily imagine that many a monk sought to improve these instruments. But as yet, no one had found means to regulate the wheel-system of a movement. In the best instruments of this period, water supplied the motive power and served as well to regulate the action."

There is a general belief that Gerbert, the monk, who was the most accomplished scholar of his age, and who later became Pope Sylvester II, was the one who first took the important step of producing a real clock, and that this occurred near the close of the tenth century — or to be more exact, about 990 A.D. This period was one of densest superstition, and expectancy of the end of the world was in the air, since many people had fixed upon the year 1000 A.D. as the date of that cataclysmic event.

*   *   *   *   *   *   *   *

It is to the monks in their cloisters that we chiefly owe the preservation of learning through the "dark ages" and from the monks, for the most part, came such progress of science and invention as was made. If Gerbert, the monk, after patient tinkering with wheels and weights in his stone-walled workshop, really achieved some form of the clock-action as we know it, he was one of the great benefactors of the human race. Still, it is not impossible that his device may only have been a more remarkable application of the clepsydra principle.[1]

The crowning discovery, which provided the mechanical regulator for timing instruments, was the discovery made by Galileo in 1581. The description of this discovery as given by Brearley is as follows :

In 1581, this youth of seventeen stood in the cathedral of Pisa. Close at hand, a lamp suspended by a long chain swung lazily in the air currents. There was nothing unusual in such a sight. Millions of other eyes had seen other suspended objects going through exactly this motion and had not given the sight a second thought. At this moment, however, a great discovery of far-reaching application — one which was to revolutionize clock construction — hung waiting in the air. Young Galileo took notice. The lamp swung to and fro, to and fro. Sometimes it moved but slightly. Again, as a stronger breeze blew through the great drafty structure, it swung in a considerable arc, but always — and this was the point which impressed itself upon the Italian lad — the swing was accomplished in exactly the same time. When it moved a short distance, it moved slowly; the farther it moved, the faster became the motion; in its arc it moved more swiftly, accomplishing the long swing in the same time as it did the short one. In order to make sure of this fact, Galileo is said to have timed the swinging lamp by counting the beating of his pulse.[2]

It is not necessary for the purposes of our discussion to follow further the inventions by which our modern timepieces have been perfected. The fact in which the psychology of social institutions is interested is that man has successfully divided the day into small units and has developed mechanisms which are common enough to make it possible for everyone to be supplied with exact information as to the conventional hour.

[1] BREARLEY, HARRY C. — *Time-Telling through the Ages*, pp. 71–73; Doubleday, Page & Co., 1919.   [2] *Ibid.*, p. 89.

Not only so, but by agreements, national and international, the whole world has been brought under a series of conventions which make it possible to compare the time of any given locality with that of any other locality. As a result, activities in different parts of the world can be made to correspond exactly in time even though they occur at hours that are wholly different in name. In order that this vast social system may be kept in perfect accord and that the infinitely numerous mechanical devices now used in all parts of the world for measuring time may be constantly corrected so as to insure exact correspondence, the support and authority of governments have been enlisted. Elaborate observations are made at national observatories and the records are interchanged. Signals are sent at frequent intervals to all parts of the world.

Perhaps the most impressive fact for the purposes of our discussion is that a great many people have been set aside to perform the services which were outlined in the last paragraph. There are, first of all, the makers of timepieces. Then there are the official observers who regulate the standard chronometers and provide for the distribution of standard signals. There are hosts of persons whose duty it is to watch other people and see to it that their activities are executed on time. All of these are society's agents in producing and maintaining the habits of punctuality.

One hardly knows whether to speak of the uses to which time measurements are put in science as by-products of the social activities which we have been discussing or as sources of the social system. Certain it is that the demand for exact time measurements came first out of man's interest in himself. The earliest makers of clocks were not students of nature, they were leaders of religious cults. In other ages they were practical mariners seeking to find a path for human enterprise where there were no guides but the stars.

Out of the original practical and religious interests, there have grown bodies of knowledge and technical devices which have been of great service to man in helping him to master the forces of nature that were in no way connected with his original observations of time. Because of the knowledge which we have of time intervals, it is possible to-day to measure among other facts of physical nature the velocity of movements and thus to master various forces which we could not control if we were not supplied with methods of exact measurement of time.

There is some danger that the extended review of historical facts which has filled the foregoing pages will obscure the psychological lessons which these facts are intended to teach. A water clock is so material a fact and a calendar is so far removed from the sense impressions and memory images which constitute the subject matter of books on psychology that the reader may feel that the psychology of social institutions deals very largely with institutions and very little with mental processes.

If such is the case, the difficulty is to be traced to the natural disposition to think of mental life in purely subjective terms. The modern man feels the urge to be prompt; this urge he recognizes as a mental fact. He cannot discover by looking into his own mind where the urge came from. He is disposed therefore to think of it as a natural disposition which he acquired through inheritance or else he thinks of it as resulting from a demand imposed upon him by industrial organization, that is, by a social system outside of his mind and consequently wholly unpsychological in character. When he reads the historical narrative and discovers that there were once sundials and water clocks, his mind stops at these material facts and is satisfied to find in them the ultimate causes of his own subjective traits.

It must by some means be brought vividly to the thinking of the reader that the sundial is itself a product of human mental effort. A sundial is not a fact of the physical world, nor a fact of the animal world. The sundial uses physical materials but these physical materials do not explain it. Back of the sundial there are ideas and human desires and long ages of coöperative experimentation. The cause of the sundial is human intelligence.

Furthermore, the causal relation between intelligence and the sundial is not to be described as a single fact. A long accumulation of psychological influences must be thought of when one seeks to discover the cause of the sundial. The minds of many men have contributed to every aspect of the completed device. Each contributing mind has passed through some act of observation and reaction and has helped by this process to achieve the final result. The processes of mind through which the successive inventors have passed are no less real occurrences in the world than are the movements of the material particles which have been brought together in the construction of the sundial. Without the successive mental acts there would never have been any such end product as there is. The reason why sundials exist is that in the minds of men process after process has taken place and each process has recorded itself in gradual improvements which have ultimately resulted in the aggregate in the finished sundial.

The long series of mental processes which are implied in the historical sketches given in the early pages of this and preceding chapters are so much more significant to the world than the mental processes of a single individual that it is almost unbelievable that the vividness and immediacy of individual mental phenomena should have so long directed the course of the science of psychology. No one doubts the reality of a visual impression of an individual who sees the sun and yet there has been no adequate recognition in psychology of the time consciousness which has been built up through generations of experience.

The psychology of social institutions does not, however, merely turn its face backward and look for the causes of the institutions which the mind of man has evolved. Every institution is a cause of future happenings. What men have invested in their inventions their children experience. Institutions arose out of the coöperation of minds and have become the vehicles which carry over the influences of mind to other personalities. By means of institutions it has become possible for one group of minds to touch and direct the experiences of minds remote in time and space. The human geniuses who discovered the planets and gave their names to the days of the week have long been forgotten. We have no knowledge of their personalities except through the institutions which they created. Their individual nervous systems and the records of their other deeds were long since utterly lost, but future generations will be trained to use the words which they coined and to base their conduct on the orderly arrangements which they planned.

There is a breadth and scope in the psychology of social institutions which is entirely lacking in any system of individual psychology. If one would understand the place of mind in the world, one must master this broader view of mental phenomena.

In the applications of psychology as well as in its formulation of fundamental explanations the broader view is highly productive. If one thinks of education, for example, and attempts to derive a formula for the guidance of the teacher, one finds little that is helpful in a mere recital of individual traits. Even the facts of individual development are comparatively meager in furnishing a basis for a program of instruction. On the other hand, a study of social institutions throws a flood of light on the processes which the schools are engaged in carrying on. Viewed in the light of the psychology of social institutions, education is seen to be an effort to fit the individual into the general plan of social coöperation. Education seeks to give the individual as much as possible of the organized experiences which generations of minds have put together. Education seeks to drill the individual in the use of those instruments of adaptation which have been perfected by earlier generations. Education aims to make it possible for the individual to master the methods of recording his own contributions to the intellectual wealth of the world.

What is true of general education is true in detail of every line of human endeavor. If one would perfect oneself in art, one must first take advantage of what the race has achieved. If nations would be well governed, they must find their place in the current of human agreements and conventions which have substituted order for individual combat. If industry is to progress, the past must supply the stepping stones to more perfect mechanical devices.

It is such conclusions as these that the detailed examinations of one social institution after another are intended to support. It is something of a handicap to thinking that social and mental evolution must thus be treated as though each of the contributing institutions were an isolated fact. If it were possible to present at one stroke the effects on human life of the invention of tools, of the evolution of commerce, and of the cultivation of the virtue of promptness, and if it were possible to show at the same time the effect on human nature of all the other social institutions, the task of the psychology of social institutions would be easier. As it is we must think now of one institution, now of another, and hope that each successive discussion will contribute to the conviction that individual mental life is what it is by virtue of powerful social influences.

CHAPTER VII

The Psychology of Precision

The effect on human thought and conduct of the evolution of number systems and time measurements is to render all human adaptations increasingly precise. The highest manifestations of this tendency appear in modern science where exactness of thought and comparison are recognized as absolutely essential. When the chemist and the physicist boast that theirs are mathematical sciences and when the biologists and students of human nature begin to collect and tabulate careful measurements rather than rely on general observations, we see the results of a long line of human evolution in which counting and minute analyses have united to change rough general thinking into detailed, precise views of the world. This line of progress would have been impossible without one other system of devices, to the consideration of which we now turn, namely, weights and measures.

Weights and measures were in their earliest stages practical devices. The constructive arts called for exact linear measure, and exchange called for measures of bulk and weight. The distances across land and sea were important to men in planning and carrying out their journeys and expeditions.

The Chaldeans seem to have made great progress in the invention of systems of measures. They seem also to have tried to unify all their measuring devices by adopting as the unit of weight a defined cubic volume of water. They also related their linear unit to fundamental astronomical

determinations.   The same is true of the Egyptians.   But
if ancient measuring systems had reached the stage of
deliberate refinement, which is indicated by such statements,
it is quite certain that the early centuries of European
history were only slightly affected by these ancient systems.   The history of weights and measures in Europe must
begin with an account of unscientific experimentation with
practical standards of the most varied types and origins.

There is an exhaustive discussion of the whole matter of
weights and measures in one of the state papers of John
Quincy Adams.   In 1821, in response to a resolution of the
Congress of the United States asking for a definition of the
function imposed upon it by the clause of the Constitution
which charges it with the duty of fixing the standard of
weights and measures, Adams prepared as Secretary of
State an elaborate document from which liberal quotations
will be borrowed.

Adams opens his report with certain speculations as to the
origin of measures in the most remote beginnings of savage
life.   His speculations are based on the meanings of the
words which are found in use everywhere in the world as
names of the common units.   After pointing out that
savages in using animal skins to make clothing will naturally
be forced to compare the dimensions of parts of their own
bodies and the dimensions of the skins, and that these same
savages in building shelters will use standards of measure
derived from their heights and arm-lengths, Adams calls
attention to the following interesting contrast :

Itinerary measure, as it needs nothing more than the prolonga-
tion or repetition of linear measure, would seem at the first view to
be the same.   Yet this is evidently not the progress of nature.
As the want of it originates in a different stage of human existence
it will not naturally occur to man, to use the same measure, or the
same scale of proportions and numbers, to clothe his body, and to

mark the distance of his walks.   On the contrary, for the measurement of all objects which he can lift and handle, the fathom, the
arm, the cubit, the hand's-breadth, the span, and the fingers, are
the instruments proposed to him by nature; while the pace and
the foot are those which she gives him for the measurement of
itinerary distance.   These natural standards are never, in any
stage of society, lost to individual man.   There are probably few
persons living who do not occasionally use their own arms, hands,
and fingers, to measure objects which they handle, and their own
pace to measure a distance upon the ground.

Here then is a source of *diversity*, to the standards even of linear
measure, flowing from the difference of the relations between
man and physical nature.   It would be as inconvenient and un-
natural to the organization of the human body to measure a bow
and arrow for instance, the first furniture of solitary man, by his
foot or pace, as to measure the distance of a day's journey, or a
morning's walk to the hunting ground, by his arm or hand.

Measures of capacity are rendered necessary by the nature of
fluids, which can be held together in definite quantities only by
vessels of substance more compact than their own.   They are
also necessary for the admeasurement of those substances which
nature produces in multitudes too great for numeration, and too
minute for linear measure.   Of this character are all the grains
and seeds, which, from the time when man becomes a tiller of the
ground, furnish the principal materials of his subsistence.   But
nature has not furnished him with the means of supplying this
want in his own person.   For this measure he is obliged to look
abroad into the nature of things; and his first measure of capacity
will most probably be found in the egg of a large bird, the shell
of a cetaceous fish, or the horn of a beast.   The want of a *common*
standard not being yet felt, these measures will be of various dimensions; nor is it to be expected that the thought will ever
occur to the man of nature, of establishing a proportion between
his cubit and his cup, of graduating his pitcher by the size of his
foot, or equalizing its parts by the number of his fingers.[1]

[1] ADAMS, JOHN QUINCY — *Report of the Secretary of State upon Weights and
Measures*, p. 7; Gales and Seaton, 1821.

The development of this natural system of measures shows a striking departure from that of the ordinary counting series which, as we have already seen, early adopts a decimal base. Adams explains as follows the reason for a base other than ten in the case of measures :

The proportions of the human body, and of its members, are in other than decimal numbers. The first unit of measures, for the use of the hand, is the *cubit*, or extent from the tip of the elbow to the end of the middle finger ; the motives for choosing which, are, that it presents more definite terminations at both ends than any of the other superior limbs, and gives a measure easily handled and carried about the person. By doubling this measure is given the ell, or arm, including the hand, and half the width of the body, to the middle of the breast ; and, by doubling that, the fathom, or extent from the extremity of one middle finger to that of the other, with expanded arms, an exact equivalent to the stature of man, or extension from the crown of the head to the sole of the foot. For subdivisions and smaller measures, the span is found equal to half the cubit, the palm to one-third of the span, and the finger to one-fourth of the palm. The cubit is thus, for the mensuration of matter, naturally divided into 24 equal parts, with subdivisions of which 2, 3, and 4, are the factors ; while, for the mensuration of distance, the foot will be found at once equal to one-fifth of the pace, and one-sixth of the fathom.[1]

The fact that measures of weight and volume are at first quite distinct can be explained psychologically by the general principle which has been illustrated in all the foregoing paragraphs. Standards originate in concrete comparisons, not in ideas about the most systematic ways of making comparisons. Weights and measures of length are in modern times classified together as instruments of precision because men have come to understand the meaning and importance of exact determination, and science teaches that all standards

[1] ADAMS, JOHN QUINCY — *op. cit.*, p. 8.

can be reduced to the same fundamental concepts of matter and motion, but for primitive man seeking ready practical means of meeting certain pressing immediate needs, weights and volumes are wholly different facts.

Adams discusses the matter as follows:

The difference between the specific gravities of different substances is so great, that it could not, for any length of time, escape observation; but nature has not furnished man, within himself, with any standard for this mode of estimating equivalents. Specific gravity, as an object of mensuration, is in its nature *proportional*. It is not like measures of length and capacity, a comparison between different definite portions of space, but a comparison between different properties of matter. It is not the simple relation between the extension of one substance, and the extension of another; but the complicated relation of extension and gravitation in one substance to the extension and gravitation of another. This distinction is of great and insuperable influence upon the principle of *uniformity*, as applicable to a system of weights and measures. *Extension* and *gravitation* neither have, nor admit of, one common standard. *Diversity* is the law of their nature, and the only *uniformity* which human ingenuity can establish between them is an uniformity of proportion, and not an uniformity of identity.

The necessity for the use of *weights* is not in the organization of individual man. It is not essential even to the condition or the comforts of domestic society. It presupposes the discovery of the properties of the balance; and originates in the exchanges of traffic, after the institution of civil society. It results from the experience that the comparison of the articles of exchange, which serve for the subsistence or the enjoyment of life, by their relative extension, is not sufficient as a criterion of their value. The first use of the balance, and of weights, implies two substances, each of which is the test and the standard of the other. It is natural that these substances should be the articles the most essential to subsistence. They will be borrowed from the harvest and the vintage: they will be corn and wine. The discovery of the metals, and their extraction from the bowels of the earth, must, in the annals of human nature, be subsequent, but proximate, to the first use of weights; and, when discovered, the only mode of ascertaining their definite quantities will be soon perceived to be their weight. That they should, themselves, immediately become the common standards of exchanges, or otherwise of value and of weights, is perfectly in the order of nature.[1]

Enough has been said in the foregoing quotations to make clear the reason why a universally accepted system of weights and measures has never been evolved even in modern civilization. There are so many different kinds of measures that it is not easy for the mind to bring all of them into a single system. The abstract notion of exactness which includes linear measures and weights is so far removed from the manifold concrete experiences which must be compared with the yardstick or weighed in the balance that civilization will for long periods be content with wholly diverse standards for the different types of exactness. Furthermore, the close relationship of some of the particular measures to the parts of one's own body will operate to delay the establishment of purely conventional social standards.

Adams writes on this aspect of the matter as follows:

With civil society, too, originates the necessity for common and uniform standards of measures. Of the different measures of extension necessary for individual man, and for domestic society, although the want will be common to all, and frequently recurring, yet, the standards will not be uniform, either with reference to time or to persons. The standard of linear measure for each individual being in himself, those of no two individuals will be the same. At different times, the same individual will use different measures, according to the several purposes for which they will be wanted. In domestic society, the measures adap-

_____
[1] ADAMS, JOHN QUINCY — op. cit., p. 10.

table to the persons of the husband, of the wife, and of the children, are not the same; nor will the idea of reducing them all to one common standard press itself upon their wants, until the multiplication of families gives rise to the intercourse, exchanges, and government, of civil society. Common standards will then be assumed from the person of some distinguished individual; but accidental circumstances, rather than any law of nature, will determine whether identity or proportion will be the character of their uniformity. If, pursuing the first and original dictate of nature, the cubit should be assumed as the standard of linear measure for the use of the hand, and the pace for the measure of motion, or linear measure upon earth, there will be two units of long measure; one for the measure of matter, and another for the measure of motion. Nor will they be reducible to one; because neither the cubit nor the pace is an aliquot part or a multiple of the other. But, should the discovery have been made, that the *foot* is at once an aliquot part of the pace, for the mensuration of motion, and of the ell and fathom, for the mensuration of matter, the foot will be made the common standard measure for both: and, thenceforth, there will be only one standard unit of long measure, and its uniformity will be that of identity.

When weights and measures present themselves to the contemplation of the legislator, and call for the interposition of law, the first and most prominent idea which occurs to him is that of *uniformity:* his first object is to embody them into a system, and his first wish, to reduce them to one universal common standard. His purposes are uniformity, permanency, universality; one standard to be the same for all persons and all purposes, and to continue the same forever. These purposes, however, require powers which no legislator has hitherto been found to possess. The power of the legislator is limited by the extent of his territories, and the numbers of his people. His principle of universality, therefore, cannot be made, by the mere agency of his power, to extend beyond the inhabitants of his own possessions. The power of the legislator is limited over time. He is liable to change his own purposes. He is not infallible: he is liable to mistake the means of effecting his own objects. He is not immortal: his successor accedes to his power, with different views, different opinions, and perhaps different principles. The legislator has no power over the properties of matter. He cannot give a new constitution to nature. He cannot repeal her law of universal mutability. He cannot square the circle. He cannot reduce extension and gravity to one common measure. He cannot divide or multiply the parts of the surface, the cube, or the sphere, by the uniform and exclusive number ten. The power of the legislator is limited over the will and actions of his subjects. His conflict with them is desperate, when he counteracts their settled habits, their established usages; their domestic and individual economy, their ignorance, their prejudices, and their wants: all which is unavoidable in the attempt radically to change, or to originate, a totally new system of weights and measures.

In the origin of the different measures and weights, at different stages of man's individual and social existence; in the different modes by which nature has bounded the extension of matter; in the incommensurable properties of the straight and the curve line; in the different properties of matter, number, extension, and gravity, of which measures and weights are the tests, nature has planted sources of diversity, which the legislator would in vain overlook, which he would in vain attempt to control. To these sources of diversity in the nature of things must be added all those arising from the nature and history of man. In the first use of weights and measures, neither universality nor permanency are essential to the uniformity of the standards. Every individual may have standards of his own, and may change them as convenience or humor may dictate. Even in civil society, it is not necessary, to the purposes of traffic, that the standards of the buyer and seller should be the same. It suffices, if the proportions between the standards of both parties are mutually understood. In the progress of society, the use of weights and measures having preceded legislation, if the families, descended from one, should, as they naturally may, have the same standards, other families will have others. Until regulated by law, their diversities will be numberless, their changes continual.

These diversities are still further multiplied by the abuses incident to the poverty, imperfections, and deceptions, of human language. So arbitrary and so irrational is the dominion of usage over the speech of man, that, instead of appropriating a specific name to every distinct thing, he is impelled, by an irresistible propensity, sometimes to give different names to the same thing, but far more frequently to give the same name to different things. Weights and measures are, in their nature, relative. When man first borrows from his own person a standard measure of length, his first error is to give to the measure the name of the limb from which it is assumed. He calls the *measure* a cubit, a span, a hand, a finger, or a foot, improperly applying to it the name of those respective parts of his body. When he has discovered the properties of the balance, he either confounds with it the name of the weight, which he puts in it to balance the article which he would measure, or he gives to the definite mass, which he assumes for his standard, the indefinite and general name of *the weight*. Such was the original meaning of the weight which we call a *pound*. But, as different families assume different masses of gravity for their unit of weight, the pound of one bears the same name, and is a very different thing from the pound of another. When nations fall into the use of different weights or measures for the estimation of different objects, they commit the still grosser mistake of calling several different weights or measures by the same name. And, when governments degrade themselves by debasing their coins, as unfortunately all governments have done, they add the crime of fraud to that of injustice, by retaining the name of things which they have destroyed or changed.[1]

Adams draws upon the Old Testament for confirmation of the various principles which he has enunciated. He writes as follows :

In the *law* given from Sinai — the law, not of a human legislator, but of God — there are two precepts respecting weights and measures. The first, (Leviticus xix. 35, 36) "Ye shall do no unrighteousness in judgment, in mete-yard (measure of length),

[1] ADAMS, JOHN QUINCY — *op. cit.*, pp. 11–13.

in weight, or in measure (of capacity). Just balances, just weights, a just ephah, and a just hin, shall ye have." The second, (Deuteronomy xxv. 13, 14, 15) "Thou shalt not have in thy bag *divers* weights, a great and a small. Thou shalt not have in thine house divers measures, a great and a small. But thou shalt have a perfect and just weight, a perfect and just measure shalt thou have." The weights and measures are prescribed as already existing and known, and were all probably the same as those of the Egyptians. The first of these injunctions is addressed in the plural to the whole nation, and the second in the singular to every individual. The first has reference to the standards, which were to be kept in the ark of the covenant, or the sanctuary; and the second to the copies of them, kept by every family for their own use. The first, therefore, only commands that the standards should be *just:* and that, in all transactions, for which weights and measures might be used, the principle of righteousness should be observed. The second requires, that the copies of the standards used by individuals should be uniform, not divers; and not only just, but perfect, with reference to the standards.

The long measures were, the *cubit,* with its subdivisions of two *spans,* six palms or handbreadths, and twenty-four digits or fingers. It had no division in decimal parts, and was not employed for itinerary measure: that was reckoned by paces, Sabbath day's journeys, and day's journeys. The measures of capacity were, the *ephah* for the dry, and the *hin* for liquid measure; the primitive standard from nature of which was an egg-shell; six of these, constituted the *log,* a measure little less than our *pint.* The largest measure of capacity, the *homer,* was common both to liquid and dry substances; and its contents nearly corresponded with our wine hogshead, and with the Winchester quarter. The intermediate measures were different, and differently subdivided. They combined the decimal and duodecimal divisions: the latter of which may, perhaps, have arisen from the accidental number of the tribes of Israel. Thus, in liquids, the bath was a tenth part of the homer, the hin a sixth part of the bath, and the log a twelfth part of the hin; while, for dry measure, the ephah was a tenth part of the homer, the seah a third, and the omer a tenth part of the ephah, and the cab a sixth part of the seah. The weights and coins were, the shekel, of twenty gerahs; the maneh, which for weight was of sixty and in money of fifty shekels; and the kinchar, or talent, of three thousand shekels in both. The ephah had also been formed by the process of cubing an Egyptian measure of length, called the *ardob*. The original weight of the shekel was the same as one-half of our avoirdupois ounce; the most ancient of weights traceable in human history.

And thus the earliest and most venerable of historical records extant, in perfect coincidence with speculative theory, prove, that the natural standards of weights and measures are not the same; that even the natural standards of cloth and of long measure are two, both derived from the stature and proportions of man, but one from his hand and arm, the other from his leg and foot; that the natural standards of measures of capacity and of weights are different from those of linear measure, and different from each other, the essential character of the weight being compact solidity, and that of the vessel bounded vacuity; that the natural standards of weights are two, one of which is the same with metallic money; and that decimal arithmetic, as founded in nature, is peculiarly applicable to the standard *units* of weights and measures, but not to their subdivisions or fractional parts, nor to the objects of admeasurement and weight.

With all these diversities, the only commands of the law for observing uniformity were, that the weights and the measures should be just, perfect, and not divers, a *great* and a *small*. But this last prohibition was merely an ordinance against fraud. It was a precept to the individual, and not to the nation. It forbade the iniquitous practice of using a large weight or measure for buying, and a small one for selling the same article; and, to remove the opportunity for temptation, it enjoined upon the individual not to have divers weights and measures, great and small, of the same denomination, in his bag when at market, or in his house when at home. But it was never understood to forbid that there should be measures of different dimensions bearing the same name: and it appears, from the sacred history, that there actually were three different measures called a cubit, of about the relative proportion of 17, 21, and 35, of our inches, to each other. They were distinguished by the several denominations of the cubit of a man, the cubit of the king, and the cubit of the sanctuary.[1]

The effort to establish systems of weights and measures by the exercise of civil authority has always encountered great obstacles. The prescription of uniformity when it comes through the dictum of a ruler seems arbitrary. There is no such natural unit of extension and weight as there is of time. Measurements of space and weight, therefore, have to pass through long stages of trial before they can be established throughout a nation.

We may draw examples of this long series of efforts to systematize measures by edict from the history of England which is reviewed in great detail by Adams. Writing of the earliest stages of England's history in this matter, he says :

In England, from the earliest records of parliamentary history, the statute books are filled with ineffectual attempts of the legislature to establish uniformity. Of the origin of their weights and measures, the historical traces are faint and indistinct : but they have had, from time immemorial, the pound, ounce, foot, inch, and mile, derived from the Romans, and through them from the Greeks, and the *yard*, or *girth*, a measure of Saxon origin, derived, like those of the Hebrews and the Greeks, from the human body, but, as a natural standard, different from theirs, being taken not from the length of members, but from the circumference of the body. The yard of the Saxons evidently belongs to a primitive system of measures different from that of the Greeks, of which the foot, and from that of the Hebrews, Egyptians, and Antediluvians, of which the cubit was the standard. It affords, therefore, another demonstration, how invariably nature first points to the human body, and its proportions, for the original standards of linear measure. But the *yard* being for all purposes of use a measure

[1] ADAMS, JOHN QUINCY — *op. cit.*, pp. 15–16.

corresponding with the *ulna*, or ell, of the Roman system, became, when superadded to it, a source of diversity, and an obstacle to uniformity in the system. The yard, therefore, very soon after the Roman conquest, is said to have lost its original character of girth; to have been adjusted as a standard by the arm of king Henry the First: and to have been found or made a multiple of the foot, thereby adapting it to the remainder of the system: and this may perhaps be the cause of the difference of the present English foot from that of the Romans, by whom, as a measure, it was introduced. The ell measure has, however, in England, retained its place as a standard for measuring cloth: but, in the ancient statutes, which for centuries after the conquest were enacted in the degenerate Latin of the age, the term *ulna*, or ell, is always used to designate the yard. Historical traditions allege that, a full century before the Conquest, a law of Edgar prescribed that there should be the same weights, and the same measures, throughout the realm; but that it was never observed. The system which had been introduced by the Romans, however uniform in its origin, must have undergone various changes in the different governments of the Saxon Heptarchy. When those kingdoms were united in one, it was natural that laws of uniformity should be prescribed by the prince; and as natural that usages of diversity should be persisted in by the people. Canute the Dane, William the Conqueror, and Richard the First, princes among those of most extensive and commanding authority, are said to have made laws of the like import, and the same inefficacy. The Norman Conquest made no changes in any of the established weights and measures. The very words of a law of William the Conqueror are cited by modern writers on the English weights and measures; their import is: " We ordain and command that the weights and measures, throughout the realm, be as our worthy predecessors have established." [1]

The way in which various measures are brought gradually into the same system is described by Adams in a brief

[1] ADAMS, JOHN QUINCY — *op. cit.*, pp. 21–22.

review of an act adopted in the time of Henry III (1266). This act declares that :

by the consent of *the whole realm* of England, the *measure* of the king was made ; that is to say : that an English *penny*, called a sterling round, and without any clipping, shall weigh thirty-two wheat corns in the midst of the ear, and twenty-pence do make an ounce, and twelve ounces one pound, and eight pound do make a gallon of *wine*, and eight gallons of *wine* do make a London bushel, which is the eighth part of a quarter.

Henry the Third was the eighth king of the Norman race ; and this statute was passed exactly two hundred years after the Conquest. It is merely an exemplification, word for word, embracing several ordinances of his progenitors, kings of England ; and it unfolds a system of uniformity for weights, coins, and measures of capacity, very ingeniously imagined, and skillfully combined.

It shows, first, that the money weight was identical with the silver coins ; and it establishes an uniformity of proportion between the money weight and the merchant's weight, exactly corresponding to that between the measure of wine and the measure of grain.

It makes wheat and silver money, the two weights of the balance, the natural tests and standards of each other ; that is, it makes wheat the standard for the weight of silver money, and silver money the standard for the weight of wheat.

It combines an uniformity of proportion between the weight and the measure of wheat and of wine ; so that the measure of wheat should at the same time be a certain weight of wheat and the measure of wine at the same time a certain weight of wine, so that the article whether bought and sold by weight or by measure, the result was the same. To this, with regard to wheat, it gave the further advantage of an abridged process for buying or selling it by the number of its kernels. Under this system, wheat was bought and sold by a combination of every property of its nature, with reference to quantity ; that is, by number, weight, and measure. The statute also fixed its proportional weight and value with reference to the weight and value of the silver coin for which it was to be exchanged in trade. If, as the most eminent of the modern economists maintain, the value of everything in trade is regulated by the proportional value of money and of wheat, then the system of weights and measures, contained in this statute, is not only accounted for as originating in the nature of things, but it may be doubted whether any other system be reconcileable to nature. It was with reference to this system, that, in the introduction to this report, it was observed, that our own weights and measures were originally founded upon an uniformity of proportion, and not upon an uniformity of identity.[1]

It may be remarked in passing that the effort to make the weight of the penny — or as it is called in modern troy weight "the pennyweight" — the standard of all measures of weight and volume failed first because of changes in coinage and second because the pound used in ordinary exchange was of another type and was ultimately strong enough to push the troy pound out of common use. The two recognized pounds of modern times have obscure histories which it is not necessary for our purposes to attempt to follow. The standards of volume measure, too, have passed through all kinds of vicissitudes. Adams presents tables to show the widest local variations in such measures as the bushel and the pound.

In regard to the units of linear measure matters followed much the same course. Professor Harkness of the United States Naval Observatory writes in regard to the early history of the English yard as follows :

The English measures of length have come down from the Saxons, but the oldest standards now existing are the exchequer yards of Henry VII (1490) and Elizabeth (1588). These are both brass end measures, the former being an octagonal rod about half an inch in diameter, very coarsely made, and as rudely divided into inches on the right-hand end and into sixteenths of a yard on the left-hand end ; the latter, a square rod with sides about half

<hr>

[1] ADAMS, JOHN QUINCY — *op. cit.*, p. 24.

an inch wide, also divided into sixteenths of a yard and provided
with a brass bed having end pieces between which the yard fits.
One end of the bed is divided into inches and half inches.   Francis
Baily, who saw this Elizabethan standard in 1836, speaks of it as
"this curious instrument, of which it is impossible, at the present
day, to speak too much in derision or contempt.   A common
kitchen poker, filed at the ends in the rudest manner by the most
bungling workman, would make as good a standard.   It has been
broken asunder, and the two pieces have been dove-tailed together,
but so badly that the joint is nearly as loose as that of a pair of
tongs.   The date of this fracture I could not ascertain, it having
occurred beyond the memory or knowledge of any of the officers
at the Exchequer.   And yet, till within the last ten years, to the
disgrace of this country, copies of this measure have been cir-
culated all over Europe and America, with a parchment document
accompanying them (charged with a stamp that costs £3 10s.
exclusive of official fees) certifying that they are true copies of the
English *standard.*" [1]

How crude the standards were even in comparatively
modern times is further attested by the formula presented
by a sixteenth-century German book on surveying for the
determination of the unit of land measure.

To find the length of a rood in the right and lawful way, and
according to scientific usage, you should do as follows: Stand at
the door of a church on a Sunday, and bid 16 men to stop, tall
ones and small ones, as they happen to pass out when the service
is finished; then make them put their left feet one behind the other
and the length thus obtained shall be a right and lawful rood to
measure and survey land with, and the sixteenth part of it shall
be a right and lawful foot.

In the eighteenth century the motive of establishing an
understanding with France led England to undertake care-

[1] HARKNESS, WILLIAM — "The Progress of Science as Exemplified in the
Art of Weighing and Measuring," *Annual Report of the Board of Regents of the
Smithsonian Institution,* pp. 597–633; July, 1888.

ful comparisons between her own standards and those of her neighboring country. The desire for comparable standards at this relatively later period grew not so much out of the practical demands of commerce as out of the growing interest in scientific determinations.

The latter part of the seventeenth century had seen great progress in the development of scientific astronomy and physics and mathematics. Measures which throughout the medieval period had been thought of altogether in terms of cloth or wine or wheat or coins now began to be used for the purpose of describing with accuracy the phenomena of nature.

Professor Harkness describes the occurrences of the middle of the eighteenth century as follows:

In the year 1742 certain members of the Royal Society of London, and of the Royal Academy of Sciences of Paris, proposed that, in order to facilitate a comparison of the scientific operations carried on in the two countries, accurate standards of the measures and weights of both should be prepared and preserved in the archives of each of these societies. This proposition having been approved, Mr. George Graham, at the instance of the Royal Society, had two substantial brass rods made, upon which he laid off, with the greatest care, the length of three English feet from the standard yard kept at the Tower of London. These two rods, together with a set of Troy weights, were then sent over to the Paris Academy, which body, in like manner, had the measure of a French half toise set off upon the rods, and keeping one, as previously agreed, returned the other, together with a standard weight of two marcs, to the Royal Society. In 1835, Baily declared this copy of the half toise to be of little value, because the original toise-étalon was of iron and the standard temperature in France differed from that in England. In his opinion the French should have sent over an iron half toise in exchange for the English brass yard, but this criticism loses much of its force when it is remembered that in 1742 neither England nor France had fixed upon a temperature at which their standards were to be regarded as of the true length.

On the return of the rod from Paris, Mr. Graham caused Jonathan Sisson to divide the English yard and the French half toise each into three equal parts, after which the rod was deposited in the archives of the Royal Society, where it still remains. Objection having been made that the original and legal standard yard of England was not the one at the Tower, but the Elizabethan standard at the Exchequer, the Royal Society requested Mr. Graham to compare his newly made scale with the latter standard, and on Friday, April 22, 1743, he did so in the presence of a committee of seven members of the Royal Society. In the following week the same gentlemen compared the Royal Society's scale with the standards at Guildhall and the Tower, and also with the standards of the Clock-maker's Company. These comparisons having shown that the copy of the Tower yard upon the Royal Society's scale was about 0.0075 of an inch longer than the standard at the Exchequer, Mr. Graham inscribed upon the Royal Society's scale a copy of the latter standard also, marking it with the letters Exch., to distinguish it from the former, which was marked E. (English), and from the half toise which was marked F. (French).[1]

The history of French standards of length begins like that of the English yard. A part of this history as given by Professor Harkness is as follows:

Turning now to the French standards of length, it is known that the ancient *toise de maçons* of Paris was probably the toise of Charlemagne (A.D. 742 to 814), or at least of some Emperor Charles, and that its *étalon* was situated in the court-yard of the old Châtelet, on the outside of one of the pillars of the building. It still existed in 1714, but entirely falsified by the bending of the upper part of the pillar. In 1668 the ancient toise of the masons was reformed by shortening it five lines; but whether this reformation was an arbitrary change, or merely a change to remedy the effects of long use and restore the étalon to conformity with some more carefully preserved standard, is not quite clear. These old *étalons* were iron bars having their two ends turned up at right angles so

[1] HARKNESS, WILLIAM — *op. cit.*, p. 602.

as to form *talons*, and the standardizing of end measures was effected by fitting them between the *talons*. Being placed on the outside of some public building, they were exposed to wear from constant use, to rust, and even to intentional injury by malicious persons. Under such conditions every étalon would sooner or later become too long and require shortening.

Respecting the ancient toise of the masons there are two contradictory stories. On December 1, 1714, La Hire showed to the French Academy what he characterized as "a very ancient instrument of mathematics, which has been made by one of our most accomplished workmen with very great care, where the foot is marked, and which has served to reëstablish the toise of the Châtelet, as I have been informed by our old mathematicians." Forty-four years later, on July 29, 1758, La Condamine stated to the Academy that "We know only by tradition that to adjust the length of the new standard, the width of the arcade or interior gate of the grand pavilion, which served as an entrance to the old Louvre, on the side of the rue Fromenteau, was used. This opening, according to the plan, should have been twelve feet wide. Half of it was taken to fix the length of the new toise, which thus became five lines shorter than the old one." Of these two contradictory statements that of La Hire seems altogether most trustworthy, and the ordinary rules of evidence indicate that it should be accepted to the exclusion of the other.

In 1668 the étalon of the new toise, since known as the *toise-étalon du Châtelet*, was fixed against the wall at the foot of the staircase of the grand Châtelet de Paris, by whom or at what season of the year is not known. Strange as it now seems, this standard (very roughly made, exposed in a public place for use or abuse by everybody, liable to rust, and certain to be falsified by constant wear) was actually used for adjusting the toise of Picard, that of Cassini, the toise of Peru and of the North, that of La Caille, that of Mairan — in short, all the toises employed by the French in their geodetic operations during the seventeenth and eighteenth centuries. The lack of any other recognized standard made the use of this one imperative; but the French academicians were well aware of its defects and took precautions to guard against them.

The first toise copied from the étalon of the Châtelet for scientific purposes was that used by Picard in his measurement of a degree of the meridian between Paris and Amiens. It was made about the year 1668, and would doubtless have become the scientific standard of France had it not unfortunately disappeared before the degree measurements of the eighteenth century were begun. The second toise copied from the étalon of the Châtelet for scientific purposes was that used by Messrs. Godin, Bouguer, and La Condamine for measuring the base of their arc of the meridian in Peru. This toise, since known as the *toise du Pérou*, was made by the artist Langlois under the immediate direction of Godin in 1735, and is still preserved at the Paris Observatory. It is a rectangular bar of polished wrought-iron, having a breadth of 1.58 English inches and a thickness of 0.30 of an inch. All the other toises used by the Academy in the eighteenth century were compared with it, and ultimately it was made the legal standard of France by an order of Louis XV, dated May 16, 1766. As the toise of Peru is the oldest authentic copy of the toise of the Châtelet, the effect of this order was simply to perpetuate the earliest known state of that ancient standard.[1]

The French standard changed abruptly, however, through the effort to carry out a proposal made by Talleyrand to the National Assembly of France in 1790. This proposal was that a new system of weights and measures be set up by adopting as a common base of all units a definite unit of space, namely, one ten-millionth of the arc of the earth's meridian extending from the equator to the pole. Weights were to be defined in terms of the weight of a cubic unit of water. The whole system was to be formulated in decimal units, the units to be designated by uniform prefixes.

The controversy between the old English system and the new French system is still being waged in English-speaking countries. The common people are so attached to the English system which readily permits the use of such fractions

[1] HARKNESS, WILLIAM — *op. cit.*, pp. 605–607.

as one quarter and one half that they have not adopted for common use the decimal system of France. In fact, even in France for a long time after the adoption of the metric system the ordinary transactions of the market kept the familiar fractional divisions which the people had always found convenient.

Our review has given us ample ground for several generalizations. The first is that measurement is a form of comparison which begins with the most concrete objects easily accessible to the observer. Parts of the body, grains of wheat, stones, and natural vessels for holding liquids are the first standards.

The second generalization is that the motives for different kinds of measurement are so various that weights and measures tend at the outset to show great diversity, with the result that different kinds of units are not thought of as belonging together. Thus weight is not determined in terms of cubical dimensions. Furthermore, the various peoples of the earth, indeed, the different localities within the same country, have different units. A late and very striking example of this is the fact that in the United States to-day the number of pounds which the statutes of the various states require for a bushel of such commodities as buckwheat and sweet potatoes vary by as much as twenty per cent.

The third generalization is that as the demands of civilization progress in the direction of precision, the standards of measurement are themselves subjected to more searching scrutiny. Put in terms of our general discussion, this can be stated as follows: When the importance of the institution of weights and measures becomes a matter of explicit recognition, attention is diverted from the uses of the institution and is bestowed upon the perfection of the institution itself. The perfection of the system is regarded by individuals and nations as justified by the superior serviceableness of the

precise weights and measures thus evolved.   In the economy
of society as a whole, it becomes an advantage to set aside
energy for the indirect and apparently abstract good of perfecting weights and measures.

The fourth generalization is that in successive stages of
an evolutionary series, the purposes which prompt men to
give attention to the system gradually change.   In the first
stages of the evolution of weights and measures the purposes were wholly practical.   In later stages the desire for
uniformity brought it to pass that the authority of organized
society was called in to regulate and systematize the institution, because men had arrived at the level where they
desired consistency as much as practical utility.   In a still
later stage the more abstract virtue of exact scientific com-
parability between all standards is demanded in order that
thought may be made general in the full sense of the word.
So long as commerce was the only incentive for securing
uniformity of weights and measures, men got on very well
with rough approximations; but when they came to think
about the dimensions of the earth and the wave-length of
light they saw that the measurements of different countries
must be made comparable and they saw also that all the
units must be made sufficiently precise to make critical
judgments possible.   Measurement becomes in these last
stages the highest form of controlled thinking.   Systems of
measurement take on a kind of sanction and a kind of fixity
which civil authority, unsupported by scientific authority,
could never give them.

In the evolution of weights and measures we have another
striking illustration of the fact that man has introduced into
his environment an institution which essentially changes his
relation to nature.   He has created by the exercise of his
genius an instrument for the guidance of his behavior which
insures economy of material and effectiveness of conduct in

the highest degree. At the same time he has set up a guide for individuals and a means of compelling the individual to conform to the practices of society, which are among the most potent factors of civilization.

It may not be amiss to emphasize once more the fact that there is absolutely no instinct in the animal world or in human nature which responds to weights and measures. It is utterly futile to attempt to bring these creations into the class of biological facts which are dealt with in the ordinary applications of the principle of biological variations and natural selection. Weights and measures constitute one of the institutions of civilization. The history which has been sketched in the foregoing pages shows what a vast amount of energy has been bestowed on the erection of this institution. The history of men's thinking which parallels the facts regarding weights and measures is a history of the transfer of attention from superficial qualities to fundamental values and exact determinations. Modern man thinks in terms of units of measurement whereas his remote ancestors thought only in the roughest approximations. Modern man thinks in terms of social equity as determined by standards which he and all his fellow men are prepared to protect and enforce. Primitive man had no such ethical notions about quantities and no such devotion to exact descriptions. Primitive man had no remotest notion of the possibilities of exact measurements of the forces and substances of nature, which even the common man of every civilized nation understands. We live in a world where the luxuries of life are delivered to us through meters, reported in Arabic numerals, and paid for in coin. Truly, civilization has left nature and primitive modes of life far behind.

Human nature has become what it is in modern times through its own reactions upon itself. The native capacity of man has not changed during the ages, but his methods of using his powers have changed. In support of this statement is cited the anthropological fact that man's skull does not seem to have changed in size and presumably there has been no change in the size and texture of his cerebrum. The fact is also cited that men of one level of civilization when brought into contact with representatives of a more complex civilization rapidly learn to take on the manners and arts of the more cultured group, thus showing that civilization depends not on some variation in individuals but on the accumulation of devices of adaptation. The reason why civilization is a higher mode of life than is savagery is to be sought in the fact that the savage has no accumulated institutional equipments, no coöperative ways of securing more than he can secure by personal effort.

CHAPTER VIII

THE INDIVIDUAL'S METHODS OF EXACT THOUGHT

The three chapters which immediately precede this have given sketches of three lines of evolution which are closely related. Weights and measures could not be perfected to any high degree before men learned to count. The measurement of time is in principle not different from the measurement of distances. All of the quantitative devices which civilization has invented converge in what we call scientific methods of exact thinking.

The fact that all these lines of evolution have contributed to a common end should not mislead us into thinking of them as psychologically alike. The mental processes involved in the use of numbers are indeed related to measurements, but numbers are quite distinct as facts of experience from yards and pounds. The comparisons which are made with the aid of balances and weights are wholly different in the conscious processes which they involve from the analytical division of the day into hours and minutes.

What has been said about the psychological differences between different modes of exact scientific thinking can perhaps be made clearer by referring to the way in which individuals acquire these different types of thinking. Each new human being who comes into the world has to go through a personal struggle to master number and acquire the art of measurement and cultivate the virtue of punctuality and its related ideas. Every individual begins life as the race began, without number or an understanding of measurement. Every individual is obliged to do what the race did, pass through a period of acquisition of number, through a period of contact with standards of measurement, and through another period of drill in punctuality. The only way to become exact is to take on the various psychological methods which make exactness of different types possible.

While it is true that both the individual and the race start without methods of exact thinking and make progress toward the general goal by mastering a number of different systems of experience, it is equally true that no two individuals follow the same path in their developments and that no individual follows the path which was taken by the race.

It will clarify our ideas about both the social processes of exact thinking and individual development if we consider in detail some of the facts which show the variety of individual methods of acquiring number and methods of measurement.

Children very commonly acquire the names of the digits before they learn the order in which these names are used in counting. A child will count in such an order as the following: one, three, seven, four, six, nine. This shows that the social device of counting has not been mastered but that one element of the device has been adopted by the child. The child has learned from his elders the various number names; what is lacking in his experience is the serial arrangement.

We know that there are marked individual differences in the ways in which children fix in their minds the number series. Some children make use of a visual image in which the numbers are arranged in a fixed order. These visual images were called by Galton, who first described them, number forms. Sometimes the number form gives evidence of being borrowed from a clockface; sometimes it is an arbi-

trary arrangement apparently made up by the individual
without external guidance.

The fact that many people do not have number forms but
are able to keep the numbers in order by merely remembering
the series of names, shows that there is more than one way
in which consciousness can operate to retain the number
series.

Other evidences that people hold numbers in mind and
think out number combinations in peculiar ways are not
lacking when one considers the revelations which are made
by the arithmetic tests.   One pupil is shown by these tests
to be thoroughly acquainted with all the combinations and
to be accurate and rapid in recalling them.   Another pupil
is competent in addition but deficient in subtraction.   One
pupil adds by counting on his fingers, another by tapping
on his desk, and another by resolving numbers so as to arrive
at combinations which make ten in as many cases as possible.

When one contrasts these personal methods of dealing
with numbers with the fact that the laws of arithmetical
combinations are regarded in logic and science as among the
most immutable principles with which the mind has to deal,
one realizes that there are two wholly different sets of facts
in the world ; there is on the one hand a fundamental system
and on the other hand the individual's assimilation of this
system.

The number system as it is presented to the individual is
a highly perfected device.   It is to be compared with some
ingeniously constructed machine which is put at the disposal
of a person who had nothing to do with its construction.
The person will, through effort and repeated experiments,
gradually become accustomed to the machine and finally
will acquire skill in its use.   There is no difficulty in such a
case in distinguishing between the intellectual processes of
invention and use.   The analogy helps to make understand-

able the difference between the racial contribution to individual thinking and the individual's progressive mastery of this racial system. The pupil in the school has presented to him by society a perfect number system. He acquires more or less skill in the use of this system during periods of practice. The pupil's skill is a fact of a totally different order from the number system and from the mental activities of the race which produced the number system.

What has been said about number can be paralleled by statements about weights and measures. Children very frequently know the names of weights and measures without having the slightest knowledge of the meaning of these names. It is true of adults as well as of children that they know many names of measures which are wholly detached from concrete experience. Most people do not know what weight is represented by the biblical name "talent." Equally indefinite is the idea which most people have of a "grain" or a "ton." When it comes to interpreting the names of measures belonging to the metric system, the confusion in most American minds is unlimited. All these facts show the difference between a social system and individual mastery of the system.

While we are justified in drawing the sharpest contrast between individual consciousness and social devices, we must not overlook the fact that the social institution acts as a constant guide to the individual while he is struggling to overtake the race in its methods of thinking. In order to make clear what is meant by this statement, one has only to consider that the Arabic number system by its very form suggests certain very important ideas and helps the individual to grasp these ideas. For example, 9 and 90 are clearly indicated to be subject to the same laws of combination by the fact that the same symbol appears in both cases even though its position is different.

In somewhat the same way, the pupil is guided in his thought about time intervals by the fact that each hour is subdivided into the same number of minutes showing that time moves at a uniform rate in spite of the subjective feeling that interesting intervals pass rapidly and empty time seems to drag on interminably.

In short, the individual is not left by the race to work out methods of exact thinking; he is asked to acquire intellectual skill as early as possible in the use of highly perfected devices which society has evolved. Not only is he offered the opportunity to avail himself of racial experience, but he finds society and its institutions ready to facilitate in every way possible his initiation into the uses of the devices which will make him competent in the methods of exact thinking.

There are some cases in which the individual finds it impossible to acquire skill in the use of a social institution. It is a well-known fact that defectives, even when they are able to cope with many of the conventions of ordinary life, find the number system too abstract and complicated for their meagerly developed intellectual powers. Here is a case where the psychological processes which have built up the number system have gone so far beyond the individual that he is not able to overtake society at all.

There are other cases in which persons of normal intelligence have for some reason or other deviated early in life from the path laid out by the social institution. The deviation may be due to emotional excitement which has created a fear of the number system or it may be due to confusion arising from the omission of some crucial intellectual step which ought to have been taken in the early stages of training. Whatever the cause, some individuals are as incompetent in the use of number as others are in the manipulation of tools. Where such a failure of the individual to learn the use of the social device continues into adult life its effect on the general intellectual attitude of the individual is often marked. What is commonly to be expected under such conditions is the withdrawal of the individual from all situations in which a mastery of the number system is essential to success. In other words society's devices are so useful as means of adaptation that the only safe procedure for a person who is not skillful in the uses of these devices is to keep out of the competitions for which his equipment is not adequate.

It is important to note that complete withdrawal from the methods of exact thinking which have been evolved by society is not compatible with successful life. There was a time when the hunter or the warrior could get on and even be a leader in his tribe although utterly unequipped with number or the arts of measurement, but the time has passed when human life can be successful without some mastery of the institutions of precision and punctuality. The institutions which are here under discussion have become compulsory. Society has occupied the world so fully that its methods must be adopted by all who seek to enjoy the advantages of coöperative life.

We shall have occasion in later chapters to describe certain institutions which society is prepared to treat as purely optional, but number and punctuality and measurement are too vital to common intercourse to be left to individual caprice. They must be cultivated in some degree by all members of civilized groups.

The degrees to which society carries its insistence in the cases of the three systems of precise thinking which are under consideration are quite as different as the individual modes of mastering these systems. One must have practically complete mastery of the time system and must be thoroughly drilled in habits of punctuality. One need have only a limited acquaintance with number combinations. The simple transactions of ordinary life which require number have been investigated and have proved to be astonishingly few. When, however, one encounters a number transaction, society insists that the individual follow absolutely the rules of the system. In the case of weights and measures less understanding is demanded, but absolute conformity to social rules is insisted upon.

These statements will serve to make clear what was meant earlier in the chapter where it was pointed out that time and number and weights and measures are distinct spheres of experience in spite of the fact that in their most highly perfected forms they are all classified together under the single term "precision." "Precision" is an abstract term. It designates a fact of human experience and social evolution which has been approached from various different directions. It is a single term covering a wide variety of facts which have come to be recognized as psychologically similar though they are totally different in their history and in the habits of life which they induce in the individual.

CHAPTER IX

THE PSYCHOLOGY OF THE ALPHABET

It is an inversion of the historical order of human evolution to discuss writing before taking up language; the same assertion holds true with regard to each of the institutions treated in earlier chapters. It is undoubtedly true that all of the social arts which man has devised were subsequent in their appearance to language. Indeed, it may be assumed with safety that man's emergence from the level of brute life is coincident with the first use of language. The justification for beginning a discussion of human institutions with a survey of tool consciousness and the other topics which have been treated in earlier chapters of this book is that these later institutions have shorter and more recent histories, and the records of their evolution are more accessible. We have, therefore, been preparing the way for an understanding of language, the oldest and most important human invention, by gradually elucidating the principles of social coöperation revealed in the more recent products of man's life in groups.

There is another justification for the treatment of the alphabet in a chapter distinct from that which discusses language; this is found in the fact that the earliest form of writing was not directly related to oral language, but was a form of communication which made its appeal to the eye and to the visual imagination alone.

A specimen of such writing is given in Figure VIII. Such writing consists in a few rough pictures. The author of this specimen was evidently possessed of little ability to make fine, regular lines; her muscles were not trained for delicate work; her implements were of the crudest kind. There was not even a clear and fully matured recognition of the form of the objects presented; no details are present, and the whole picture is nothing more than a rough approximation to the original. But rough and crude as these drawings are, they appealed to the savage's memory and imagination enough to communicate to him certain ideas. What

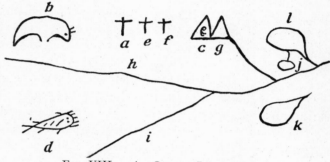

FIG. VIII. — AN OJIBWA LOVE-LETTER [1]

could be more natural than that these lines and figures intended for the eyes should reproduce that aspect of objects which appeal to the eyes, namely, the form? Primitive writing was throughout a matter of visual interest and visual recognition.

Starting from this primitive picture writing, human

[1] The Ojibwa love-letter reproduced in the figure is recorded and explained by Garrick Mallery in the *Annual Report of the Bureau of Ethnology, 1888–89*, p. 363. The writer, a girl of the Bear totem (b), summons her lover, who belongs to the Mud Puppy totem (d), along the various trails indicated, to the lodge (c) from which the beckoning hand protrudes. The enclosed figures at l, j, and k are lakes. The crosses indicate that the girl and her companions are Christians. "The clear indications of locality," writes Mallery, "serve as well as if in a city a young woman had sent an invitation to her young man to call at a certain street and number."

evolution moved in two different directions. In the first place, man began to take more and more interest in the reproduction of form. The details of objects began to receive more attention and to be more accurately and fully incorporated into the reproductions. This refinement of form very soon began to go beyond the limits necessary for the communication of ideas, and an art developed, the chief interest of which was the complete treatment of form.

The second line of development which began with primitive picture writing is the one in which we are interested in our present discussion ; it is the line of development of writing proper. Here we must recognize a greater devotion than in art to the communication of ideas. The figures used in writing are of interest only in so far as form stands for some kind of meaning. The result of this chief interest in meaning rather than in form is that the outline drawings are reduced to their simplest terms. There is, indeed, a point beyond which the form cannot be simplified without danger that it will lose its power of communicating a distinct idea. Thus, if the savage wishes to make a distinction between horses and cattle, he must keep enough of the distinctive details to insure the communication of the right idea. He accomplishes his end in this particular case by retaining the horns as the distinctive mark of his drawing for cattle. But while form cannot be lost sight of entirely, it is so unimportant that purely external causes may contribute to the corruption and simplification of the forms of the drawings. One such outside consideration is to be found in the fact that straight lines are easier to draw than are curved lines. The result is that forms were much simplified in the early stages of writing, in the interest of ease of production.

Some excellent illustrations of corruptions in form are given to us by students of Chinese writing. Chinese writing is not like our own, made up of various combinations of a few phonetic elements. It has a separate symbol for each word. The word for sun, for example, is a single symbol rather than a series of three letters as in our writing. The modern Chinese symbol for sun looks like a ladder with three rungs. At first sight this does not seem to have any relation so far as its form is concerned to the object for which it stands. But if one compares this modern symbol with a symbol of more ancient origin, the modern form is immediately recognized as due to the general principle that straight lines are easier to draw with the brush pen of the Chinese than are curved lines. The ancient form for the

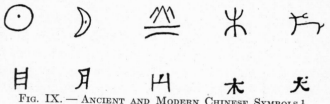

FIG. IX. — ANCIENT AND MODERN CHINESE SYMBOLS [1]

sun is an outline picture consisting of a circle with a dot in the center. The dot of the ancient symbol is the middle rung of the modern ladder-shaped symbol. The sides and the top and bottom rungs of the modern figure are the final rectilinear remains of the circumference of the ancient circle.

Figure IX reproduces a number of ancient and modern Chinese forms which bear out the same conclusions as those reached in the discussion of the symbol for the sun.

Form-writing thus developed gradually into what may be called convenient or simplified form-writing. The convenient writing would not have been possible unless there had been accompanying mental emphasis on meaning rather than form. This fact of greater and greater emphasis on

[1] The characters signify, reading from left to right : sun, moon, mountain, tree (or wood), dog.

meaning ultimately results in reducing the characters used in the writing to what we call symbols or mere signs.

Interest in symbols, that is, the attitude that meanings are more significant than are forms, makes possible a wide range for development. Symbols, freed largely from references to objects of like form, came very soon to have two or three meanings, some very remote from the original signification. Thus, in Egypt the figure of the owl came to mean not only the bird itself but also, as with us, night, and, still more indirectly, silence and wisdom. Among our American Indians, the animal which the Indian chief painted on his totem pole came to stand for the man, and sometimes for the whole tribe. Symbolism of a highly developed type thus became common.

At this point there set in another line of development which was slowly worked out in Egypt and Phœnicia, and which has had the greatest possible influence on the development of our present form of writing. As soon as symbolism had reached a high development, it naturally came into mental association with oral speech which is another symbolic mode of representing objects for the purposes of human intercommunication. It needs no long discussion to show that speech is a kind of symbolism. A given sound arouses in the imagination an idea which is quite remote from the sound itself.

To make clear the way in which the symbolism of picture writing and the symbolism of speech came together, let us sketch the process of evolution which took place somewhere among the Semitic tribes. When the primitive man of these tribes looked at a given object, he received a direct impression. If after having received a direct impression, he wished to arouse in a companion a recollection of such a direct experience, he could do it in one of two ways, either by making a symbolic mark or by making a symbolic sound.

The symbolic mark and the symbolic sound had at first no connection except as they both referred to the same object. But very soon the sound symbolism began to assert its superiority. The sound name of an object was so fully developed and so thoroughly familiar that it took precedence as the means of expressing thought. Men did not even stop to recall in full the direct impression made by the sight of the object. They began to think in words, as we do, and to let the objective appearances drop into the background. Just as soon as this happened, the written symbol was forced into relations with the superior sound symbol.

The first steps of this growing relation between sound and written symbols were of a type with which we are all quite familiar. There is a kind of puzzle called a rebus in which the first personal pronoun, "I," for example, is represented by a picture of the organ of sight, which has a name similar in sound.. The verb "can" may likewise be represented in a rebus by that convenient tin article of household furniture with which we are familiar. We are thus well on the way to a sentence. The sentence, "I can see a house," is easily completed in the same general way, so far as the verb "see" is concerned, by a picture or symbol of the ocean; and then all that is needed as a representation of the word "house" is a written symbol or a true picture of the house itself.

This kind of rebus writing actually appears in some of the old Egyptian records, and shows how sounds and written symbols began to be related. Thus, the Egyptians had a word, the name of one of their gods, which was pronounced *Hesiri*. They also had two distinct words, *hes* and *iri*, exactly like the two syllables of the name *Hesiri*, so far as the sounds were concerned, but in no way related in meaning to the name of this god. The two separate words, *hes* and *iri*, meant, respectively, a seat and an eye. When the

Egyptians wanted to write the name of the god, they did not draw his picture, but they evidently thought of his name, and then, thinking of the sounds only, they made this double pun that he was a seat-eye god. After that the representation of the god was easy, for they drew first the seat and then the eye and let it go at that. Another illustration from Egypt is the use of a basket to mean lord. This usage is perfectly clear as soon as we know that the word for basket and the word for lord were both pronounced *neb*.

Written symbols acquired through connection with sound words a wider range of usefulness than they had before. The picture of a basket, for example, came to stand, not only for the basket itself, and for the act of carrying, and for the idea of plenty, but also, through the association with sound, for the word "lord."

After the perfection of this form of rebus-writing, the sound association went forward another step. Instead of the symbol calling to mind the total sound which it represented, the symbol began to stand for the first sound contained in its name. Thus, to invent an illustration using our own English words, suppose one wanted to write the word "monkey." A monkey being an animal hard to draw, the writer would divide the word into two syllables, and would then look around for some object with a name the first syllable of which is the same as the first syllable of "monkey." *Mon-* is the common syllable for the words "money" and "monkey." The picture of a coin is used to stand for the desired syllable *mon-*, and the word "monkey" is half written. The last part of the word "monkey" can be easily represented in the simple rebus fashion by the picture of a key.

This way of breaking up words so as to extract the first syllable is a very laborious device; we can hardly understand how the race had ingenuity enough or patience enough to complete the task. But a race which had no other de-

vice for recording its experiences would naturally keep at
the task of analyzing words for the sake of the results secured in fluency and completeness of writing.

The illustration which we invented to explain the way
in which symbols came to represent single sounds is paralleled by real historical facts in abundance.   Thus in the ancient Egyptian language the name of the owl began with
the sound which we represent to-day by the letter "M."
The Egyptians used the owl as a symbol for this "M"

FIG. X. — ORIGIN OF THE LETTER M [1]

sound ; and, as little as one would guess it from the form of
our letter "M," this letter is the direct historical descendant
of the Egyptian symbol of the owl.   Figure X will make
clear how the line of descent is traced.   The series of forms
in the figure shows again the fact to which we earlier called
attention, namely, the fact that as interest in the form of

[1] The figure shows the derivation of the letter M from the Egyptian hieroglyphic owl.   The four forms in the upper part of the figure are Egyptian
forms.   The first on the left is the usual hieroglyphic picture of the owl, or,
as it was called in the Egyptian language, *mulak*.   The three remaining upper
forms are found in the writings of the Egyptian priests.   The first form on the
left of the lower series is an ancient Semitic form.   Then follow in order an
ancient Greek form, and two later Greek forms. (Adapted from Isaac Taylor,
The History of the Alphabet, pp. 9–10, Charles Scribner's Sons, 1899.)

the symbol grows less and less intense, the form becomes increasingly simple and convenient. It is finally reduced, as are all our letters, to comparatively simple groups of lines, not resembling even remotely the object from which the figure was first derived.

The historical succession shown in Figure X can advantageously be made a subject of detailed study. The second figure in the upper line is evidently a simplification made in the interests of ease of production. The third and fourth figures carry the matter a step further. It is obvious that the simplified figures make a demand on the reader which the full figure does not make. The reader of the simplified figure must be ready to respond with an interpretation to a mere suggestion. This greater readiness of interpretation depends on familiarity with the symbols or, putting the matter in other terms, on training. The priests who were constantly dealing with written records were, as contrasted with the ordinary observer, highly trained in recognition of symbols; they were competent to use freely therefore the abbreviated or simplified symbols.

We have now traced the history of writing down to the point at which it began to be a means of representing sounds rather than direct visual experiences. We have seen that the primitive attitude of mind was one of attention to form, that the gradual emancipation of attention from form and its transfer to meaning were complicated by the necessity of subordinating written symbolism to the more fully developed sound symbolism of speech. All this evolution was very ancient. The Greeks emerged from their early association with the Oriental world fully equipped with a sound alphabet, which was, doubtless, borrowed largely from the Phœnicians. The Romans learned the same alphabet from their Italian ancestors and later modified it through their own use and through contact with the later Greek forms.

The forms of our own letters are derived in very direct lines of descent from the Roman forms, so that we may confine our attention to the Roman alphabet and the later European alphabets derived from the Roman.

The earliest Roman letters were used on monuments, and owe their form very largely to the hard materials on

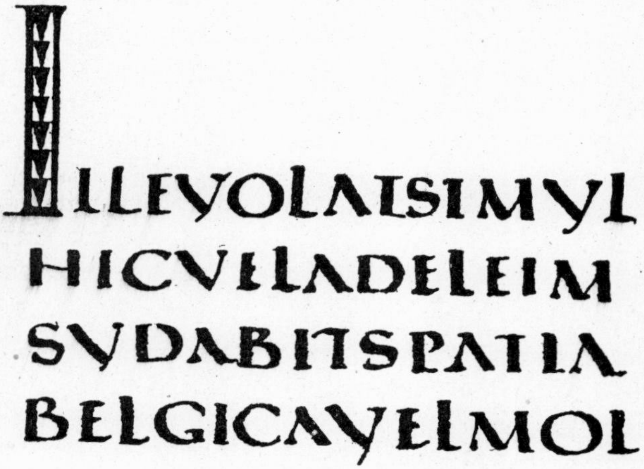

FIG. XI. — ROMAN CAPITALS [1]

which they were traced.   The letters were made up almost entirely of straight lines and sharp angles.   They were all very nearly uniform in height, and were written without connections between the successive letters and without breaks

[1] The specimen of Roman capitals is from a manuscript of Vergil's *Georgics*. The letters here reproduced show the first parts of four successive lines and are to be deciphered as follows :

Ille volat simul . . .
Hic vel ad Eleim . . .
Sudabit spatia . . .
Belgica vel mol . . .

Arndt, Wilhelm Ferdinand — *Schrifttafeln zur Erlernung der lateinischen Palæographie*, hrsq. von Wilhelm Arndt; besorgt von Michael Tangl, Berlin, 1903–06.   107 facsimiles in 3 portfolios.

between words.   Figure XI gives an illustration of this earliest type of writing, as used even in some of the later Roman manuscripts.   One needs only to look at the letters to recognize at once that in the modern world many of these same Roman capitals are still doing service where straight, angular letters of great legibility are desirable and possible.

The Roman capitals represent what we may call the maximum of legibility.   It would be difficult to improve upon these forms if mere legibility were the only consideration in the formation of letters.   But there are considerations other than mere legibility.   The capitals are very clumsy letters to write.   One cannot write rapidly when one has to make those sharp angles and separate letters.

The demand for a more rapid form of writing must have made itself felt very early.   Indeed, we have evidence from a few business records belonging to the beginning of the Christian era that even the early Romans had a rapid running hand which was used for ordinary business records.

Figure XII reproduces a specimen of this early Roman cursive, as it is called.   This cursive differs from the capitals in a number of characteristics.   The letters tend to run into each other.   In some cases in even the earliest cursive, there are connecting lines or ligatures between the letters. These ligatures are regular and pronounced characteristics of all the later forms of cursive.   Their less frequent appearance in the early forms is due to the fact that this writing was done for the most part on very unpliable wax tablets, and was, consequently, by no means as free and easy as was the later writing which was done after better materials had been discovered in papyrus and vellum on which one wrote with pen and ink.   Finally, it must be noted that this early cursive writing is by no means as regular or legible as is the writing made up of capitals.   Something of the regularity of form and of the clear-cut legibility of letters is always sacrificed when rapidity of execution becomes the chief consideration.

The contrast between capitals and cursive is the ever-recurring contrast between forms of legible writing and forms of rapid writing. As one comes down through the later periods of the history of writing, one finds a succession of forms devised like the capitals for legibility and beauty, and on the other hand one finds other forms devised for rapid and easy writing. The tendency of the beautiful and very

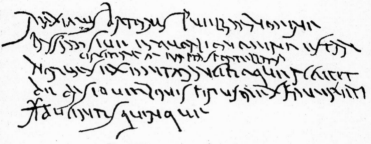

FIG. XII. — ROMAN CURSIVE [1]

legible forms is to become more and more regular and difficult to make, and the tendency of the rapid forms is to become more and more difficult to read.

After the Roman capitals and the early cursive, there grew up a kind of compromise form which was less angular than the capitals, and hence easier to write. It was used, however, only by the book-making scribes, for it was still

[1] The figure shows early Roman cursive found on a wax tablet written in the year 139 A.D. It relates to the purchase of a slave girl. It is to be deciphered as follows :

> Maximus Batonis puellam nomine
> Passiam sive ea quo alio nomne est, an
> circiter plus minus empta sportellaria
> norum sex emit mancipioque accepit
> de Dasio Verzonis Pirusta ex Kaviereti
> ⌗ ducentis quinque. (Arndt's *Tafeln*.)

too difficult for ordinary use. This form is reproduced in
Figure XIII and is the so-called uncial form. A typical letter in this form is the letter *e*, which is no longer angular as it
was in the capitals, but is much more like our lower-case
letter. The derivation of this round *e* from the square
capital is sufficiently direct to be obvious. The motive for
inventing this new form is also obvious. The round letter
is much more economical in the number of movements which
it requires. In the square capital, the upper and lower
horizontal strokes and the one vertical stroke, all had to be
made separately. In
the round letter, one
uninterrupted curved
movement was substi-
tuted for the three sep-
arate movements just
mentioned. The single
curved movement is,
therefore, to be looked
upon as a concession to
the demand for fluency.

quoscumcog
nossesapien
tisesitumue
roprospicere

FIG. XIII. — UNCIALS[1]

But the concession would never have been possible without
a change from the earlier writing materials. The conditions
favorable to this change are explained by an eminent authority in the following sentence: "To the substitution
of a soft surface for a hard one, of the pen for the graving
tool, we undoubtedly owe the rounded forms of the uncial
letters."[2]

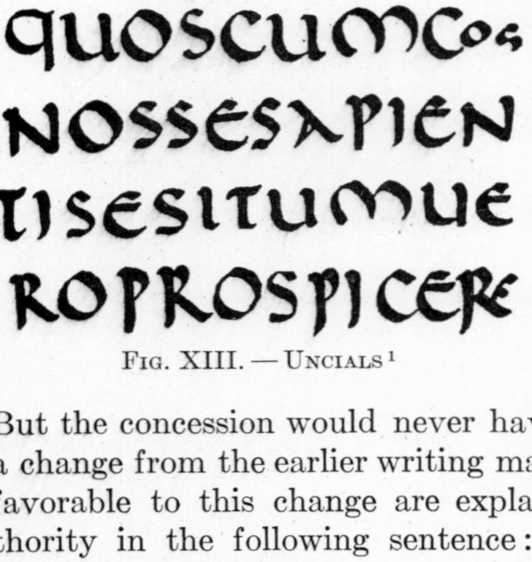

[1] The figure shows uncials from a manuscript of Cicero's *De Republica*.
The manuscript was probably written in the third century. The lines are to
be deciphered as follows:

quoscumque cog   tis est tumue
nosse sapien   ro prospicere   (Arndt's *Tafeln*.)

[2] THOMPSON, E. N. — *Encyclopædia Britannica*, Ninth edition, XVIII,
p. 145; Cambridge University Press.

One may say that the process which shows itself in the development of this *e* is the typical process of compromise which has been going on since the Roman period even down to our own time. There is a constant and growing concession to the demand for easier movement on the one side, and a clear effort on the other side to preserve the legibility and beauty of the letter. The great variety of forms invented since that early date are nothing more nor less than the experiments of the race in legibility and beauty, and ease and fluency of writing.

During these experiments almost every conceivable form has been tried. The widest extremes have been reached and most of the forms tried have been abandoned. The cursive grew so illegible in the thirteenth century, we are told, that Frederick II was obliged to prohibit its use. The tendencies toward elaboration among the careful and artistic writers went to such extremes that months were spent on a single letter.

With the invention of printing there entered a factor which tended to put a stop to experimenting with forms. The makers of types began to select from among the various scripts used by the scribes of the time, and the alphabet began to settle into its final form. The German printers, for example, selected the forms which we know as the Gothic letters. The world has decided that the German printers made a mistake, and most civilized nations, and even some of the better German printers of to-day, are using the much simpler and more legible forms of the old Roman capitals and later uncials.

The invention of printing also fixed our English script. We borrowed the style of letter that had been made permanent by an Italian printer. Before we turn to that matter, however, let us glance at one or two forms of medieval script which will show us what we escaped. Figure XIV reproduces one of the most elaborate and fantastic of the early scripts. It is without the virtues of beauty or legibility, and it was too elaborate to survive in a busy world. On the other hand, the specimen of Anglo-Saxon writing shown in Figure XV certainly is beautiful and legible; its cardinal and fatal fault is its elaborate and unwieldy form.

We are fortunate in the form of script which was finally adopted in England. We are fortunate as compared, for

FIG. XIV.— MEROVINGIAN CURSIVE [1]

example, with the Germans, who are even to this day continuing to use an elaborate and angular form of writing. It is to Italy that we owe our script. In the days of Queen Elizabeth, the educated Englishman went to Italy to gain polish from contact with an older civilization and from Italy he brought back a simple, beautiful, running script. This script was borrowed from the form of printed letters which we call italics. The very name " italics " shows that

[1] The figure shows a specimen of Merovingian cursive from the year 688 A.D. The part here reproduced is the end of the first line of the manuscript. The four lines which appear below the letters and extend into the writing are the upper loops of some of the letters of the line just below the one here reproduced. The letters are to be deciphered as follows :

Ideoque vestra cognuscat industria quod nos

(Arndt's *Tafeln*.)

the type was made in Italy. The story goes that the famous printer Manutius Aldus, who did his work early in the sixteenth century, copied the handwriting of the great scholar Petrarch, and that Pope Julius, in recognition of the beauty of his new type, granted Aldus the exclusive right to use it. This type of Aldus became our italics, and undoubtedly was one of the most influential factors in determining our modern form of script.

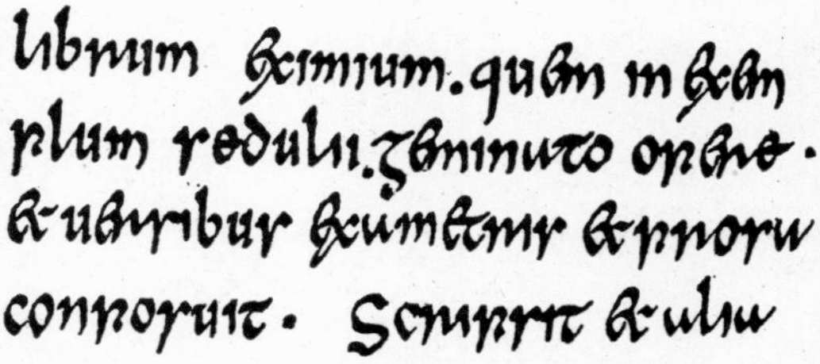

There are a number of supplementary discussions which may be added to this

FIG. XV. — ANGLO-SAXON WRITING OF THE EIGHTH CENTURY [1]

main outline of the evolution of writing in order to throw much light on the way in which the mind of man works in evolving institutions. Taylor points out that the invention of alphabetic symbols can be traced back in Egyptian history to a very early date, but the invention was not fully utilized. Taylor's discussion of this matter is as follows:

Thus we see that from the times of the earliest known monuments the hieroglyphic writers possessed a sufficient number of true letters to enable them to write alphabetically. They seem, however, not to have dared to trust themselves with their own great invention, by confining themselves, as they might have done, to the magnificent simplicity of the alphabet which they had potentially discovered. They thought it needful to interpret the mean-

[1] The letters in the figure are Anglo-Saxon from an eighth-century manuscript of Beda's History. The lines are to be deciphered as follows:

librum eximium, quem in exem
plum Sedulii geminato opere,
et versibus exametris et prosa
conposuit. Scripsit et alia   (Arndt's *Tafeln*.)

ing of their alphabetic symbols by perplexing additions of ideographic and syllabic signs. We find a word spelt out alphabetically, a needless syllabic sign is then added, and this is followed by an unnecessary ideogram. The plan is so cumbrous as to seem to us almost inconceivable. We have letters, syllabics, and ideograms piled up one on another in a perplexing confusion. So many crutches were thought necessary that walking became an art of the utmost difficulty.

But all the same, in the tangled wilderness of the hieroglyphic writing the letters of the alphabet lay concealed. All that remained to be done was to take one simple step — boldly to discard all the non-alphabetic elements, at once to sweep away the superfluous lumber, rejecting all the ideograms, the homophones, the polyphones, the syllabics, and the symbolic signs to which the Egyptian scribes so fondly clung, and so to leave revealed, in its grand simplicity, the nearly perfect alphabet of which, without knowing it, the Egyptians had been virtually in possession for almost countless ages.

But this great achievement, simple and easy as it seems, was beyond the power of Egyptian conservatism to effect. The step was so easy as almost to be impossible. It was left to another people to take up the unsolved problem, and to effect the grand discovery — a discovery at once so fertile in its results, so weighty in the history of the progress of human culture. The triumph of this great conception was reserved for the gifted Semitic race. To the sons of Shem we owe the two most precious possessions of mankind. The first of them is the Alphabet: the second is the Book, and the Religion of the Book.[1]

Conservatism, or hesitation in modifying a mode of behavior after it has once been set up is typical of human nature in all ages. If there were need of further illustrations of this, they could be readily supplied out of very recent history. English spelling is known to be unneces-

[1] TAYLOR, ISAAC — *The History of the Alphabet*, I, pp. 68–69; Charles Scribner's Sons, 1899.

sarily complex.   The letters used in our writing are many
of them mere historical remnants.   Are we willing to drop
them?   Only very reluctantly.   The older generation has
learned the clumsy combination of letters which spell the
word " though " and is quite unwilling to abandon its usual
mode of spelling and seeing this word for the simpler form
" tho."

In seeking an explanation of the changes which have taken
place in written forms, Taylor makes a very suggestive comment on one of the most important conditions under which
conservatism can be overcome.   Regarding the relation of
Chinese to Japanese writing he makes the following statement :

> The monosyllabic nature of the language of the Chinese enabled
> them to elaborate the *rebus* into a graphic system so complete as to
> make it possible to dispense with any advance towards an alpha-
> betic method.   In a monosyllabic language the interval which
> ordinarily separates the *rebus* from syllabic writing does not exist.
> Hence it was possible for the Chinese system of verbal phono-
> grams to remain essentially unchanged for a period which their
> tradition fixes at upwards of 4,000 years.   But in Japan the con-
> ditions of the problem were wholly different.   About the 3rd cen-
> tury, A.D., at the time of the great Eastern extension of the Bud-
> dhist faith, the Japanese came into contact with the civilization of
> China, and obtained a knowledge of the characters in which the
> Chinese literature was written.   The Japanese language being
> polysyllabic, the Chinese characters, which are verbal phonograms,
> could only be used for the expression of the polysyllabic Japanese
> words by being treated as syllabic signs.[1]

Later Taylor generalizes on the matter thus :

> In the creation of the Japanese and Annamese syllabaries out
> of the Chinese ideograms, we have instances of a very general law
> which governs the development of graphic systems.   During a

[1] TAYLOR, ISAAC — *op. cit.*, I, p. 34.

period of four thousand years the Chinese, left to themselves, were unable to advance beyond ideographic writing. But this important step was, as we have seen, readily accomplished when the Chinese writing had to be adapted to a language of another type. As a rule it is found that the advance from one stage in the development of writing to the next is only attained by the transmission of a graphic system from one nation to another. The transmission of the Aztec Hieroglyphs to the Mayas of Yucatan, of the Egyptian Hieroglyphs to the Semites, and the thrice repeated transmission of the Semitic alphabet to Aryan nations — to the Greeks, to the Persians, and to the Indians — are instances in point. Each of these transmissions was accompanied by important developments in the art of writing.[1]

Such statements are full of significance for the student of social institutions. They show that the higher types of institutional adaptation are not mere continuations of the lower types. The step in evolution which is taken when a new institution appears is long and difficult. Conditions must be favorable for what may be described as a radically new departure. Such favorable conditions have often been partly ready for a long period before the conscious step became possible which consummated the change.

The point to be emphasized in this discussion is that progress depends on change rather than on mere continuation. The history of China shows conclusively that mere perpetuation of an institution and additions of uniform elements often lead to the production of a stagnant rather than a progressive condition. Taylor points out that the Chinese system of writing became after long ages of use too clumsy to serve as a means of national progress. He says:

It is plain that to acquire an exhaustive knowledge of such a cumbrous system of writing would be a very formidable task. But even to obtain such an acquaintance with it as to be able to

[1] TAYLOR, ISAAC — *op. cit.*, I, p. 39.

write a common business letter, or to read an ordinary book, it is necessary for a Chinese student to commit to memory some 6,000 or 7,000 of these groups of characters. This by itself constitutes a serious tax upon the memory, and the tax on the faculties of attention and accuracy is even greater, for many of the characters being necessarily very much alike, it is most difficult to distinguish them without mistake, as will be seen by the inspection of the columns of any Chinese book. The result is that at the age of twenty-five a diligent Chinese student has barely acquired the same amount of facility in reading and writing which is usually attained by a child in an English village school at the age of ten. It may fairly be said that with the Chinese method it takes twenty years instead of five to learn to read and write.[1]

How far the conditions here described go to explain the static condition of Chinese civilization until recent times, is difficult to say, but it is quite certain that in its writing and in all of its other social institutions, China shows at once the virtues and defects of uninterrupted growth in a single direction.

Turning from the study of the origins of writing to present-day conditions, we find that ability to read and write is so essential to the maintenance of a democratic state that the institutions of popular government may be said to be absolutely dependent on the spread of literacy. It has been asserted that no nation has ever risen to the level of self-government in which the percentage of illiteracy exceeds twenty. Certain it is that a striking object lesson of the dangers of illiteracy is given in the chaotic political conditions in Russia and Mexico. The great majority of the population in these countries cannot read or write. They cannot be reached through newspapers and books and as a result the spread of rumors and superstitious prejudices prevents the creation of a wholesome public opinion.

[1] Taylor, Isaac — op. cit., I, pp. 32–33.

In those countries where the population is highly literate there has been in recent times a vastly increased breadth of public understanding of governmental and social policy. This evolution of general political intelligence is directly paralleled by an increase in the popular mastery of the arts of reading and writing.

In the middle of the last century the communities of the United States were hardly more than isolated groups of rural provincials. Their knowledge of national policies and their interest in matters outside their own narrow circle of direct oral communication were small. During the last three quarters of a century the situation has undergone a radical change with respect both to general interest in public policy and to general diffusion of literacy.

A knowledge of the extent to which writing has gained ground as a common art in the United States in the last three quarters of a century can be obtained from an examination of the statistics of the post office. If we add together the money paid for letter postage in 1843 and assume that it was spent for the cheapest letter that could be forwarded through the mails, it will be found that the average letter-writing of each inhabitant during the full year amounted to less than four letters of one sheet each. This estimate is altogether extravagant because the lowest letter postage of that date, namely, six cents, would carry only one sheet of paper within a radius of thirty miles. If letters went more than thirty miles, or were made up of more than one sheet, they cost more, reaching a maximum at four hundred miles or more, when each sheet cost twenty-five cents. Letters sent at rates of postage higher than the minimum would reduce the average computed. It is fair to assume, therefore, that letter-writing in 1843 was not a common practice.

Other facts of the same import are as follows: In 1840

the revenue of the post office for all classes of mail was twenty-seven cents per year for each inhabitant of the United States. This amount had not doubled in 1870, when it was forty-nine cents. It rose to the point where in 1890 it was $0.97; in 1900, $1.35; and in 1910, $2.43. Not all of these expenditures were for letters, but the figures show that reading and writing are much more commonly used to-day than they were a generation ago. This conclusion is overwhelming when account is taken of the steady reduction in rates which has taken place during the period under discussion.

Such statistics emphasize the fact that modern civilization has adopted writing as one of its most important instruments for the promotion of coöperation. The accelerated pace at which the institution has come into prominence shows that men are placing less reliance on earlier modes of adaptation and are emphasizing this which is a highly evolved social convention.

If this rapid spread of writing and reading had not occurred it is difficult to see how there could have matured on this continent the type of civilization in the midst of which we live. Anyone who tries to explain our civilization must find in the arts under discussion factors absolutely essential to the explanation of our industrial, social, and political life.

The attitude of modern society on the matter of writing and its corresponding art, reading, is entirely different to-day from that which appears at an earlier period in our national history. It is within the personal knowledge of people still living in the United States that writing was not thought of as essential to the practical equipment of a man. If we consider only the most highly authentic figures on this matter, we find that, in 1880, 17 per cent of our population could not write or read. Back of this date the statistics are largely matters of speculation, but it is certain that the percentage increases rapidly. We find, for example, in a message of Governor Campbell to the legislature of Virginia in 1839 the statement that "almost one-quarter part of the men applying for marriage licenses were unable to write their names." If we go a little farther back, the proportion of illiterates undoubtedly puts in the majority those who did not command the arts of reading and writing.

The attitude of modern society is such that a percentage of illiteracy as high as that of 1880 is wholly intolerable. To-day no man will willingly admit that he cannot read or write. The expectation of the nation is that all of its members will come under the influence of the established institution of writing to an extent which will make them ready participants in the intellectual life of the generation.

With regard to reading, modern expectations are even more far-reaching than are those with regard to writing. Public signs are used on every hand on the assumption that all who make use of the streets are able to follow written directions. The man who cannot read can hardly take care of himself in a crowded city.

The rate at which the expectation that people will read in order to share in the common ideas of the nation has established itself can be judged from a series of statistics collected some years ago by the Bureau of the Census showing the number of issues of newspapers and periodicals published in the United States in different years. A graph made from the figures is shown in Figure XVI. The corresponding graph for increase in population is shown in Figure XVII.

A comparison of these graphs and attention to the sudden change which took place in the rate of publication of newspapers and periodicals subsequent to 1880 cannot fail to impress the student of American intellectual institutions. It is perfectly clear that reading became a very much

more common fact in the years following 1880 than it ever
was before.   It is also clear that the impetus toward extensive reading has continued to operate since 1880 with
constantly increasing effect.

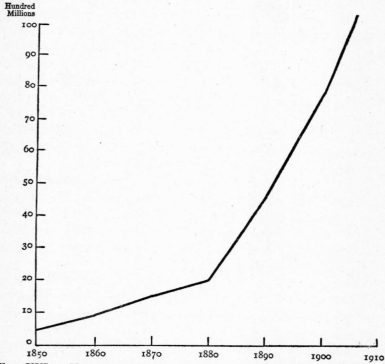

FIG. XVI. — NUMBER OF ISSUES OF NEWSPAPERS AND PERIODICALS PUB-
LISHED IN VARIOUS YEARS

The importance of this fact as describing the special character of the civilization of the United States is further
brought out by the statement that in 1910 there were published in this country more than 18,000 periodicals of all kinds.
Of this number 2,226 were daily papers.   The total number

of periodicals published in the world during that year was less than 50,000. Germany had 7,000; Great Britain 9,000; Japan 4,300; and other countries, smaller numbers.

Some of the objective facts connected with the development of American periodical publications are mentioned

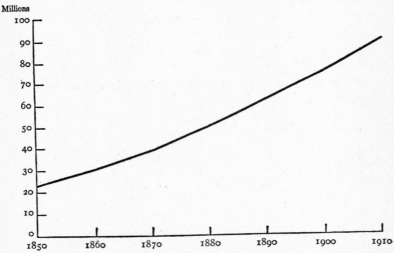

Fig. XVII. — Number of Inhabitants in the United States According to Decimal Census

by the author of the special census report on newspapers and periodicals. He writes:

This sketch of the rise and development of the American newspaper has now reached the period of time which marks the commencement of the third and present era in its history. It is not possible to assign the beginning of this era to any particular year or event, its coming being due to a variety of causes, which may be enumerated in the following order: First, the establishment of the penny press; second, the development of railroads as a means for the distribution of newspapers, the transmission of news reports, and the reduction of heavy postage rates; third, the discovery of telegraphy, and its immediate application to the purposes of journalism; and fourth, but not less important than other causes, the improvements of the printing press, which have rendered it possible to print large editions of newspapers in a short time.[1]

In the paragraph just quoted we see a disposition to lay stress on the mechanical appliances which make printing possible and to disregard the psychological factors contributed by human nature as though they were to be taken for granted. Literally interpreted, the paragraph seems to say: If newspapers are produced cheaply and in large numbers, human beings will consume them; human beings will devote time and energy to acquiring ability to read and they will turn away from the direct pursuit of food and comfort which are the fundamental and natural goals of animal and primitive human endeavor. All this redirecting of the personal energy of human beings does not seem to the author of the quotation to be at all remarkable. It is not remarkable that the inventor of the cylinder printing press used his genius to satisfy a human demand. The only facts remarkable in the situation are that steel and iron came together and railroads were constructed for the distribution of papers; copper wires and wooden poles covered the land and telegraphing began; power from coal was applied to rollers and printed sheets were produced.

To the student of the psychology of social institutions the explanation of printing by reference to its material manifestations is thoroughly unscientific. The cause of all these material changes is to be found in the human mind. Newspapers do not increase in number because presses are built for their production. Newspapers increase in number and presses are perfected because human beings have through

[1] NORTH, S. N. D. — "History and Present Condition of the Newspaper and Periodical Press of the United States"; *Tenth Annual Census*, VIII (1884), p. 446.

long ages been working out a method of intercommunication which has proved to be so important in binding together national groups that printing has become a human necessity. The nation that makes the most rapid progress in this intellectual institution finds that it has more of the good things of life than have other nations. Human nature is stimulated by such discoveries to devote more and more of its energy to the perfection of its method of communication. By its economic system of giving compensations to genius which satisfies its desires, the modern nation has set aside individuals who devote all their time to perfecting the arts of writing and reading. Children are taught that they must acquire these arts. Great material resources are put at the disposal of those who serve society in the preparation of printed matter. In short, human nature has given itself over to a new plan of life and action. Is it not crude and short-sighted to neglect all these facts and to say that the much reading which appears in the United States from 1880 on is caused by railroads and telegraph and a new kind of printing press?

CHAPTER X

LANGUAGE, THE FUNDAMENTAL INSTITUTION

There is very little advantage for our purposes in asking the question when and how language originated. There is no known tribe or people so low in the scale of life that it does not possess some form of language. All the inventions of the types which have been discussed in earlier chapters, except possibly the most primitive tools, imply the existence of a fairly well-developed language. Trade of every kind is not conceivable except among people possessed of words; certainly numbers, time measurements, and weights and measures would be impossible without language. Even the simplest technical arts could hardly have flourished except in social groups where men had learned the lesson of communication.

Assuming the existence of language from the earliest stages of human life, we turn to the task of outlining some of the more important improvements which men have produced in this instrument of social organization. By this discussion we shall discover the relation of language to the higher forms of mental life.

Before entering on that task, we may pause to comment on a very striking fact with regard to American books on psychology. They omit almost entirely any discussion of language. In his two large volumes, James gives in the aggregate less than six pages to the subject of language and a large part of what he has to say directly on the topic relates to the way in which a dog learns to bark. Elsewhere he mentions words only incidentally in his treatment of the processes of thought. The fact that James thus slights language has left its mark on the whole group of younger writers who have prepared the textbooks which have issued from his example. They, too, treat language in a few paragraphs at most, as though it were a psychological phenomenon of little or no moment.

The American writers who have concerned themselves with a scientific study of language have been chiefly those who were interested in the history of words and grammatical forms or those who were absorbed in literature as either critics or contributors. Language, in so far as it has been a subject of serious study, has therefore come to be thought of as something detached from the minds which have refined it and made it into the fundamental instrument of social control.

It is the purpose of this chapter to counteract so far as possible this tendency to neglect the psychological consideration of language. The discussion of language has been postponed to this point in the hope that the conclusions reached through the examination of the more concrete social institutions have prepared the way for a full understanding of the character and importance of this universal and highly evolved instrument of social coöperation.

When one thinks of the form which human consciousness takes on in all its operations, the cardinal importance of language is at once evident. No modern man or woman could think in the way he or she does during every moment of waking life if there were no words. The names of the objects about us are the mental counters with which we operate in all our conscious efforts to adapt our behavior to these objects. Social relations are thought out and arranged through the use of words.

An appreciation of the part which language plays in

human life can be gained if one asks such questions as the following: What part of the mental energy of a modern human being is devoted to the use of words? If one is absorbed in the observation of something that is going on before one's eyes, what is the most natural way of expressing one's absorption? If one is aroused to an emotional attitude, how does the emotion ordinarily come to the surface? If one meets a fellow being, what is the mode of behavior induced by the meeting? If one is in need of information or even of physical coöperation from someone else, what instrument is employed in securing it? The answers which we must give to these questions ought to guide psychology in its attitude toward language. If we include reading and writing as forms of language, and certainly we should, a very large fraction of life will have to be assigned to the use of words.

The institution of language is so universal and so intimately related to all aspects of mental life that an infinite variety of languages and dialects have appeared in the course of human history. Each of these has competed for a broader recognition than that which it had at the time and place of its inception. Like tribes and nations, the less well organized languages have in many instances perished in the competition and the better languages have survived. There is no single language which has virtues so conspicuous as those possessed in its field by the Arabic numeral system and consequently there is no universal agreement even in our day of highly developed international coöperation as to the words which shall be used in trade and in personal intercourse.

One of the conspicuous reasons why the competition between languages has not run its full course, as did the competition between numeral systems, is that languages are the carriers of literatures. Literatures in turn are embodiments of the national history of the peoples who produced them. Literatures are to society what individual memory is to each one of us. It makes relatively little difference, therefore, how superior some other language may be in its vocabulary and in its grammatical forms; the vernacular of a people will tend to survive because of that which it carries in the way of traditions and popular ideals.

We find ourselves, accordingly, confronted with a task which is doubly difficult when we turn to the discussion of language. We are dealing with an institution that is at once universal and particular. It is universal in the sense that in some form it is absolutely essential to all mental operations; it is particular in the sense that there are a great many different forms in which this institution appears.

The selection of suitable illustrations which can be made the basis of a systematic psychology of language as a social institution is for the reasons cited a complicated task. Fortunately the labor required has been performed by one of the leading minds of the generation which has just passed. Wilhelm Wundt, the great German psychologist, devoted the later years of his productive life to a series of volumes on what he called *Voelkerpsychologie,* or the psychology of peoples.[1] The first two volumes of this monumental work contain a minute analysis of language. Following in the main Wundt's teachings, we may adopt his examples and his conclusions as the basis of a number of generalizations which will carry forward our understanding of intellectual institutions.

The most primitive languages are those which resemble in structure gesture language, a mode of expression which we know to be simpler than speech. That gesture language

---

[1] WUNDT, WILHELM — *Voelkerpsychologie;* Erster Band, *Die Sprache.* Erster Theil, pp. xv + 627, Zweiter Theil, pp. x + 644, Leipzig, Wilhelm Engelmann, 1900.

is of a lower level than are other modes of communication is attested by the fact that it is resorted to by anyone who is driven to seek a medium of communication for which he has no preparation in past experience. Thus if one is lost in a strange country and must communicate with men who do not understand one's words, the resort to gestures is natural and immediate.

The characteristic fact with regard to gesture language is its directness and intimate connection with concrete objects. One points to the object referred to if it is present, or outlines a picture of it if it is not in sight. One has to forego discussion of abstract notions except in so far as objects or acts of a depictable type will suggest such notions. A striking example of the concrete character of gestures even when they express abstract ideas can be borrowed from the language of the Dakota Indians. When the word "truth" is to be expressed, the index finger is pointed from the lips directly forward. The gesture might be translated "straight talk." When, on the other hand, the idea of "falsehood" is to be expressed, the index finger is moved to the right or left across the lips so as to express the idea of "oblique talk." It is an interesting evidence of the close relation of this mode of expression to direct experience that the form of gesture used by the Dakota Indians is the same as that employed by deaf mutes in Europe.

The grammar of gesture language, like its vocabulary, is altogether concrete. If one wants to say "the tall strong man" in gesture language, the first sign to be used must represent the man, not his attributes. The attributes have nothing to which they can attach themselves if they are depicted before the object to which they belong.

As it is with gesture language, so also is it with the simplest known languages. The words of these simple languages, such as certain African languages spoken on the Sudan, are

monosyllabic names of concrete facts in the environment.
The monosyllabic sounds are in a sense less concrete than
gestures, but they vary in such a way as to make a direct
appeal to the senses and are to this extent both natural and
direct.   Thus if a certain sound means "large," the same
sound spoken at a different pitch means "small."   "Large"
and "small" are thus treated as parts of a single series.
"There far away" is a low tone; "there at some distance"
is a tone of middle pitch; and "right here" is a high tone.
Even such contrasted ideas as "sweet" and "bitter," or
"passive receptivity" and "vigorous activity," are expressed by changes in pitch.

In our complex modern speech we sometimes adopt this
same method of expression.   When one is telling fairy stories
to children, the giants are always spoken of in tones of
low deep pitch and the fairies are always spoken of in high-
pitched tones.   The same natural antithesis is adopted
when one addresses large animals and small.   No one would
speak to a horse and a kitten in the same pitch.   The variations thus retained in highly evolved languages are for the
most part related to emotional experiences and are to be
thought of as more like primitive types of expression than
are the words and sentences used in deliberate discussions.

The sentence forms, if they may be called such, in simple
languages are, like those of gesture language, dependent on
a succession of ideas coupled together without any inflexional
elements.   Each word in such a series gets its final value
from the total mental picture to which it contributes.   There
is no distinction between noun and verb forms.   Indeed, the
same sound serves now as a noun and again at a later time
as a verb.

Some of the shadings of meaning which in highly developed languages are provided by inflection are secured in these
simpler languages by devices which illustrate clearly the

difficulty of expressing ideas with monosyllabic words. Thus when the Togo tribes want to make a distinction of tense in their verbs they have to resort to repetitions of the same sound. "I eat" is the present tense. "I eat eat" means I have eaten.

Languages of the primitive type are sometimes driven to adopt very complex expressions in the effort to find a series of words that will cover an idea which is somewhat abstract. When the Togos want to express the idea "to bring," they have to break it up into its three stages. They say "take — go — give." The steps of the process are here given in detail. The bringer must first take up the thing; he must then go with it, and he must finally deliver it. Another example from the same tribe is the expression for the west; it is "sun — sit — place."

The crudities and inadequacies of primitive languages prove that men had to experiment for long ages with the processes of thinking before they could refine their methods of recording and arranging ideas. Words and sentences are not modes of reaction by means of which human beings adjust themselves to material surroundings. They are not instructive modes of reaction; they have to be invented and perfected through use. They are the means by which members of a social group exchange ideas and through this exchange help one another to arrive at clearer and more productive sequences of thought. Words more than any other social devices are the means by which minds react upon themselves and control and refine their own operations. Words constitute a world apart from the world of things. As men grow expert in making combinations and recombinations in this separate world they find that they can prepare for practical manipulations of material realities in such a way as to make their actions enormously more effective at the same time that they get the advantages of

economy of time and energy. It requires, however, long
practice to secure the advantages of a fully evolved system
of expression.

The motives for energetic experimentation with language
are very strong. In addition to the advantages which a
social group derives from the solidarity that language brings
to the group and from the mastery of things which results
from intelligent planning of action, there is an internal motive in language itself which makes for improvement. Inadequate expression and ambiguous expression create a
feeling of restlessness on the part of both speaker and audi-
tor. Under such conditions one of two results will appear.
Either the deficiency will be tolerated and the people will
continue through inertia or lack of intelligence to use the
inadequate language or else invention will be stimulated to
produce a less ambiguous expression. What has always
happened in the long run is the latter. Somewhere in the ages
of human communication, there have always been geniuses
ready to overcome every ambiguity. These geniuses have
worked slowly and with cumulative effect. Their motive
has usually not been a desire to benefit the race, but the
direct selfish motive of avoiding mistakes. This purely
utilitarian attitude has, however, accomplished more than
the individual intended. Because men live together and
act upon one another, the advantage of a better way of expressing ideas has always redounded to the advantage of
those who heard the expression as well as of him who devised
it. The effect of personal effort has thus been carried over
to the group.

Some of the directions in which inventive genius worked
in developing language may be enumerated. First, the
number of expressions for different objects and different
qualities had to be very greatly increased. An example
taken from modern life will serve to illustrate the point.

Most men have a very meager color vocabulary. This fact reflects the ordinary masculine attitude toward shades of color. Women, on the other hand, being more devoted to the use of colors for purposes of personal adornment need to have a much larger stock of names with which to discriminate the fine distinctions which they find important. They exercise their genius, therefore, in inventing color names and what is more they cultivate a fluent mastery of these names and of the ideas which they represent which is altogether incomprehensible to the masculine mind.

Another striking illustration of the method of enriching one's stock of words and thereby guiding all future thinking can be derived from the history of the invention of the word "gas." The Dutch chemist, Van Helmont, working in his laboratory in the seventeenth century found it desirable to distinguish that form of matter which is not liquid or solid, and so he used this new word. He said that it was suggested to his mind by a Greek word which is, however, different in form.

When the world was young, the opportunity for inventing new words must have been unlimited. Even in that faraway age, however, the inventor's task was less than half accomplished when he had emitted the new sound. Before he could regard his task as complete, he must induce his neighbors to use the sound as he had used it. Here again we may draw on modern experience. The child playing in the sand invents a word for the pebbles that fill its hand. The new word is "pocos." Does society adopt this word because it has been duly invented? Not at all. Society has an expression of its own for the designation of pebbles, and it does not look with favor on the exercise of further inventive genius. So the child's word "pocos" lingers for a time in the tolerant memory of the immediate family and then passes into oblivion.

Where society was made up of persons of different levels of distinction, the invention and selection of words were obviously the prerogative of the upper classes. Indeed, the upper classes were those who more than the lower classes needed the larger equipment of sounds in order to carry on their more elaborate modes of thought. The thinking and the vocabularies of the common man followed those of his leader. It has ever been so with social institutions. It was not long since in our generation that the word "molly-coddle" came into common use by the same method.

The period of sheer invention of words is past. If a new idea turns up these days and needs a verbal label, we usually go back to the languages of antiquity and borrow a combination of sounds that approximate in their meaning the new idea. Our vocabularies are thus increased with little expenditure of mental energy.

In the early days of the race the procedure was different. Invention was necessary in the full sense of the term because there were no languages of earlier date from which to borrow. Still it cannot be assumed that the earliest word makers set themselves consciously at the task of invention. It must be assumed rather that there was something natural in what they did, something so spontaneous that the whole tribe would follow the example of the inventor because the word suited their natures as well as that of the first user.

Wundt has brought together a long array of facts to prove that the earliest words invented by the race are those in which the organs of speech make a natural movement from which the sound flows as a secondary rather than a primary consequence. What he means can be illustrated by such an English word as "zigzag." The movement of the tongue in producing this word is in a very direct sense an imitation of the idea expressed. The sound comes to have meaning because in making it the tongue puts one in the zigzag attitude. There are other examples such as the words "crack" and "explosion." The naturalness of these sounds is readily recognized, but it comes from the muscular sensations which the making of the sounds induces.

It is a fact of human nature which the poets have always recognized that the sound and the pronunciation of words can be made to comport with meaning in a way which is much more subtle than we usually recognize when we think of words as symbols of ideas. Tennyson was a master of such combinations. Read the following lines from his *Lotos-Eaters* and note the way in which the sounds of the words fit into the spirit of the poem.

> In the afternoon they came unto a land
> In which it seemed always afternoon.
> All round the coast the languid air did swoon,
> Breathing like one that hath a weary dream.
> Full-faced above the valley stood the moon;
> And like a downward smoke, the slender stream
> Along the cliff to fall and pause and fall did seem.

The foregoing discussion of the way in which words originated will prevent us from falling into the misconception that language is chiefly a series of sound impressions. Language has to be produced and therefore can be fully explained only when it is realized that man made words as an expression of his indirect social reaction to the world in which he lived. It is a well-known fact of the history of language that words which imitate natural sounds, such as "bow-wow" for "dog," are relatively late. It was only after man had learned the art of speech and was well drilled in its uses that he began to pick up by imitation the sound-words which his environment suggested. The earliest words are all reactions explicable as expressions of human attitudes, not as sound imitations.

Perhaps the most striking examples which can be cited in further confirmation of such statements are the words which children first use. The first words in all infant speech are such words as "pa-pa" and "ma-ma." In all languages these words recur with some variations in the consonant elements. The interesting point for our discussion is that these words are natural only in the sense that they issue from the infant as the easiest sounds to produce. The meanings attached to these early efforts of infancy are not derived from the child's intention. They come rather from the child's adult attendants. The parents have learned the value of words and urge on the child who contributes the sounds, certain interpretations which are adopted by the whole group and turn the natural sounds into conventional words.

The efforts of primitive men to build up vocabularies adequate to the world in which they lived must have led very early to the invention of enough words to tax the memory of speakers and listeners. The condition which is here referred to became all the more acute because primitive man's constant devotion to concrete facts made it extremely clumsy for him to express some of the ideas which soon became essential to his thinking. Recurring to the example given in an earlier paragraph where it was stated that the idea of bringing required the use of three expressions equivalent to the ideas "take-go-give," we see how the cumbersomeness of primitive language would begin to impede rather than facilitate thought. The cumbersomeness of early language due to the great variety of responses to concrete situations had to be overcome through long ages of use during which various devices were invented for simplifying and systematizing expression. In this process of perfecting language we can trace, as in the first invention of words, the operation of certain laws of mental life.

In order to illustrate what is meant by the statement that language is systematized and simplified let us consider some of the obvious facts about our own forms of words. Take all the words ending in *er* and *or* which refer to persons who are agents of various types of performance. Such words as "banker," "driver," "reaper," "actor," "confessor," are all alike in their general reference to persons who do something. The suffixes *er* and *or* can be traced back to early periods of the Teutonic and Latin languages. They show that whenever the minds of users of words are in the general attitude of thinking of persons, there is a tendency for expressions to take on a common form. It is not to be assumed that people started using the *er* and *or* endings with the conscious purpose of systematizing their language. Minds tend to associate ideas which are related and will bring this tendency into operation without being explicitly aware of its existence. The common sound factor is a natural device of mental economy.

Sometimes the common sound element in words of cognate meaning is much more clearly recognized than in the examples just cited. Thus the ending *ed* has come to be accepted as the mark of the past tense of verbs. A moment's consideration of the verbs of English make it perfectly evident that the device of ending past tenses with the same letter is relatively modern. The oldest verbs in the language are those which the grammarians call strong or irregular verbs; they show by their form that our ancestors made a wholly different sound when the situation changed from the present to the past. The past tense of the verb "to go" is one of these ancient forms. The various forms of the ancient verb "to be" illustrate the same fact. Intermediate forms, which are not as irregular as "went" and "was" but are not regular, are almost innumerable. For example, "swim" and "swam," "have" and "had," "fly" and "flew," "buy" and "bought," are enough alike to keep the mind fixed in each case on the same kind of an act, but different enough to make it clear that the situations referred to have elements which distinguish them.

The slow approximations of words of like order to common forms are illustrated again by the differences between the positive and comparative forms of ancient adjectives and by the similarity in structure of positives and comparatives of recent origin. The comparatives of such old adjectives as "good" and "bad" have no resemblance whatsoever to the positive forms. A case of what might be called double usage is seen in such pairs of words as "large" and "huge," which are wholly different in sound and structure, and "large" and "very large," where the common element is explicitly brought out.

All these examples show that languages have in their long history been rendered more usable by being systematized. The psychological law that is here at work may be expressed by saying that words which involve the same fundamental idea tend to take on the same form. This process of relating similars goes on whether the psychological impulse is explicitly recognized or not.

The history of language is replete with illustrations of the operation of this law. One of the ideas which man very early had to mark with distinctive sounds was the idea of the plural. Here, again, our own language yields abundant illustrations of the divergence of the ancient method of making plurals from the uniform modern method of adding an s to the singular. "Man" and "men," "child" and "children," "ox" and "oxen" are all examples of the primitive tendency to parallel differences in thought by differences in words. A study of primitive languages adds a long list of devices which were employed while men were experimenting with the art of making plurals. One very natural method was that of making the same sound twice to indicate a plural. Thus the Sahaptin Indians say *pitin* for girl and *pipitin* for the plural. In Samoa the natives say *fulu* for hair, and *fulufulu* for the plural.

There are cases where the more primitive word is the plural rather than the singular. Modern examples of this kind are to be found in such collective words as "army" and "mob." Here the unit out of which the collective group is made can be designated only by some phrase which tends to break up the collective whole. If we want to relate the word "soldier" to the word "army," we must use some such combination as "private in the army." Wundt's comment on this situation is as follows :

It is characteristic of much primitive thinking that plurality is not thought of as a sum of individual objects but as a collective whole. The same word in such cases sometimes serves for both the individual and the group, the special significance being left to be inferred but without any special verbal expression. Naturally such usage will be most common when the words refer to inanimate objects which are of minor value. There are African languages in which the nouns are plural throughout and can be used as referring to singular objects only by adding some form of limiting suffix. The cases here referred to are paralleled by others in which the singular becomes plural by adding a prefix of a type indicating collective reference to a group. A combination of the two forms of expression appears in the language of the Bari negro tribes in which those objects which naturally appear in groups and are seldom attended to as individuals are spoken of in the collective. Such objects are the fingers, flies, bees, and monkeys. The noun stem has a singular meaning, on the other hand, in the words "roof," "river," "house," "day," "wolf," and the like which designate objects commonly attended to as single things. In the case of the plural words a singular is made by adding a demonstrative suffix; in the case of singular words a suffix with a broadening significance is used in making a plural.[1]

[1] WUNDT, WILHELM — *op. cit.*, Bd. I, Th. I, pp. 32–33.

Leaving the devices for making plural nouns, we may consider next the facts of inflection known as case forms. Our own language is so little supplied with case forms that it furnishes no adequate series of examples to illustrate this particular device of expressing ideas. We have a possessive case which has been gradually reduced to such uniformity that it is a mere vestige of earlier more elaborate forms. The abandonment for the most part of case forms in English represents the completion of a long cycle of language experiments which began curiously enough without case forms and has passed through stages where these forms were very numerous.

The first languages, as has been pointed out, were without structural elements. Words were monosyllables. The Mande negro tribes are even now at this stage. If they want to express any of the ideas which are expressed in the highly developed languages by the locative case, they combine words which are wholly independent. Thus if they want to say that a thing is "behind" another, they mention the two objects and put between them the word for "back." If they want to express the idea "above," they use the word "air" or "heavens"; if they want to express the idea "under," they use the word "earth" or "ground." We see in these combinations language at the stage where all ideas are concrete and expressed only through direct reference to the observed facts of the environment.

The next stage of development is one in which spatial relations began to be thought of in a more abstract way and the sounds that express these relations lost their direct reference to objects and were used as symbols of pure relationship. Abstract particles expressing position are known to us in English in such words as: " on," "under," "above," "below." The isolation of these words of relationship was the work of long ages of language evolution. Before the isolation could be accomplished in full, the stage of case inflection had to be lived through. Case inflection appears in the fact that when a noun is to be used as part of a phrase expressing some relation, such as that of location, it will be modified in structure so as to distinguish it from the same word when it is used in a sentence which expresses another relationship, such as ownership. It is a further fact of language history that the idea of location usually is not specific enough without the use of another word distinct from the noun to specify the particular location. Thus it comes about that Latin both inflects its nouns and puts prepositions before them in order to express exactly the relations of space.

The number of case forms which have been used in the history of languages is very great. As languages matured, the more significant relations came to clearer recognition, and incidental relations were left to be expressed by separate words. The languages of the Greeks and Romans had reached the stage of a few well-defined cases and many prepositions. The language of Germany reduces somewhat the number of cases. English has, with the exception of the possessive ending, come to the expression of all of the relations by the use of separate words.

The difference between the separate words used by English and those which were used at the beginning of language development as illustrated by the language of the Mande negroes, cited in an earlier paragraph, is that our English prepositions are wholly abstract. They have been developed for the express purpose of making clear a relation rather than an object.

English must substitute some device to make up for the loss of the advantage which inflected languages have in the fact that they use a characteristic sign both at the end and at the beginning of a phrase. This double use of a characteris-

tic expression insures the phrase against ambiguity. English uses order of words as a substitute for inflection. To
make this case clear let us consider the different ways in
which English and German express a locative idea. When
a German speaker wants to say that something is going on
in the house, he changes the forms of the article and of
the word "house" from the nominative to the locative. He
says "*in dem Hause.*" The nominative of the article is *das*
and of the noun *Haus.* The German locative is furthermore
introduced, as indicated, by the preposition "in." In English the declension forms are lost but the order is retained,
thus making clear the relation of the noun to the preposition without changing the form of the noun.

The systematization of verbal forms which has been illustrated in the foregoing paragraphs shows that the conscious associations of men's minds are constantly operating
to determine the forms of language at the same time that
words are guiding thought. It is not alone in matters of
form that the operation of gradually changing associations
can be traced ; the same kind of development takes place with
regard to meaning. New meanings attach to familiar words
and new words appear in response to the need for more
adequate methods of expression.

The history of literature and language is replete with examples that show the intimate parallelism between expanding
thought and corresponding change in expression. There are
certain lines in *Hamlet* which are usually misunderstood by
twentieth-century readers because the printed words of the
text have remained unchanged while the processes of mental
evolution have gone on and have completely changed the
mental associations attached to the words which Shakespeare
used. Hamlet has been discussing with himself the possibilities of suicide and comes to the consideration of the uncertainties that lie beyond death. It is these uncertainties, he

says, which make "us rather bear those ills we have than fly to others that we know not of." Now comes the line often misunderstood. Hamlet says : "Thus conscience does make cowards of us all." The interpretation which usually arises in a present-day reader's mind is not that intended by Shakespeare at all. Shakespeare did not mean to say that most of us are guilty of some wrong-doing somewhere in our lives and therefore afraid of the future and its possible punishments. The word "conscience" meant to Shakespeare about what the words "thoughtful meditation" or "conscious consideration" mean to a modern user of English. If one looks up the matter, one finds that "conscience" in Elizabethan English conveyed just these ideas. Thus Hobbs, the philosopher, writes : "The same passion (for glory) may proceed not from any conscience of our own action, but from fame and trust of others." Stubbs, writing on medieval and modern history, says : "The characteristic of the long medieval centuries, the conscience that war is justifiable only by law . . ." What Hamlet says, therefore, is that we are all prone to think matters over before taking the risks of a future which we do not know, and as we consider all the hazards involved, we have less and less courage to take the final step.

The example is a striking case of a gradual psychological change which has detached from a word the interpretation which earlier generations associated with it, and has substituted for the older meaning a new and more specialized meaning. There has been a shift, in other words, in the mental world, and this shift makes of the word "conscience" a new fact in human life.

The history of English is full of examples of words that have changed their psychological relations and have gradually come to have meanings that are sinister. One of the modern examples of this is the word "graft." The verb "to graft" meant at first merely to work. The specialized meaning of digging seems to be implied in the Anglo-Saxon form from which the modern word is descended. Early colloquial English used the word in such questions as "Where are you grafting?" meaning "Where do you live or work?" From this perfectly respectable beginning the word has gradually gone down hill. The work of which the grafter is accused to-day is not of the general sort originally expressed; it is of a sort which fills the name "grafter" with opprobrium.

Changes in the meanings of words of the type illustrated in the foregoing examples can be grouped under a number of general statements. Let us consider some of them.

First, when two objects serve analogous functions, there is a tendency to use the same word to describe them. Thus we speak of a "foot of the mountain" or the "foot of a ladder." We speak of the "mouth of a river" and the "neck of a bottle." We have such verb forms as the "river running into another" and a "reputation falling." In each of these cases the minds of the speaker and listener set aside all concrete relationships and for purely psychological reasons bring together situations that are alike only in the abstract.

Second, words which express feelings are readily transferred; thus one speaks of a "bitter disappointment" or a "burdensome task." In both these cases purely subjective attitudes are expressed as belonging to situations which in reality have no sensory qualities of the sort described but do arouse attitudes like those attaching to the experiences referred to. A disappointment has, of course, no taste, but it is associated with a particular kind of feeling which is not unlike that of an unpleasant taste.

Third, a word brought into various contexts will take on in each case a particular shade of meaning. The word "country" conveys one idea in the phrase, "My country, 'tis of thee" and an entirely different meaning in the phrase "country cousin." The word "right" stands for one meaning when contrasted with "left," and a wholly different meaning when coupled with such a word as "civil" or "political."

Fourth, words which express certain kinds of facts are sometimes retained with changed meanings when the conditions of civilization change to such an extent that the original connotations are no longer appropriate. Our word "arrive" is a striking illustration of this kind of a change. It is derived from the Latin preposition *ad* meaning "to" and the word *ripa* meaning "shore." Under the conditions of Mediterranean maritime life, the only arrivals were those who came in boats and landed on the shore. As conditions of travel changed, a word was needed to indicate the arrival of travelers by other than water routes. The sound was retained which had served in the first situation, and the meaning was altered to suit the new mode of life.

It is certainly impossible to review such facts as have been detailed about language without carrying away a vivid impression of the enormous amount of human ingenuity which has been expended in its improvement. One is similarly impressed when one thinks of the fact that each individual born into the world is obliged to acquire anew the complex forms of behavior which are necessary in order to use language. A type of action which consumes to this extent the time and energy of a race will surely leave its impression on the race itself. In dealing with language we are not dealing with some trivial addition to man's repertoire of behavior. We cannot be satisfied to think of language as a late addition to the instinctive tendencies; it is a new and major aspect of human life.

The relation of language to civilization and to individual experience can be described in terms which are familiar to the reader of this book. Language is a social institution.

It has evolved through the coöperation of countless generations. It becomes a guide to the thought and effort of
every member of the race. The child strives to become a
part of the social group by mastering this conventional
mode of behavior. In doing so he has his attention turned
now in this direction, now in that. Each word which he
learns controls for the moment his thought. Each sentence that he hears shapes for him a succession of ideas and
holds them in a certain order. After the individual has
been under the influence of language for a time, he will
begin to do most of his thinking by using the distinctions
and relations which society has given him through its established modes of communication. Language is a mode
of mental procedure. It is not something which we use from
time to time; it is the method of our whole mental existence. An individual can no more get away from language
than he can empty his mind of ideas.

Perhaps the import of these statements can be made
clearer by referring to science and its terminology. When
we begin to think scientifically about an animal, we find that
it is necessary to distinguish between the parts of the animal's body. We find we must note certain stages in the
animal's growth. We must describe certain of its habits
of life and its contacts with other beings in the world. For
each observation which we make we find it desirable to have
some kind of a mental marker. A series of markers for ideas
about animals has been devised in zoölogical terminology.
The more specific this terminology, the clearer will be our
thinking. Teachers, therefore, take great pains to drill
students in the exact and discriminating use of a specific terminology. Is all this drilling undertaken merely in order
that the observer may tell someone else about what he has
been thinking? Certainly not. The exact terminology is a
guarantee that the one who possesses it will turn his think-

ing directly and with full regard to detail to those centers of observation which study has shown to be important. A scientific term is a guide to thinking; it is an instrument of discrimination.

More than this, general scientific terms hold together the results of long trains of research. When the zoölogist uses the term "vertebrate," he is not merely calling attention to the fact that the animal has a backbone. He is introducing his students to the long line of scientific studies which preceded the establishment of the final classification to which the science of animal life has come as a result of its investigations. The term "vertebrate" is a carrier of a great scientific generalization. Words carry in epitomized form all the rich body of associations which entered into their first development.

To be sure, there are serious hazards involved in the indirect forms of thinking which words make possible. There is the danger to which attention was called in the example borrowed from Shakespeare's *Hamlet*, that in the course of years the mental complex aroused by certain words will undergo radical change. There are other like possibilities. The teacher may give the student a word which is full of meaning derived from a long succession of scientific investigations; to the teacher the word may convey all the rich content that has been loaded into it during the history of science, but the student may repeat the sound and have little or none of the stock of experience which the sound is intended to carry. The same sound may have wholly different values in two such cases.

What has been said with regard to scientific terminology can be enlarged upon when we begin to think of other systems of experience which the race has accumulated. Consider, for example, the importance of words in recording national history. Since the earliest dawn of human life, men have gathered about the campfire to hear of the exploits of their heroes. The story-teller and the bard have contributed through words to a social pride and social determination to make further progress which have been of the greatest significance in directing the lives of individuals and groups. The development of national pride and group solidarity would be impossible if there were no common elements in the experiences of individuals. Language supplies common elements of thought by compelling individuals to go through mental processes which are alike. Language is not merely a vehicle for the transmission of ideas from mind to mind; it is a compelling institution which forces men to become alike in their associations of ideas. The learning of a word is a process of socializing the individual and of making his conscious world like that of others who use the same language.

We see from such considerations as these why language is so fundamental to society. In order that men may live together in groups they must have common ideas on all essential items. Common interests and joint modes of action are essential to the very existence of a community. Social unity can be secured only when some method is provided for holding individuals to the same inner patterns of thought and desire. Animals live in groups at times when some external circumstance forces them together, or at times when some strong common motive of action coincides with individual desires. A drought is said to drive all kinds of wild animals to live for a time under a natural truce at the watering place. A pack will hunt together and join in defending one of their number against an enemy, but these animal groups are not communities. Primitive man found the secret of a more permanent union. In order to effect this union he had to find a means of making its members alike in their inner desires and experiences. That device for producing a common way of thinking was developed in language. By constantly keeping the members of the tribe in communication and by gradually enriching the vocabulary which records common ideas and purposes, man has controlled the thinking of all the members of the group until now the ideas and ideals of a nation compel the attention of every newcomer and guide his or her thinking to the point where it is like that of those with whom the individual lives and associates.

We have spoken of a nation's history. Consider in like terms the folklore and the literature which express the peculiar ambitions and aspirations of a given people. Think of the effect which is produced on the minds of the children of a family by the constant reiterations of certain modes of thought. These are not examples of trivial or incidental facts; they are examples of the way in which through language common modes of thinking have been cultivated and common modes of action have been induced.

Professor McDougall, to whose works on social psychology we have had occasion to refer in earlier chapters, has contributed in his recent book, entitled *The Group Mind*, a number of observations which are of interest in this connection. In the main, McDougall is convinced in this as in his earlier work that the problems of national life are to be solved by a consideration of the inherited equipment of its members. To his mind certain nationalities which have a fundamental group of mental traits are likely because of these traits to become leaders in the world. Yet even while defending this thesis and while neglecting altogether to undertake any analysis of such social institutions as language, McDougall is driven by his survey of the historical facts to make statement after statement which confirms the position that is defended in this chapter.

We may quote at length from one of McDougall's chapters:

Let us consider now very briefly in relation to the life of a nation a second essential condition of all collective mental life — namely, that the individuals shall be in free communication with one another. This is obviously necessary to the formation of national mind and character. It is only through an immense development of the means of communication, especially the printing press, the railway and the telegraph, that the modern Nation-State has become possible, and has become the dominant type of political organisms. So familiar are we with this type that we are apt to identify the Nation and the State and to regard the large Nation-State as the normal type of State and of Nation, forgetting that its evolution was not possible before the modern period.

In the ancient world, the City-State was the dominant type of political organism; and to Plato and Aristotle any other type seemed undesirable, if not impossible. For they recognized that collective deliberation and volition are essential to the true State. Aristotle, trying to imagine a vast city, remarks — "But a city, having such vast circuit, would contain a nation rather than a state, like Babylon." The translator there uses the word "nation," not in the modern sense, but rather as we use "people" to denote a population of common stock not organized to form a nation. The limits of the political organism capable of a collective mental life were rightly held to be set by the number of citizens who could live so close together as to meet in one place to discuss all public affairs by word of mouth.

The great empires of antiquity were not nations; they had no collective mental life. Although the Roman Empire, in the course of its long and marvelous history, did succeed in generating in almost all its subject peoples a certain sentiment of pride in and attachment to the Empire, it cannot be said to have welded them into one nation; for, in spite of the splendid system of roads and of posting, communication between the parts was too difficult and slow to permit the reciprocal influences essential to collective life. As in all the ancient empires, the parts were held together only by a centralized, despotic, executive organization; there was no possibility of collective deliberation and volition.

All through history there has obviously been some correlation between the size of political organisms and the degree of development of means of communication. At the present time those means have become so highly developed that the widest spaces of land and sea no longer present any insuperable limits to the size of nations; and the natural tendency for the growth of the larger states at the expense of the smaller, by the absorption of the latter, seems to be increasingly strong. It seems not unlikely that almost the whole population of the world will shortly be included in five immense States — the Russian or Slav, the Central European, the British, the American, and the Yellow or East Asiatic State. The freedom of communication between the countries of Europe is now certainly sufficient to allow of their forming a single nation, if other conditions, such as diversities of racial type and of historical sentiments, would permit it.[1]

Later McDougall describes in the following terms the problem of England in building up an empire :

To-day England is contemplating a task never before attempted, the fusing into one nation of the peoples of the mother-country and her distant colonies. Whether or no she will succeed depends upon whether the enormously increased facilities of communication can overcome the principal effects of physical barriers that we have noted — namely, lack of intermarriage and divergence of occupation with the consequent divergence of mental type and interests. The task is infinitely more difficult than the establishment of such an Empire as the Roman ; not because the distances are greater, but because the union must take the form of nationhood, because it must take the form of a collective mind and not that of a merely executive organisation. But, in the considerations which have shown us that membership in and devotion to a smaller group is by no means adverse to membership in and devotion to a larger group, we have ground for believing that the task is not impossible of achievement.[2]

[1] McDougall, William — *The Group Mind*, pp. 181–183; G. P. Putnam's Sons, 1920.   [2] *Ibid.*, p. 185.

These statements undoubtedly express profound truth. One can hardly overlook the fact, however, that they seem to deal with communication as though it were possible without long antecedent preparation of the communicating minds. McDougall seems to say that newspapers and the telegraph are important facts. The more fundamental view is that newspapers and the telegraph are outgrowths of a gradually growing demand on the part of collective groups for intimate and uninterrupted contacts. These devices for enriching human associations were invented by men who have learned to desire association and have enjoyed the advantages which are derived from less complete methods of communication. It is not newspapers and the telegraph which make a nation, but community of interest and like ideas.

Communication is not something objective and superficial. A word cannot pick up an idea and carry it over to another mind. Ideas become effective in a group only in so far as all the members of the group have learned forms of thought which are common. The slow evolution of social units has been due to the necessity of making men over into collections of minds capable of common modes of thought. Language does not accomplish this task without the aid of many other institutions. The form of government under which people live, their religious beliefs, their modes of dress, their types of food, and their occupations must be gradually brought to conform to unified patterns before there can be complete mutual understanding and sympathy. But none of these secondary institutions can be perfected except as there is a ready means of general expression of ideas. Language is the fundamental institution. Men start with a few words and phrases and as soon as they master these they deposit the results of their common thinking and common behavior in institutions such as religious belief or customs of courtesy. With this start they invent new verbal distinctions and work them over until by a long series of social compromises the group reaches manifold common ways of thinking and speaking.

In this process of gradual assimilation of mind to mind, written words to which the reader may come back again and again serve one purpose, while the intense expressions of some orator making a plea for public adoption of a new idea serve a somewhat different purpose. Either instrument for the promotion of social solidarity requires time in order to produce its full effect.

There are barriers to the establishment of common modes of thought. Some of these are material, such as distance; some of them are psychological, such as rigidly fixed patterns of thought which have been built up through long ages of isolation. Communication can in the long run overcome these obstacles if it is persistently cultivated, but communication is not in itself the final fact. Communication must set up common modes of mental reaction. This is the reason why in the last analysis language should be thought of as a system of social control. This is the reason why the history of language should be studied not merely for the forms of words but also for the ideas which are associated with the words.

Some discussion of education as the device for cultivating common ideas belongs in this chapter, though it will be necessary to postpone to a later part of the book a full discussion of the institutions of education. Nations have expended no small part of their resources in educating the younger generation in those practices and ideas which are necessary for the preservation of the group. The first education was practical; the Indian boy was trained in the art of hunting; the Spartan boy was trained for war; but gradually the center of attention in the educational system of nations has shifted from the practical arts of hunting and war to language, which has come to be the center of the modern school system. The reason for this is apparent from what has been said. The preservation of the modern nation is not a matter merely of food getting and defense against enemies; it is far more a problem of developing unity of ideas and solidarity of beliefs and ambitions. It is much more important for Americans to understand public policies and to think alike than to be able to perform any particular acts of skill. Language and other social institutions have produced a kind of coöperative life which is so utterly dependent on community of ideas that the major energy of society in its organization of education is given to the promotion of community of ideas rather than to the cultivation of the trades, however important they may be.

One final comment naturally suggests itself at the conclusion of this chapter. Language in its current changes is an impressive example of human evolution. We do not need to go back to the origin of language to discover what is meant by human evolution. We can very properly infer what kinds of changes were going on in far-away periods by tracing the processes which are going on now. The accumulation of new ideas and the marking of these ideas by words and phrases are daily experiences in the lives of all nations and individuals. The simplification and systematization of the vast collections of ideas which are in the possession of the group are going on under our direct observation. The influence of individual minds on the thinking of the group and the powerful influence of the group in directing the thinking and behavior of the individual are illustrated in everyday life and require no antiquarian research to reveal the methods and centers of emphasis of human evolution.

At the risk of wearing out the reader's patience, but with

a view to keeping the unique character of human evolution constantly in the foreground, the conclusions of earlier chapters may be reiterated in the presence of the facts derived from a study of language. Human evolution is not a matter of instincts. Out of instinct has grown something new. Gregariousness among the animals is not an instrument of perfect control of the individual as are language and other social institutions. Language has as far superseded gregariousness as the technical instruments of modern civilization have superseded teeth and claws.

Human evolution is by no means at an end; indeed, the most significant stages of the process may certainly be thought of as lying in the present and the future. Up to this time the race has been engaged in perfecting a method of adaptation. This method is so radically different from anything which has preceded it in the history of the animal kingdom that upward movement has been delayed by frequent interruptions and backslidings. The methods of adaptation have finally reached a fairly high state of perfection. Language and science and technical discovery are now ready to be used with a degree of conscious purpose which was impossible at earlier stages of civilization.

The psychology of civilization is, therefore, not a record of past happenings; it is a study of present-day forces which are gathering momentum and are in need of consideration in the interest of such guidance as men are ready and able to give to their own futures. Civilization is a moving, living fact; its elements, which are the institutions that have been evolved up to this time by man's genius, are at once the products of this evolution and the controls which are to direct its further course.

CHAPTER XI

THE ART OF MUSIC

It is characteristic of the institutions which have been considered thus far that they command universal conformity. No one can live in modern society without submitting himself in some degree to the industrial and monetary systems. The use of number, the adoption of standards of measurement, and a ready comprehension of spoken and written language are requisite to even the most modest degrees of success in life. In sharp contrast with one's relation to these compelling institutions is one's relation to the fine arts. If we consider the art of music, we find that one can get on very well in modern social groups with little or no appreciation of music and with absolutely no ability to participate in the production of the elaborate harmonies to which the higher evolutions of the art have attained.

The contrast becomes even more impressive if we study the history of music. In its earliest stages music was distinctly a social art. The primitive tribe performed its religious rites to the sound of such music as it had learned to produce. The primitive work-song is also an example of a method of social compulsion which is common among peoples of the lower levels of civilization. As music has evolved out of these most primitive forms, it has become less and less a universally mastered art. It has passed through many stages of development and has exhibited many new forms and taken on many new applications, and in doing so it has lost in some measure its universal social appeal. To some it

is a source of the highest enjoyment, while to others it is an
entirely dispensable luxury. This history is almost exactly
the reverse of that which was uncovered in tracing the evolution of number or of systems of exchange. There the
power of the institution over the individual steadily increases as the institution matures.

We must seek an explanation of this contrast. We shall
find it in the fact that the higher levels of musical art appeal
to the individual's emotions. The emotions are subjective
and incapable of complete social control. Now and then,
to be sure, a group can be swayed by a common emotional
appeal and every individual in the group will be similarly
moved in his purely subjective experience. Such cases are,
however, rare; when they occur, they grow out of accidental
conditions which create a group sympathy and community
of emotional anticipation, as when a company is aroused by
some emergency in national life and is prepared to be impressed by a national anthem. Even in such cases it is
to be assumed that there are various shades and types of
emotional response. The experiences of individuals are
here very much more variable than are the responses to
number expressions or even to language. When the common emotional preparation is lacking as it is under the
ordinary circumstances of life, the variability of individual
responses to music becomes so great that the social character of the art is largely if not wholly lost.

When the art of music was primitive, the possibilities of
easy participation by every member of the group were almost
unlimited. With every step upward in its evolution, music
has left behind some member of the group and finally in its
perfected forms it is fully appreciated only by those who have
kept pace in their technical and emotional development with
the progressing art.

The fact that anyone can occupy a nonparticipating rela-

tion to music while he must learn to use money and number
and language in order to survive in modern society makes
it perfectly clear that the emotions stand in a relation to
society wholly different from that held by intellectual experiences.   The emotions are no less real than are the
facts of number, but they are of a different order.   They are
related to survival in an entirely different way.   We shall
have occasion in several of the subsequent chapters to enter
into a fuller discussion of the place of the emotions in social
economy.   We shall undertake in this chapter to lay an
empirical basis for our discussion through a study of the
art of music.

The earliest music is inseparably connected with the
group dance.   The group dance in turn can be understood
as a manifestation of the tendency inherent in the nervous
organization of all individuals to derive satisfaction from
rhythmical movements.   The successive contraction and
relaxation of a muscle is physiologically the most wholesome
method of action of this organ.   Any long-continued contraction of a muscle without the relief of relaxation is felt
as an unpleasant strain.   Any long-continued inactivity
of a muscle leads to an experience of restlessness.   The
natural life of a muscle is that in which a normal succession
of contractions and relaxations keeps the internal condition
well-balanced.   What is true of the muscles is equally true
of the nerve cells.   They thrive best when they pass through
a succession of periods of activity and recuperation.   The
dance furnishes an opportunity for these natural physiological successions to take place in the freest possible fashion.
When the individual is engaged in the pursuit of game or in
any of those forms of behavior which aim at some definite
end, the succession of contractions and relaxations is con-
strained and their period is dictated by external conditions.
The dance, on the other hand, is controlled by inner im-

pulses. This is what makes it an art as distinguished from labor.

Early in the history of the race, the purely personal forms of rhythmical action which are natural in moments of excitement or of joy were welded by social sympathy into group performances. One of the first means of establishing social uniformity of action is a series of sounds which mark time and result in uniform rhythm throughout the whole company. Even to-day the clapping of hands is one of the common methods of securing social uniformity. Primitive man went further in that he adopted a variety of noise-making devices as accompaniments of the dance. Two sticks were beaten together, or if the dancers were warriors carrying shields and spears, these were struck together in unison with the dance movements. The first music was nothing more than this rhythmical series of noises. As the ears of the dancers were stimulated by the sounds, their nervous systems were aroused to action in the same tempo and the group fell into the same rate of muscular reaction.

The pleasurable effect of rhythmical sounds and the interest in making this effect as pronounced as possible led primitive man to devote some time and attention to the perfecting of instruments with which to accompany the dance. He also associated with his construction of sound-producing instruments all of the mythical notions that were characteristic of his life. He made drums of various kinds and personified them. In each he found an answering spirit.

The extent to which primitive peoples worship their drums is indicated by the following quotations from Rowbotham's *History of Music*.

The great seat of Drum Worship was South America. Even at the present day it is to be found in full vitality in the interior of Brazil, but a hundred years ago it could be said that "the Drum was the only object of worship from the Orinoco to the La Plata."

This is two-thirds of South America, and as it is more than probable that Patagonia — as we shall see hereafter — should be added in too, this would make the area of the cult nearly co-equal with that of the continent. The precise form of the fetich, though it belongs to the genus "Drum," is yet strictly of the Rattle species. The Maraca, as it is called, is a hollow gourd, with small stones or hard cornseeds inside it, generally the former, which rattle when it is shaken. It is fixed on a staff, which is stuck in the ground, and the people fall down before it and worship it. It is supposed to be able to predict the future, and is consulted on all occasions of importance, such as the celebration of festivities, or the eve of a battle ; and the actions of the people are regulated by the replies which the rattle makes.[1]

A modified form of Drum worship obtained through the length and breadth of Lapland as late as two hundred years ago — so little modified, however, as to argue incontestably an anterior stage when the pure form of the cult prevailed. Though when we first get accounts of the Lapland sorcerers, they had ceased actually to *worship* the Drum, had already learnt that their fetich was something weaker than themselves, which might be controlled and made to do their bidding, yet the supernatural powers which they supposed to dwell in the instrument, and the excessive veneration with which they regarded it, clearly point to some antecedent stage not unlike the Maraca cult of the Brazilians.[2]

Rowbotham points out the analogy between these savage practices and beliefs and the attitude which exists in more recent times towards bells.

The History of the Bell is a perfect counterpart to the History of the Drum. And whoever cares to peer into the records of that era of naïve credulity which we call the Middle Ages shall find the same superstitions, which were connected with the Drum, reappearing inconnection with the Bell. He shall read of Bells being thought to speak, of Bells thought to be alive, of Bells dressed, and

[1] ROWBOTHAM, JOHN FREDERICK — *A History of Music*, I, pp. 7–8 ; London, Trübner and Co., 1885.　　[2] *Ibid.*, p. 10.

arrayed with ornaments not unlike the Fetiches we are now considering. Maracas could influence the " fertility and sterility of the ground," and Bells were rung *pro fructibus terrae*, " to make a good harvest." The Natchez used rattles to conjure the weather, and our own forefathers hung bells in their churches " to break the thunderbolt and dispel the storm." The American and Jakutskoi medicine men covered their dresses with little rattles in order to spread the magic virtue over their persons; and the medieval clergy adorned their copes and tunicles with little bells because there was something " canny " in their " tinkling " — the " tinnitus " was " salutifer" says the monkish biographer of St. Hilary of Arles. The drums beaten at Lapp sacrifices may show us well where the sacrificing bell of the mass has come from ; and the Healing drums of Koreki sorcerers appear again in the handbells that curates used to ring in the Visitation of the Sick.[1]

The dance with its accompanying noise reaches a most elaborate development among primitive peoples. One anthropologist describes his observation of rhythms among the Greenlanders. These primitive people become such masters of the art of producing rhythms that they can beat more than one rhythm at a time. They tap with the feet at one rate and with the hands at another. This is a feat which requires much training because the natural tendency of the nervous system is to act as a unit and to stimulate all the motor organs with a single impulse.

The production of various noise-emitting instruments could not go very far without stimulating invention in a direction other than that of mere attention to rhythm. The different objects used in making noises produced sounds of different quality. A rattle made of a hollow gourd produced one kind of noise while a hollow log made a wholly different kind of noise. Men began to seek out objects which were capable of giving variety to their sensory experiences.

[1] *Ibid.*, pp. 17–18.

Furthermore, as they turned attention to the qualities of sounds, they began to cultivate skill in fitting to their various moods the sounds produced by such crude instruments as they had.

The Esquimaux use their Drum " *to express their passions by* "; the Manganjas use it " *to express their joy and grief* " — the grief of a savage no doubt but still the grief of a man, and every bit as pure and every bit as true as that which mixes in the civilized emotions of ourselves. " Hear my Drum " cries the North American brave to his absent love, " though you be at the uttermost parts of the earth, hear my drum " — for he believes he can show the depth of his affection by the music of its beating. " Do you *understand* what my Drum says? " cries he again in the enthusiasm of the Wabeno, for he believes his Drum can utter definite thoughts.[1]

The production of a variety of tones engaged the attention of certain primitive peoples to a degree which shows how fascinating is the sheer discrimination of sound. The Chinese have gone further than have other peoples in this respect. A series of passages from Rowbotham will illustrate this matter :

THE SOUND OF SKIN has eight varieties, and there therefore are 8 different kinds of Drums, which vary in minute points of construction, as in having a longer or a fuller barrel, or in general bulk, or even in the method of beating, for the 8th variety has two different names, according as it is struck by the right hand or the left. But this 8th variety has another peculiarity ; for while the others give the sound of SKIN alone, it qualifies the sound of SKIN with the sound of RICE — which is a subordinate sound of Nature, and does not come into the universal gamut. And this is how the Sound of Rice is given. The barrel of the drum is filled with the husk of Rice, which has been beaten from the grain in a mortar ; and being filled full of this, it gives the sound of the Rice when it is beaten, as well as the sound of Skin.

[1] ROWBOTHAM, J. F. — *op. cit.*, pp. 30–31.

*   *   *   *   *   *   . *   *

THE SOUND OF STONE is extolled by Chinese theorists as one of the most beautiful of all the sounds. It is said to give a sound midway between the Sound of Metal and the Sound of Wood, " and it is less tart and rasping than the Sound of Metal, and much brighter than the sound of Wood — more brilliant and sweet than either." To make the stone instruments, of which there are two varieties, the Tse-King and the Pien-King, both being comprised under the general name, King, the stone is sliced into thin plates, about the size and something of the shape of a carpenter's square.

*   *   *   *   *   *   *   *

THE SOUND OF BAKED EARTH was first extracted by striking a flat piece of baked earth against some hard substance. But the sound thus produced was very harsh and unmelodious. The next attempt to extract it was by infringing on the domain of the Drum, and the sound of baked earth was got by stretching a piece of tanned skin over a vase of baked earth. Then vases of baked earth were made in the shape of drums and struck with drumsticks. But these and similar experiments proved unsatisfactory, and since it was found impossible to get the sound of baked earth from an instrument of percussion, it was decided to attempt it from an instrument of wind. A certain quantity of earth was therefore taken, the finest that could be got. It was made still finer by washing it in several waters, and then worked into the consistency of liquid mud. Two eggs, one of a goose, the other of a hen, served as the models, and the liquid mud was thrown over these and allowed to set. And then the egg on the inside was broken and picked out, and an exact mould of the egg remained. The opening made at the end for the purpose of extracting the egg was next enlarged to serve as a mouthpiece, and 5 holes were pierced in the bowl, 3 on the front, and 2 on the back ; and 5 Musical Notes were now able to be produced, each giving the desired sound of Baked Earth.

THE SOUND OF SILK has two leading varieties, and seven minor varieties. The sound of silk was produced by twisting silken threads into cords and twanging them with the fingers. Little by little it began to be noticed that the sound of silk gave definite musical notes, and the cords were then pegged down on a flat board, and the number of threads in each cord counted so as to preserve the note unaltered for the future.[1]

When the desire to discriminate tones had reached this stage, we are well beyond the earliest or drum stage in the evolution of music. In the meantime, other motives had undoubtedly contributed to experimentation in the production of sounds. The desire to produce a loud sound which could be used as a signal in warfare led to the invention of various forms of trumpets and horns. Here we may quote again from Rowbotham.

When Orellana went on his expedition down the Marañon, the savages who from time to time attacked him almost invariably preluded their onset by a tremendous din of horns and trumpets. The Muras, who were the scourge of the colonists in South America, would always perform a wild overture on horns before commencing their attack. The people of the Orinoco used horns for a similar purpose. The Samoans blow conch-shells as a prelude to the war. The savages of Guiana commence their attacks with a screech of horns and trumpets.

Now this use of the Horn in warfare is plainly an infringement on one of the uses of the old Drum; for the Drum was supposed " to give victory over enemies," and doubtless the Horn was used with similar intention. But let us notice how much more rational is the use of the new instrument than the old. For how was the Drum supposed to confer victory? By a piece of pure Fetichistic superstition. It was rubbed on the thighs of the warriors previous to their entering battle, and this was supposed to endow them with irresistible strength. But with the Horn there was no magic concerned; for Gideon is not the first man in the world's history who has routed a host by a sudden blast of the trumpets.[2]

For our purposes the impressive lesson to be drawn from these examples is that men not only evolved a series of

[1] ROWBOTHAM, J. F. — op. cit., pp. 287–291.   [2] Ibid., pp. 37–38.

musical instruments but also trained themselves in the discrimination of tones and built up a most elaborate series of associations. Some of the ideas which they cultivated were purely fantastic but these ideas came to be a part of the accepted social belief. The social group was led by this belief to supply the necessary energy to cultivate the art to higher and higher levels.

The form which this devotion to the musical arts took on very early in the history of civilization was a kind of division of labor. Society set aside certain specialists who produced the sounds to which the rest of the group responded. The earliest Egyptian monuments give evidence of large groups of musicians employed on all kinds of public occasions. The march of an army, the banquet of a king, were not complete without an elaborate musical accompaniment. Every religious ceremonial was introduced by musicians, often in great numbers. The common people, as contrasted with these specialists, were to respond to the music but not to produce it. Music began thus to break away from the life of the common man. He was allowed to enjoy music and to participate in its effects, but he was no longer a producer after instruments were perfected.

There remains one natural sound-producing instrument which the common man always commands, that is, the voice. There are two kinds of contributions which men made to music with their voices. Probably at the same time that men were trying the first experiments with the drum there was natural emotional shouting accompanying the other movements of the dance. Parallel with this was the work song intended to keep a group of workers in harmony in their action just as modern sailors are kept together when they sing at their tasks or as soldiers are kept in step by singing as they march. The other vocal contribution to music was the chanting intonation which the story-teller

cultivated when he modulated his voice to fit the meaning
of his narrative.   This was a form of music more subdued
than was the war song or the shouting at the dance ; it was
perhaps more like the work song.

The intonations of the voice were, however, in the course
of time brought into association with the sounds produced by
musical instruments.   The chant came to have an instrumental accompaniment and the war song was guided by the
rhythm if not by the pitch of the drum.   It is a long history
during which the voice and musical instruments have been
gradually attuned to one another.   It was probably the
stringed instruments which were most commonly employed
in developing this relation.   The stringed instruments were,
however, at first so different in tone from the voice that accompaniment was not what it is in modern music.   Even
the professional bard who chanted the hero stories did not
parallel his vocal performances with the sounds from his
harp.   He struck the harp at the beginning of the chant and
punctuated the pauses in his vocalization with instrumental
strains.   It was not until relatively recent times that the
voice and the instrument attempted pitches of the same order.

In the slow process of adjusting voices and instruments
to one another, the instruments had the advantage of supplying tones which are fixed.   The instrumental musician can
come back again and again to exactly the same note, but the
singer lacks both the muscular precision and the memory
for tones which are necessary for a return to exactly the
same note.   If the voice is to attain anything like the stability of the instrument, there must be a long and arduous
training of the singer.   Not only so, but the range of possible tones which can be produced with precision by the
instrumental musician is indefinitely wide, while the limits
of precision of the voice, even of the trained voice, are soon
reached.

The voice, on the other hand, contributes largely to the development of music because it is so intimately associated with the human experiences which music aims to express. The emotions of the singer will enter into the pitch of his singing and also into the rate.

The history of music can be described as a gradual accommodation of human perceptions and powers of imitation to the instrumental production of tones. The instruments employed in this long evolution have been of every possible variety and have brought into music certain physical regularities which do not appear at all in early music. There is thus a kind of artificiality in developed music which can be understood only when it is recognized that modern music is instrumental as well as human.

The history of the musical scale is shrouded in obscurity because the recording of music is a very late art. The great probabilities are that the most primitive music sought a certain variety by sounding in succession tones of different pitches, but the intervals between such varying tones were not fixed. They depended on the accidents of the situation. Anyone who hears a child amusing himself with a primitive succession of tones in which he sounds first a high tone and then a low, repeating the pair over and over, is probably listening to the earliest musical scale. The variety can be increased by adding a third pitch to the succession. From this point on the scale is increased to a series of five pitches. Here it stops for a great many peoples. The Orientals have a scale limited to five notes. The weird effect produced on American ears by music limited to fewer than our developed number of pitches is sufficiently well known to require nothing more than a mere reference here.

The subdivision of the scale into its present number of intervals is the work of the Greeks and of the European nations which followed in the path of Greek civilization.

The Greeks studied the science of music as well as practiced its arts. They knew even in the days of Pythagoras the relation between the length and tension of a vibrating string and the tone which it produces.

Much of the mythical philosophy which Pythagoras taught about numbers was derived directly from his experiments with sounds. All the systematization of music which came through Greek civilization tended to make of the art a highly cultivated form of experience. Rowbotham, in commenting on the evolution of music, even in Egypt, before it passed over into Greece, comes to the following conclusions :

We left Music a Life Speech. We find it an *article de luxe*. What was once the common property of all has become the prerogative of a chosen few. It should seem that in this matter Music, Joy, and Freedom have fared alike.

The Barbarian's birthright — which are these three things — is made so little account of now, that the toiling masses, in their stern conception of life, yield it up without a murmur to the idlers who flirt with it. There has been a sad dwindling in the estimation of Music since Civilisation set in, if the greater part of men can now make shift to do without it, and the rest are content to make its acquaintance by deputy. And the reason of this dwindling must plainly be that Music no longer answers any practical purpose in life. History, religion, morals, law have left the old channel through which they flowed ; and the scribes, philosophers, jurists, and others whom the disintegration of knowledge has brought into being, would laugh at the idea of chanting their lucubrations — and with reason too, for the pen has taken the place of the Lyre, and has been found a much more manageable instrument. Joy and freedom can no longer fill the vacuum, for they have been banished from the majority of lives, and their fortunate possessors are too much bewildered with the numberless ducts of happiness at their disposal to concentrate its flood on catgut. The old channel therefore is quite dried up, and until something is directed into it again, lies unused and worthless.

Music must therefore be content to drag on an uneventful existence until better days arrive — of no more account than tapestry and embroidery, perhaps not so much.[1]

The historian of music expresses the belief that after losing its first natural character his art will take on in its later evolution a new and more productive relation to human experience. Be that as it may, it is very impressive to the psychologist studying the changes in human experiences that the history of one of the most widely cultivated of the modern arts shows a distinct break between mature art and the art which was natural and primitive. Modern music and even Greek music are cultivated arts. Men can be brought to a full appreciation of the meaning of cultivated art only through training. The fact is, of course, that for a great many individuals this special cultivation of musical appreciation is lacking. It is not forced upon one by the practical necessities of life as is the use of language and number. Music in its fully developed modern forms is to be compared to the higher reaches of literature or to the special demonstrations of higher mathematics; these are the possessions of the few, not the property of the common group. Nor is it likely that music can ever become, as it is sometimes called, the common language of the emotions, for the reason that the emotions are not matters of general social participation. They are subjective and personal to a degree which forever excludes them from the kind of social compulsion that must of necessity attach to the major conventions, such as language and number, on which ordinary intercourse is dependent.

We have followed music to the point where it has become a highly developed scientific art, and, as such, separated from the ordinary life of the common man. We may now

[1] ROWBOTHAM, J. F. — op. cit., pp. 197–198.

outline briefly what may be called a second cycle of the evolution. In this second cycle the art is worked over into a form in which a new type of appeal is made and a new type of training is instituted in the social effort to unite men at a higher level in the appreciation of the art.

Although Greek music became a highly intricate and elaborately instrumented art, it was far below the level of present-day music. It produced melodies or sequences of tones, but does not seem to have arrived at the point where it could master the harmonies which are characteristic of the modern art. The higher evolutions begin with the use of music in the ancient and medieval church.

Briefly outlined, the steps of this evolution are as follows: At first the church service which was participated in solely by the clerics was intoned and an elaborate system was evolved by them which was based on the ancient practice of chanting, but was much more highly perfected than the chant of the bard. After intonation came a later stage when the clerical conductors of the service were assisted by choirs which answered with a contrasting tone and with appropriate verbal responses.

From this participation of various voices in the service, there soon followed an effort to harmonize the several voices. This required a new adjustment and led to the form of music known as counterpoint. At this stage each voice carried its own melody, but the various melodies were timed so that there was a correspondence of note to note, making a tonal combination which was simple in rhythm though complex in pitch.

A long period of experimentation with counterpoint was necessary before the laws of congruent tones were discovered. The instrumentation of this more complex form of music also had to be mastered and this introduced an element of physical combination which had not been present at the earlier stage when the different tones merely succeeded one another in simple melodies.

While this development was going forward under the influence and support of the church, there was growing up a body of popular folk songs and professional music of a secular character which later joined with the church music and the two together produced, following the sixteenth century, the great variety of forms which constitute modern music.

It will be well in order to make this outline clear to add an account which describes some of the experiments that were necessary in order to perfect the modern art. A number of summary paragraphs may be quoted from Pratt's *History of Music:*

From the 4th century the strong accent upon unity of organization, fixity of creed and uniformity of liturgy led steadily to a demand for richness and stateliness. Costly edifices become common, ministrants were multiplied, and the whole ritual of worship tended to become ornate. This involved a new attention to music.

The first center of activity was Constantinople, where Greek music was the established type of artistic song. Thus the tradition of the ancient unison melody was handed on to Italy and the West. The evolution that followed is only imperfectly traceable in detail, but in the end it provided the mediæval Church with a large and striking body of melodies, fitted to a variety of prose texts and even to metrical poetry. We must suppose that these ritual melodies grew out of manifold experiments at different places, which were only gradually wrought into a general and uniform system. Even after the system was codified, its usages continued to accumulate, and from time to time considerable modifications in style appeared. . . .

Since the Gregorian style originated for liturgical reasons, its home was the metropolitan cathedral or the monastic chapel, whence it spread to parish churches generally. Being cultivated only by ecclesiastics, to the common people it was remote and abstruse. Its direct influence upon the general progress of music was

therefore limited. To some extent there arose an antipathy between it and secular music, which was heightened by the fact that
church song was always in Latin. In the general evolution of
music it has always remained a somewhat peculiar specialty, representing the persistence for a particular purpose of a style which
is essentially antique. Yet it must be confessed that in its ideal
perfection, as it stood in the early Middle Ages, it was a remarkable example of melodic invention and beauty.[1]

*   *   *   *   *   *   *

The positive achievements of the centuries following 1200 stand
in striking contrast to the timid experiments of those before.
From this point onward the art of music becomes interestingly
interwoven with progress in other fields, being a phase of the general intellectual awakening of Europe that preceded the Renaissance. . . .

The distinctive feature of the period in music was a profound
alteration in the aim of composition. In Greek music and its
successor, the Gregorian style, the one desire was for a single
melodic outline to enforce and beautify a verbal text. All music
was a specialized outgrowth or derivative of poetic speech. A new
era came in when it was seen that music might have beauty and
meaning more or less independent of its words, being built up into
a fabric or edifice of tones by massing and interweaving two or
more voice-parts like strands or threads.

The transition to this new idea involved two lines of effort, which
for convenience may be taken up separately. These were (a) the
reduction of melodies to regular rhythmic form, with such accen-
tual and durational values of the tones that their motions could be
accurately measured and mutually adjusted, and (b) the discovery
of ways in which melodies could be simultaneously combined so
as to be concordant, or, if discordant, still satisfactory and effective. The former effort led to a theory of "time," the latter to a
theory of "counterpoint," and the two were mutually interdependent at every point.[2]

---

[1] Pratt, Waldo Selden — *The History of Music*, pp. 64–65; G. Schirmer,
1907.   [2] *Ibid.*, p. 77.

From his doctrines of salvation by faith, the right of private judgment, and the universal priesthood of believers, Luther deduced radical conclusions regarding public worship, including special emphasis on congregational participation in the service in the vernacular language (instead of Latin). Although holding closely to the outlines of the Roman service, he undertook to reduce some features that he held objectionable and to make the people's part conspicuous. He seized upon common song as indispensable, and in 1523 and 1526, with the aid of Walther and others, issued orders of service with this element emphasized. The hymns provided were as a rule specially written in metrical form. For them melodies were either borrowed from favorite folk-songs or part-songs or were newly written in similar style, thus linking the new type with forms already universally popular. These melodies were later called "chorales."

Though at first the musical treatment of chorales was more or less contrapuntal, with the melody in the tenor, before 1600 the style advanced to a definitely harmonic form, with a solid progression of chords, the melody in the treble and the lines sharply defined by cadences and controlled by a coherent tonality.

The chorale became the nucleus of Protestant church music generally, and it is of historic importance because its wide acceptance hastened and popularized the new tendency to base composition on harmony rather than counterpoint, and because from its extensive literature German organ music later derived an inexhaustible fund of suggestion. What the treasures of Plain-Song had been to Catholic music, the new treasures of the chorale style became to Protestant music. This innovation, then, contained the germ of great subsequent developments.[1]

No one can read such statements without being impressed by the fact that civilization has expended in the refinement of the art of music an enormous amount of energy. Like all human institutions this art has grown through ages of experimentation and in the long process has absorbed the

[1] *Ibid.*, p. 129.

thought and efforts of many men. The impression that society has evolved the art through great effort is heightened if one reads the later history of music and becomes acquainted with the lives of the composers who have contributed to music since the sixteenth century saw the dawn of modern music.

Music like every other human institution is thus seen to be the result of a gradual accumulation of what may be called social capital. No single individual, whatever his personal capacity for the appreciation of tones, can be regarded as the source of this art. The Greeks derived their instruments and their ability to appreciate the relatively simple music of which they were masters, from Ionia and Egypt. The medieval church took what Greece contributed and elaborated it into something incomparably more complex than had been the art of the ancients. Modern musicians borrowed in turn what the medieval world produced, and are still in process of refining and amplifying it. Everywhere we see evidence of the highest degree of social coöperation.

Not only has music grown through gradual social coöperation, but it has always held a position of high esteem in the social mind. Although there have been individual instances when exponents of the musical arts suffered from neglect, the major fact is that, in general, society has accorded its highest rewards to those who have contributed to music. The honor paid to musicians and the support which society has given them while they were doing their work are evidences of the most substantial kind that society is willing to coöperate in the development of the art.

Especially is it important for the psychology of social institutions to note the fact that many persons join in contributing indirectly to music even though they personally have very little direct knowledge of the institution to which they are contributing. It is enough for the plain man that the leaders of society think highly of this composer or that. He will fall in line and contribute in some degree to the social and material support of the composer even though his personal delight in listening to music is small. This means that the social mind is determined in its estimates of values not by personal tastes and appreciations but by certain aggregate judgments. Social interdependence has become so compact that even if an unmusical individual does not go to the opera himself, he is glad to know that his city is supporting it. He can understand social respectability, even if he does not fully participate in the experiences on which it rests.

The relation of music to social life in general can be comprehended most readily if the principle of limitation of individual attention which was expounded in an earlier chapter is kept in mind. It was pointed out that the hunter and the arrow maker specialize because the human mind is incapable of including in its range of activities a great variety of interests. The division of labor in the field of industry does not permit individuals to forego altogether productive industry but it does permit each person to follow his particular bent within the general economic system. Specialization of interest is not permitted by society to any such degree as will allow the individual to omit the cultivation of language or of punctuality or of some degree of precision. Society demands of all of its members the fundamentals of social intercourse. Given these, society is obliged to recognize the limitations of individual energy and time and is complacent when the members of the group seek enjoyments and recreation in different lines. Music is one of the recognized forms of human experience which society leaves to the individual taste, to be cultivated or neglected as each member of the group sees fit.

In spite of the absence of social compulsion, there have been motives for the perfection of the art of music sufficiently strong to lead to the bestowal on this art of a great deal of effort.   Music as a device for making ceremonials impressive, music as a source of occasional stimulation, music as a source of refined enjoyment by the selected few will never disappear for lack of cultivation.   It is one of society's luxuries, but so long as society has surplus energy and an adequate satisfaction of its imperative needs the luxuries will be sought.

CHAPTER XII

NATIONAL STANDARDS AND NATURAL STANDARDS IN GRAPHIC ART

There is a group of fine arts which have to do with the arranging of materials in space in such a way that they will appeal to the human eye as agreeable. These fine arts are closely allied to certain practical arts. For example, architecture is concerned with such matters as the ability of a foundation to carry the weight of a superstructure; and also with the æsthetic effects produced by a building because of the lines which it marks off against the background of the landscape and the sky. Similarly in thinking of clothing we may emphasize the decorative effect of color and form and speak of design, or we may think merely of comfort and utility. In the first instance, we are dealing with fashion; in the second, with something to wear.

The fine arts of this group, including besides architecture and costume designing, pottery, metal working, drawing, painting, landscape gardening, and a host of others, all have histories which it would be illuminating for the student of civilization to study. They all reveal the inner nature of man in his struggle to master the outer world and at the same time gratify his own taste. They all show how each generation has based its actions and its tastes on the experiences of its predecessors, evolving thus a gradual accumulation of standards which control the individual to a very pronounced degree. For example, the periods of national architecture make it perfectly evident that the individuals who designed temples and churches in various countries and epochs did so not in response to purely individual ideals but under the control of patterns handed down from social experience.

Perhaps the most striking illustrations of the control of tastes by standards evolved by the group are to be drawn from the succession of fashions in dress. No modern man would venture to appear on the street with a costume of the sixteenth century. Men have found that in the exacting demands of modern business competition, it is better to cover up one's personal preferences for form and color by adopting the drab monotony of conventional male attire. Social experience shows that a man can do business with less distraction in such a garb. Women, on the other hand, are engaged in cultivating a different kind of contact with the social world, and their costumes are accordingly of a different type. Even here, however, competition has dictated that there shall be a reasonable limit set to variability.

What is true of architecture and dress is true of all of the arts. There is a style of drawing and painting in China and Japan which is sharply in contrast with the style of drawing and painting of occidental civilization. We find that each individual artist in these contrasted areas is better satisfied with the style of his social environment than he would be with the style of the group foreign to him. He is surrounded and controlled by the style which belongs to his people. This is clear evidence of social domination of taste and technique. Example after example of the same type can be drawn from the history of every nation and every period.

There is another fundamental fact common to all of the arts here under consideration. It is that "good form" from the point of view of taste very often turns out to be "good form" from a mechanical point of view. A column of marble is most beautiful when the diameter of its shaft and the size of its capital are exactly adequate to the weight which the column has to carry. This correspondence between the human demand and the demand dictated by physical law has often impressed writers on æsthetics. They find in such facts evidence of a great underlying unity of being which includes human nature and all of the natural objects in the world.

The psychologist is confronted with the problem of uniting in a single system a series of facts which at first seem to have little or nothing in common. Art is national and at the same time art is natural. Art grows out of the free expression of human preferences, and at the same time those objects are found to be the most artistic which obey most fully the laws of mechanics.

The purpose of this chapter will be to gather up certain observations which apply to drawing and painting in the effort to supply a general formula of explanation for all of the arts dealing with space relations. The two graphic arts are chosen because they more than others of the space arts have been subjected to comparative study. The reason for this fact is probably to be found in the ease with which drawings can be preserved and reproduced. They are more readily accessible to the student than are any other art materials.

The most primitive drawings of the race, that is, the drawings made by savages and children, are not accurate or detailed representations. They are mere outline sketches reproducing usually only a part of the object's contour. Sometimes they are hardly more than a scrawl of lines showing that the drawer is thinking of something tall or something broad. The drawings are mere devices for reminding the artist or the onlooker of something which he has seen and in which he has been interested. The primitive artist draws animals and men but not inanimate objects, evidently following his intimate interests rather than the impressions which the environment offers to his eyes.

Without attempting to reproduce all of the figures to which reference is made, we may borrow the account given by Wells of the drawings found among the remains of some of the earliest inhabitants of Europe.

It greatly aids us to realize their common humanity that these earliest true men could draw. Both races, it would seem, drew astonishingly well. They were by all standards savages, but they were artistic savages. They drew better than any of their successors down to the beginnings of history. They drew and painted on the cliffs and cave walls that they had wrested from the Neanderthal men. And the surviving drawings come to the ethnologist, puzzling over bones and scraps, with the effect of a plain message shining through guesswork and darkness. They drew on bones and antlers; they carved little figures.

These late Palæolithic people not only drew remarkably well for our information, and with an increasing skill as the centuries passed, but they have also left us other information about their lives in their graves. They buried. They buried their dead, often with ornaments, weapons, and food; they used a lot of colour in the burial, and evidently painted the body. From that, one may infer that they painted their bodies during life. Paint was a big fact in their lives. They were inveterate painters; they used black, brown, red, yellow, and white pigments, and the pigments they used endure to this day in the caves of France and Spain. Of all modern races, none have shown so pictorial a disposition; the nearest approach to it has been among the American Indians.

These drawings and paintings of the later Palæolithic people went on through a long period of time, and present wide fluctuations in artistic merit. We give here some early sketches, from which we learn of the interest taken by these early men in the bison, horse, ibex, cave bear, and reindeer. In its early stages the drawing is often primitive like the drawing of clever children; quadrupeds are usually drawn with one hindleg and one foreleg, as children draw them to this day. The legs on the other side were too much for the artist's technique. Possibly the first drawings began as children's drawings begin, out of idle scratchings. The savage scratched with a flint on a smooth rock surface, and was reminded of some line or gesture. But their solid carvings are at least as old as their first pictures. The earlier drawings betray a complete

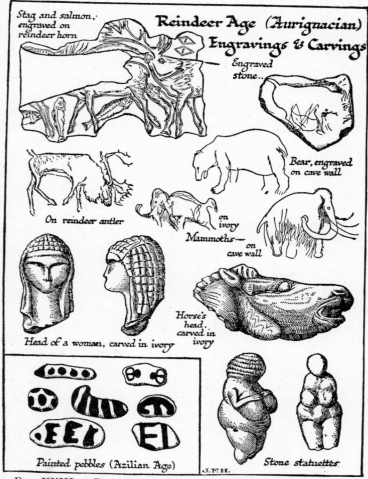

Stag and salmon, engraved on reindeer horn

Reindeer Age (Aurignacian) Engravings & Carvings

Engraved stone..

Bear, engraved on cave wall

On reindeer antler

on ivory

Mammoths— on cave wall

Head of a woman, carved in ivory

Horse's head, carved in ivory

Painted pebbles (Azilian Age)

J.F.H.

Stone statuettes

FIG. XVIII. — DRAWINGS AND CARVINGS OF PREHISTORIC MAN.
(From Wells.)

incapacity to group animals. As the centuries progressed, more skilful artists appeared. The representation of beasts became at last astonishingly vivid and like. But even at the crest of their artistic time, they still drew in profile as children do ; perspective and the fore-shortening needed for back and front views were too much for them. They rarely drew themselves. The vast majority of their drawings represent animals. The mammoth and the horse are among the commonest themes. Some of the people, whether Grimaldi people or Cro-Magnon people, also made little ivory and soapstone statuettes, and among these are some very fat female figures. These latter suggest the physique of Grimaldi rather than of Cro-Magnon artists. They are like Bushmen women. The human sculpture of the earlier times inclined to caricature, and generally such human figures as they represent are far below the animal studies in vigour and veracity.

Later on there was more grace and less coarseness in the human representations. One little ivory head discovered is that of a girl with an elaborate coiffure. These people at a later stage also scratched and engraved designs on ivory and bone. Some of the most interesting groups of figures are carved very curiously round bone, and especially round rods of deerbone, so that it is impossible to see the entire design all together. Figures have also been found modelled in clay, although no Palæolithic people made any use of pottery.

Many of the paintings are found in the depths of unlit caves. They are often difficult of access. The artists must have employed lamps to do their work, and shallow soapstone lamps in which fat could have been burnt have been found. Whether the seeing of these cavern paintings was in some way ceremonial or under what circumstances they were seen, we are now altogether at a loss to imagine.[1]

These primitive people drew the objects with which they were best acquainted. Their world of art represented the world of their most absorbing interests. Furthermore, they

[1] WELLS, H. G. — *The Outline of History*, I, pp. 92-95; Macmillan Co., 1920.

drew these objects as they thought of them, not as they appeared in nature. No primitive art is realistic. Only after long ages of experimentation do men learn how to concentrate attention on details and on such realistic facts as perspective and natural color.

Perhaps it may be well to digress a little from the consideration of primitive drawing and establish sympathy for the early artist by pointing out some of the limitations of ordinary adult experience. One begins to understand why the first artists neglected perspective when one thinks of the train of experiences which one has in watching an approaching fellow being. Under such circumstances the fact is that the approaching figure casts in the eye an image of ever-increasing size. The man one hundred yards away casts an image on the retina which is half the size of the image cast when he is fifty yards away. The ordinary observer does not, however, think of the approaching man as increasing in size. Experience has taught that men do not change suddenly in their dimensions. The change in size of the retinal image is interpreted not in terms of actual sensory experience but in terms of what one knows about men. When an amateur tries to draw the man, therefore, he does not make him of different sizes to represent his appearance at different distances, but always of the same size. This is the psychological reason why mathematical perspective comes into drawing very late. Primitive artists were concerned with what they thought about objects, not with what they actually could see.

Examination of the drawings of primitive peoples emphasizes in various ways what has been said about the lack of reproductive detail in primitive drawing. A drawing of a fish or of a man will show only the head. The reason for this is that the artist was interested only in what was for him the most conspicuous part of the object. This is an

illustration of the principle of selection under the guidance
of interest.   Sometimes a profile face will be supplied with
two eyes.   This is an illustration of the fact that the first
drawings are "out of the head" of the artist.   He knows that
men have two eyes, so he puts them into his drawing quite
regardless of the fact which careful observation will show,
that when a face is seen in profile only one eye is visible.
In like fashion primitive artists in trying to depict a man
mounted on a horse will show both of the man's legs on the
visible side of the horse.

The other characteristic of primitive drawings to which
reference has been made is that they are always mere outline sketches.   There are no details, no lights and shades.
When colors are used, the pigments are selected not because
they conform to the colors of objects but because they help
to make the pattern stand out more clearly.   The coloring
of the Sunday comic supplement is strictly in accord with
the most approved savage tastes in these matters.   The
colors are all selected because of their striking character
and because of the contrasts which they can provide.   Each
figure is given its color in great flat surfaces in order to help
those who look at the picture to pick out easily the parts
of the picture which have different meanings.   Outlines are
sharp and distinct.   There is no shading or blending of
surfaces.   Contrast and easy selection are the dominant
motives of the artist.

As soon as one notes these characteristics of primitive
drawings, one recognizes that they are nothing more nor less
than projections of the experience of the observer.   The
drawing is not at first the reproduction of an object.   It is
the reproduction of an idea.   Its limitations are the limitations of the idea.   What it contains by way of positive
features is what the mind tends to emphasize.

Coming back to the statement quoted from Wells, we may

point out that these early men, who were absorbed in hunting animals for food, did not draw landscapes and trees. In fact, as Wundt has pointed out in a passage to be quoted at length later, landscape drawing and painting are very late in their appearance in the history of art. Men take the landscape for granted at first and bestow their whole attention on the animals and men, who are the centers of prime interest.

Starting from primitive outline ideas, men have made progress through social coöperation in a number of directions dictated by the interests which their drawings were intended to serve. Thus when communication or the making of records was the dominant purpose, that evolution was worked out which was recorded in the chapter on the alphabet. The alphabet is a series of simplified drawings which ultimately came into association with sounds and lost their function of informing the eye with regard to the shape of objects and took on the function of reminding the observer of names.

In another case simple outline drawing was developed into decorative design. Men noted that certain animal forms fitted gracefully into certain spaces, and they devised repetitions of the form to make a border or surface which seemed to them interesting. In such a case the animal form was very frequently modified so as to emphasize balance and symmetry of parts to a degree that departed radically from nature. The head of the animal sometimes was made as large as the body in order that the two parts of the animal should contribute to the design in equal degree. Figure XIX gives some examples of this evolution. The alligator form has been conventionalized and transformed into an ornamental design.

Decorative design, hardly less than the alphabet, leads away from the observation of nature. The motive here is not to follow closely that which is presented to the eye when the object is seen but to rearrange lines so that they shall mark rhythmical successions.

The third direction in which men moved in maturing the graphic arts of drawing and painting was that of reproducing more accurately figure and color. This led to representative drawing and painting. The motives for the cultivation of realism in art are so obvious that we need not attempt to describe them. We are interested here more in

FIG. XIX. — ALLIGATOR DESIGNS.   (From Holmes)[1]

the method by which realism has been evolved than in its motives. Let us take a case out of ordinary modern life which will give us insight into the process that has gone on in human history.

Suppose that the ordinary man wants to draw a sphere. He will be able to make a very good start by drawing a circular contour. He may even go a step further and fill in his circle with black or some color so as to set it off clearly from its background. The drawing will remain, however, absolutely flat and will be unsatisfactory because of its com-

---

[1] HOLMES, W. H. — *Ancient Art of the Province of Chiriqui*, vi, 1888, p. 173; Ethnological Report, Washington.

plete lack of perspective. The ordinary observer is helpless to improve his drawing because he does not know what to look at in the natural sphere in order to discover what is needed to improve his drawing. His attention is usually absorbed in the contours of the object and of the drawing. So far as he can see, they agree. The same is true of the coloring. What the ordinary observer has not noted is the play of light and shade. Some day an observer more keen than others will note that there is always a bright spot on the side of a sphere and that this shades off into darker areas. This keen observer puts a bright spot on his circle and it begins to stand out. Once the keen observer has taken this step and recorded it, others can see what they did not see before, and the art of representing spheres will have been advanced to a higher level. Individual genius and social coöperation will have operated to improve at once observation and art, bringing both of them into closer harmony with nature.

Too much emphasis cannot be laid on the fact that realism in art is not an expression of purely æsthetic impulses. Realism in art is an aspect of growing realism in ideas. Primitive man does not note all objects of nature in detail any more than does modern man. If one is not interested in trees, and most persons are not, one does not look at trees in detail. The result for drawing is that most people cannot reproduce trees with any high degree of realistic detail. The way to make progress in the accurate drawing of trees is to observe them closely. Conversely, one of the best ways to induce careful observation is to set the observer the task of drawing trees.

The progress of realism in graphic art can be divided into a number of sharply distinguishable phases. First came closer attention to the details of contour; then came attention to color; and finally, came attention to light and shadow.

This last refinement was part of the very late mastery of the technique of representing perspective.

In the course of this progressive attention to detail, the individual observer is sure to be guided by the modes of life of his tribe. The hunting tribe will have one group of realistic interests; the herders will have another. The Greeks brought to the highest perfection representations of the human figure. The Orientals have perfected flower forms and animal forms.

We see from these statements why it is that art takes on the character of a national mode of thought and expression. The Chinese and Japanese, for example, have never attempted the fullest development of perspective. The beauty ·of their art is the beauty of a balanced and harmonious surface. The attention of these peoples is controlled by the interest which their national tastes selected for emphasis. Once a trend of observation and of art becomes established, it dominates all of the individuals who come into intimate contact with it.

The history of European art is sufficiently recent and completely recorded so that we can trace with precision the progress in the mastery of perspective drawing. In the late medieval period the paintings of the European artists were centered on human subjects. Since decorative art was cultivated chiefly in connection with ecclesiastical edifices, it was the saints and martyrs and episodes in the life of Christ which engaged the attention of artists. The dominant human figures were in many cases the only objects in the works of art. In other instances, an attempt was made to give local character to the portrait, and a background was undertaken along with the representation of the human figure. The first efforts of this type are altogether lacking in perspective. Usually the human figure is of colossal size as compared with the building or landscape in the background, and it is thrust into the front of the picture in such a way as to destroy altogether the unity of the scene. Colors conforming to nature were also lacking. All kinds of experiments with the background and with the coloring of the human figures were tried, many of them following wholly conventional lines.

During the sixteenth and seventeenth centuries the Renaissance brought a movement of return to nature. Browning has given a vivid account of this movement in his poem entitled "Fra Lippo Lippi." The monk is justifying himself to the constable who has caught him truant from the cloister and falls into a discussion of his art. He tells how he began as a beggar urchin to take careful note of people and things and how he was later allowed to begin painting on the cloister walls. He tells how he followed as closely as he could his observations of real people and how the monks were filled with admiration at his realism, but the prior came with serious doubts. The prior belonged to the older school of conventionalists and doubted very much the morality of realism.

The following are Browning's lines:

> The monks closed in a circle and praised loud
> Till checked, taught what to see and not to see,
> Being simple bodies, — "That's the very man!
> Look at the boy who stoops to pat the dog!
> That woman's like the Prior's niece who comes
> To care about his asthma: it's the life!"
> But there my triumph's straw-fire flared and funked;
> Their betters took their turn to see and say:
> The Prior and the learned pulled a face
> And stopped all that in no time. "How? what's here?
> Quite from the mark of painting, bless us all!
> Faces, arms, legs and bodies like the true
> As much as pea and pea! It's devil's-game!

Your business is not to catch men with show,
With homage to the perishable clay,
But lift them over it, ignore it all,
Make them forget there's such a thing as flesh.
Your business is to paint the souls of men —
Man's soul, and it's a fire, smoke . . . no, it's not . . .
It's vapour done up like a new-born babe —
(In that shape when you die it leaves your mouth)
It's . . . well, what matters talking, it's the soul!
Give us no more of body than shows soul!
Here's Giotto, with his Saint a-praising God,
That sets us praising, — why not stop with him?
Why put all thoughts of praise out of our head
With wonder at lines, colours, and what not?
Paint the soul, never mind the legs and arms!
Rub all out, try at it a second time.
Oh, that white smallish female with the breasts,
She's just my niece. . . . Herodias, I would say, —
Who went and danced and got men's heads cut off!
Have it all out!"   Now, is this sense, I ask?
A fine way to paint soul, by painting body
So ill, the eyes can't stop there, must go further
And can't fare worse!   Thus, yellow does for white
When what you put for yellow's simply black,
And any sort of meaning looks intense
When all beside itself means and looks nought.
Why can't a painter lift each foot in turn,
Left foot and right foot, go a double step,
Make his flesh liker and his soul more like,
Both in their order?   Take the prettiest face,
The Prior's niece . . . patron-saint — is it so pretty
You can't discover if it means hope, fear,
Sorrow or joy? won't beauty go with these?
Suppose I've made her eyes all right and blue,
Can't I take breath and try to add life's flash,
And then add soul and heighten them threefold?
Or say there's beauty with no soul at all —

(I never saw it — put the case the same —)
If you get simple beauty and nought else,
You get about the best thing God invents :
That's somewhat : and you'll find the soul you have missed,
Within yourself, when you return him thanks.

Later, Browning tells his theory of art in Fra Lippo's
appeal to the common sense of the constable in the following
lines :

You be judge !
You speak no Latin more than I, belike ;
However, you're my man, you've seen the world
— The beauty and the wonder and the power,
The shapes of things, their colours, lights and shades,
Changes, surprises, — and God made it all !
— For what ? Do you feel thankful, ay or no,
For this fair town's face, younder river's line,
The mountain round it and the sky above,
Much more the figures of man, woman, child,
These are the frame to ? What's it all about ?
To be passed over, despised ? or dwelt upon,
Wondered at ? Oh, this last of course ! — you say.
But why not do as well as say, — paint these
Just as they are, careless what comes of it ?
God's works — paint anyone, and count it crime
To let a truth slip. Don't object, " His works
Are here already ; nature is complete :
Suppose you reproduce her — (which you can't)
There's no advantage ! you must beat her, then."
For, don't you mark ? we're made so that we love
First when we see them painted, things we have passed
Perhaps a hundred times nor cared to see ;
And so they are better, painted — better to us,
Which is the same thing. Art was given for that ;
God uses us to help each other so,
Lending our minds out.

This story of the realism of the Renaissance is a story of the way in which natural colors were substituted for conventional colors and perspective was gradually perfected through observation.

In his *Voelkerpsychologie*, Wundt has commented on this movement in terms which may be put in English as follows:

The struggle to secure perspective is a matter of importance in the evolution of artistic imagination not only because of its own direct achievements but also because it reflects a change in the whole mental attitude of men toward art and its objects. Briefly put, the matter can be sketched in the following terms. The painting of the Renaissance is dominated, as was that of the immediately preceding period of Christian art, by religious ideas. The Renaissance sought its materials, however, in real life. It aimed to express in concrete ways such ideals as piety, humility, religious ecstasy, mother-love, and childish innocence in every possible form and color. Sometimes in order to bring out the virtues it resorted to contrasts. The people and the happenings which were used to convey these ideals in art were always taken from reality. Devotion to reality led the artists to strive more and more to reproduce as exactly as possible the form and color and shadings of the objects which they represented. In order to give his picture depth, the artist added to the single human figure or to the group which he painted some kind of a background; at first this was made up of walls of a building, and later a landscape. In the Italian art of the middle Renaissance the background is evidently put into the picture with no motive other than that of contributing to the lifelikeness of the human figures. The background was required especially where the human figures were in action or where the biblical narrative represented in the picture called for a setting of some kind. The background, however, as soon as it began to appear, emphasized the need of perspective as the human figures never had done. It is out of this demand for a mastery of landscape perspective that there grew the artistic device of finding and using a vanishing point for all pictures. As soon as landscape painting with the device of perspective had been worked out in the effort to give the human figures a true spatial setting, there was a tendency to carry over to the human figures and to the other objects in the painting all that had been discovered in the perfection of the landscape.

In the meantime the human interest which was the center of the painting exercised an influence on the selection of the background. The idea which was in the mind of the artist as characteristic of his human figures furnished the motive for the selection of a congenial background which would express the same general feeling tone. Thus the landscape which was originally put into the picture in keeping with the biblical narrative as, for example, the temple at Jerusalem or the Garden of Gethsemane, was depicted in such a way as to conform to the meaning of the picture or at times was changed with a view to making the impression more vivid through the development of a contrasting feeling tone. With all these additions the Italian art of the Renaissance is essentially an art of human figures, exhibiting as its only real object human nature in its various manifestations and its relations to God and men. Even with the greatest Italian masters the landscape is simple, almost sketchy. Their landscapes show no seasonal variety, and that most impressive element of landscape perspective, namely, atmospheric perspective, is shown, when present at all, only in the coloration of distant mountains on the horizon.

The employment of landscapes as significant backgrounds prepared the way for the development of landscape painting as an independent phase of art. It was necessary that landscapes should exhibit the power of art to express sentiments and emotions first as a part of a picture including human actions before they could be used independently as means of expressing human experiences. The emancipation of landscape painting from its earlier restricted form is the achievement of Dutch art. The stimulating character of this new type of art arises from the fact that it is entirely independent of human beings and of those particular conditions under which human life produces emotional values. Landscape painting thus becomes an essential element of modern painting coördinate with two other forms of art which arose at the same time. One of these is portrait painting, which gives expression

to the psychological character of an individual without any reference to religious or historical considerations. The other is the
so-called *genre* or familiar art which portrays a domestic interior
or a village scene and exhibits thus the joys and sorrows of common life. These were developed along with landscape painting.

The discovery that landscape taken by itself is the purest and
most effective means of expressing all kinds of human moods from
the highest exaltation to the profoundest depression is one of the
greatest discoveries of all time in art. As a means of expressing
human emotions and sentiments, landscape painting takes a place
among the representative arts analogous to that taken by pure
harmony in music when it became detached from singing and dancing. This discovery of the value of landscapes could never have
been made except through the use of landscapes as backgrounds for
human life, any more than music could have been evolved without
its connection in primitive life with singing and dancing. Furthermore, in the degree in which landscape painting aroused and cultivated a feeling for nature, nature itself became an object of
æsthetic enjoyment. As the art of the Greeks discovered the
beauty of the human figure, so modern painting was the means
of bringing to attention the beauty of nature.[1]

This lengthy quotation from Wundt teaches by direct
reference to historical facts how it is that the art interests
of one generation grow out of the interests of an earlier
age. Painting is a product of social coöperation.

Our study has supplied explanation of the first fact which
was noted at the opening of this chapter, namely, the fact that
art has a national character. We turn now to a consideration of the second fact. Art, in order to be of the highest
type, must conform to natural law.

Lipps, a German writer on æsthetics, has based his theory
of spatial æsthetics on an examination of the Doric column.
His contention is that an observer looking at this column is
drawn into sympathy with it much as one is drawn into

[1] WUNDT, WILHELM — *Voelkerpsychologie*, Bd. II, Th. I, pp. 278–281.

sympathy with a human being who is seen trying to lift a heavy object or carry a heavy weight. The sympathy which is felt for the column or the man includes as one of its most important elements certain reactions giving rise to sensations of strain. One feels one's own muscles grow rigid as one contemplates a person trying to lift a heavy object. The reaction is a part of the process of perception. If the impression given by the column or by the fellow being is that of adequacy to the situation, the strain is slight or even replaced by a feeling of relaxation. If, on the other hand, the bearer of the burden seems to be inadequate, there is an accumulation of strain which is in the nature of an effort on the observer's part to help carry the weight. The sympathy which comes when the weight is adequately carried is a sympathy of pleasure and success. The sympathy which is felt when one has to help carry the burden is a sympathy of distress.

The explanation propounded by Lipps is in complete accord with the accepted views of modern psychology regarding the nature of perception. It is fully established by laboratory studies that recognition of any object is dependent not merely on sensory impression but on the character of the reaction which is aroused in the observer. Let us consider in detail an experiment which will support the explanation given by Lipps. If a person picks up a bottle of mercury, he will grossly overestimate its weight. The reason for this is that ordinary bottles filled with ordinary liquids have been lifted again and again by every mature person. As a result of all of these experiences, each of us has acquired a certain tendency to strain the muscles to a familiar degree every time he starts to pick up a bottle. When we reach for the bottle of mercury, we set our muscles as experience has taught us to set them for bottles in general. This time the set is wrong. The bottle does not respond as we had expected, and, impressed by the disparity between our expectations and the facts, we overestimate the weight. Overestimation is here the result of a shock of disappointment.

The mercury illustration opens the way to the consideration of a whole series of interesting questions. How does the mature observer of a Doric column come to have the right tension? How does his sympathy respond with accuracy to just the right diameter of the column and to just the right size of the capital? How far can one go astray in such matters?

A part of the answer to these questions is to be found in the fact that, in a great many instances, human tastes do not properly adjust themselves but do as a matter of fact go astray. The supposed accuracy of untrained human sympathies is very largely a fiction. The reason why people live with perfect composure in hideous houses and enjoy furniture which is overornate and top-heavy with upholstery and inharmonious in color; the reason why people think well of cast-iron statuary on their front lawns is that their reactions have developed along with their perceptions in unæsthetic surroundings.

It is true that in matters of symmetry and balance all human beings are fairly agreed as to what is proper and what is not. This is due, however, not to the fact that we were born with æsthetic bents in favor of symmetry, but rather to the fact that from the first days, experience has put before our eyes and into our hands objects which are symmetrical and objects which nature compels us to balance if we are to hold them at all. Every move that the infant makes is in a world governed by the laws of mechanics. Naturally, his muscular tensions will be trained under the control of these laws. Now and then experience will mislead, but, in the main, nature is uniform enough so that we may safely rely on our cultivated habits of tension.

The facts which stand out very clearly when we analyze æsthetical experiences are that we are agreeably impressed with those objects and situations which correspond to the strains and tensions which we have acquired, and that we are distressed when the strain induced by the perception of an object is in any way inharmonious with our expectation and training. The fundamental fact is not the æsthetic appreciation of the moment but the long line of experiences which have drilled our nervous systems.

Examples without number could be adduced of the fact that perception is controlled by training. Take so simple a matter as the recognition of the direction of straight lines. The world is full of vertical and horizontal lines. Every time an observer runs his eye up and down a tree or the edge of a building, he gets a lesson in verticality. Every time one looks along the horizon or sees a log lying on the ground, one gets a lesson in the recognition of horizontal positions. To be sure, there are all sorts of other experiences which present lines at various angles. The branches of every tree and the sloping hillsides offer to the eyes of the observer examples of angles of which one line is oblique while the other is horizontal or vertical. The oblique lines extend in a great variety of directions, however, and gradually the vertical and horizontal lines are emphasized because of their frequent recurrence. In the dark room of the laboratory when there is nothing with which to compare the lines, we can recognize horizontals and verticals with a degree of exactness not remotely approached by our recognition of lines in other directions. Does this prove that our eyes are peculiarly adapted at birth to vertical and horizontal lines? Not at all. Experience has drilled us in adjustment to these two most common directions, and we know them best because our environment has been our teacher.

The conclusion just reached is impressively reënforced if

we consider the æsthetic habits which are cultivated by men and women in the presence of artificial objects such as articles of dress. One needs only to look at an old photograph to see how curious are the forms of dress indulged in a few years ago. Yet in that earlier day the accepted fashion was not impressive for its ugliness. Indeed, it looked altogether becoming and excited the admiration of many a beholder. Perception was trained by familiarity.

Perception and æsthetical appreciation are trained by the landscape in which one spends one's life. The familiar hills of a New England landscape are sometimes so deeply impressed on the æsthetical memory of one who grew up in that environment that the even stretches of the prairies seem desolate and barren. On the other hand, after one has lived on the open plains, the hills which shut in the view seem intolerable.

The reactions of pleasure or displeasure which have thus been recorded in the individual are reactions which have been trained in the presence of the natural objects which constantly conform to mechanical laws. One's personal sympathies thus come to reflect more or less faithfully the uniformities which exist in the physical world.

The demands of mechanics are more imperative than are any others in guiding our perception. There are accordingly certain æsthetic tendencies which may properly be described as derived from contact with the physical world and others which are derived from the surroundings which have been arranged for us by those who build our houses and bridges and plan our parks and gardens. The latter have great latitude. It is here that national examples and the work of individual artists have taken control. Sometimes the national choices have been guided by environmental facts which are not out of harmony with mechanics but are unrelated to them. The arches of the Gothic cathedral, suggested by the forest, represent a devotion of forest-loving peoples to their natural environment which is not mechanical in any sense of the word. The lotus-flower capital of the Egyptian column is another example.

Thus it comes that taste is guided by mechanical and also by other controls. There is a human type of beauty which springs from the absorbing interest of every man and woman in the other members of the race. How subtly the lines of the human figure have reached into our drawing and the proportions of the human body have affected ornament and recognition of bilateral symmetry can be fully realized only by those who have analyzed art to find the sources of that which we call appreciation.

Turning from the discussion of the history of the graphic arts, we may close the chapter by considering briefly the experience of individuals as they attempt to cultivate personal mastery of these arts. In the graphic arts, as in music, there appears a division of human effort. There are those who are highly trained in the recognition of form and color and are absorbed in experimentation with new combinations. There are others who can do no more than follow the lead of these specialists. Sometimes the following is from afar. The specialist always sees the advantage of putting before those who are little trained concrete and repeated examples of that which is æsthetically preferable. The art specialists are constantly asking for opportunities to exhibit that which is typical of national taste and that which best comports with the demands of mechanical symmetry and balance. All of this goes to show that the artist knows that taste grows by constant contact with that which controls it.

The distinction between the common man and the artist is somewhat less obtrusive in the field of æsthetics of space than in the field of music. To be sure, the distinction exists, but spatial objects have a constancy and stability which permit the artist and the ordinary observer to reach somewhat the same level of taste because of the repeated opportunities to come in contact with the same kinds of experience. The artists in the field of space are somewhat more insistent than are the artists in music that there be universal conformity to that which they regard as good.

In spite of the universal character of space experiences, it remains true in this sphere of graphic art as in music that individuals exhibit a wide range of variability and are readily permitted to depart from national standards. A man may have a false scale of appreciations of art and his neighbors will tolerate him when they would not allow him to have a false weight or measure. A man may be eccentric in his tastes and he will not be openly reproved, whereas if he adds and subtracts incorrectly, society will make its disapproval of his ways manifest in unmistakable terms.

Here, as in the case of music, it is to be noted that there are strong motives for the development of the art even though society does not insist that every individual take a large share in this development. The permanence of the products of graphic and constructive art and the consequent possibility of cumulative judgments of praise or condemnation have done more to establish standards here than in those arts which are less accessible to general observation.

CHAPTER XIII

Institutional Religion and Personal Religion

Religion more than any other institution has changed its status during the progress of civilization. Among barbarous tribes the sanctions and dictates of religion were more binding than were any of the other controls exercised by the group. Indeed, institutional religion was the device to which rulers and the wiser members of the community constantly resorted as their chief means of governing individuals. This original condition of complete domination of all members of the community by religion persists even to-day in many parts of the world. Among highly civilized nations, however, it has come to pass that religion has in the course of time given over to custom and law its authority in many matters with which it was formerly concerned and has become in large measure a body of personal beliefs, emotions, and practices.

Anyone who is at all familiar with the Old Testament will recall the minute detail in which the religion of the Hebrews prescribed the diet, hygienic practices, and property rights of all classes of society, as well as the social customs to be observed in all matters touching the life of the group or the family. There is no line which can be drawn between the tribal government and religion. Every regulation was attributed to divine authority and was enforced by agencies which were recognized as representatives of this authority.

What was true of the Hebrews is true of all early nations and without exception of semibarbarous peoples. The hunting tribes are bound by all kinds of religious restrictions.

The warriors of primitive peoples are guided and directed by the priests. Every major undertaking of the individual is initiated with the most elaborate religious ceremonials. Religion touches every aspect of life.

Highly institutionalized religions are undoubtedly preceded by practices which derive their sanctions from the natural demands of human association. In many matters of hygiene, diet, and family life it is possible to trace religion back to certain instinctive tendencies in human nature. The thesis has often been defended that religion is the most fundamental natural expression of human consciousness. For our present purposes it is not necessary to reach any decision regarding the origins of religion. Whether religion came from the needs and instincts of the individual or from some other source, the fact is that at the dawn of history it was present as a rigid body of social regulations. It was protected and transmitted by a priestly group set apart by society for these specific duties. Penalties for the infraction of its requirements were so severe that any individual who ventured to depart from religious requirements was dealt with most severely, not uncommonly to the extent of torture and execution. On the other hand, rewards of the most unlimited kind were promised to those who obeyed.

There can be no doubt whatsoever that the presence in tribal tradition of a perfectly clear formula of action was a source of great relief to many a primitive man when he was faced by a crisis. He was told by his religion what to do and he was promised a great reward whether he succeeded or not in his effort. This simplified matters enormously and removed the inhibitions which might otherwise have held him in check. One almost envies primitive men the kind of definiteness of belief which expresses itself in the fanatical confidence of the adherents of primitive religion who torture themselves before their idols or even give up their lives in complete faith that they are to gain unlimited rewards for themselves and their descendants.

While religion thus takes its place as one of the most powerful and primitive of human institutions, it becomes obvious from a study of its manifestations that the social machinery by which its injunctions are enforced is in no sense of the word instinctive or individualistic. Religion is the product of group collaboration; it has been throughout the history of the world a check upon individualistic instinctive action; it has achieved its highest results by transforming individual modes of behavior rather than by fostering instinctive action.

The history of the race records again and again the transforming effects of religion on whole tribes and nations. Sometimes the transformation is accomplished through the teachings and example of some missionary who goes to a partially consolidated social group and influences its members to turn their practices in the direction of industry and justice. Sometimes religion is forced by military power upon a reluctant conquered tribe. In all such cases the final stage of religious belief has been a compromise between that which was in the minds of men before the new religion came and that which the teacher or conqueror regarded as an ideal form of institutional practice.

If the matter needs illustration, let one look up the history of the modern celebration of Christmas. It is quite certain that the early Christian church did not set the date of the nativity in December; some of the churches observed this festival in April or May, some in January. The fact which operated to establish the December date now universally accepted is that all the northern tribes of Europe look on the winter solstice as the most important point in the year. The Teutonic tribes held their great feast known as Yule at this time to mark their joy at the return of the sun. These tribes believed that during the fortnight following the turn of the sun they could trace with especial clearness the powerful influences of their great deities in the affairs of men. When the Christian missionaries sought to bring over the barbarians from their earlier religion to Christianity, they adopted the Yule festival as the occasion for special emphasis on the life and birth of Christ. They prepared special manger songs and carols. They later established the practice of dedicating the Christ tree and decorating it with gifts.

If we think of that which went before Christianity as the natural tendencies of the Teutonic tribes, we must think of that which was brought about by the missionaries as an institutional transformation of these natural tendencies. The teachings of the new religion were at variance with the warlike traditions of the northern barbarians and as such could not be forced at once into their minds. By making some concessions in externals to the earlier barbaric customs, the Christian teachers were able to inculcate the essentially new form of belief and action and to bring about the result that the warrior tribes were lifted out of their earlier tendencies and led to adopt wholly new modes of behavior. Even when it seems to concede to natural tendencies, institutional religion is thus seen to be establishing itself as a new and powerful social control.

This is not the place to attempt an evaluation of religion in human history, but it is appropriate for the student of the psychology of social institutions to point out that among the factors which have been powerful in building up modern states and nations, none is more significant than religion. The science of geography may describe the effects of climate on human life. Economics may describe trade routes and the influences of raw materials and money, but more fundamental than all these are the alliances based on religion and the wars which have grown out of the incompatibility of conflicting systems of belief. Mankind has governed itself at every stage by religious institutions. For our study it is not the details of particular systems of religion that are significant, but the general prevalence of this institutional method of control which in one form or another has appeared as the dominant influence in every period of history.

The change which has come in modern times is not so much in the fact of social control as it is in the kind of sanction to which appeal is made in support of the dictates of the group. If modern life is less under the control of priests and less attentive to the special ceremonials of the religious system than was primitive life, this is due in large measure to the fact that the practices which used to be enforced by religion are now enforced through other institutions. We may describe the evolution which has taken place by saying that ethical principles have been extracted from religion and have assumed the status of independent social institutions. These principles are in many instances made effective through government, in others through public opinion.

The ten commandments of the Hebrews are not by any means inoperative in modern society even where they are not thought of as dictates of some mysterious supernatural power. The social force of the command not to kill is as great or even greater than it was in the days of Moses, but that force depends to-day on a recognition of the rationality of the injunction and on its reiteration in statutory law. A wild half-civilized tribe emerging from a long period of captivity had to be impressed with the necessity of respecting human life. All the appeals to fear of eternal punishment which its leader could command were needed to make effective the injunction against murder. To-day there is a general respect for human life. The generations which have lived under the Mosaic law have established a social attitude in this matter which primitive man never exhibited.

The present social attitude finds its support in the habits of thought and action of civilized communities and in their legal enactments and requires no constant reference to the supernatural.

What is true of the explicit command of the Decalog against killing is true of a multitude of minor precepts of personal hygiene and social intercourse. The half-civilized tribe needed to be told in authoritative terms how to keep clean and what to do in periods of contagion. These same people had to have their weights and measures defined to them in terms which it was understood that the priests would enforce. As the centuries have passed, and social sanctions have gradually become democratic, the appeal to supernatural authority has undergone a series of modifications. First, the injunction was changed from that of deity to a command of deity's representative. The representative gradually grew more and more secular and less and less infallible. The necessity of rational explanation and justification of social conventions was conceded with increasing freedom. The consequences of infraction of society's injunctions were made less drastic and more appropriate to the offense. The individual as a result began to govern his own attitudes by principles rather than by subservience to arbitrary injunctions. Religion evolved into rational systems of conduct which retain all that was good in religious institutions and are purged of much of the unnecessary and artificial ceremonial which surrounded the older practices.

There remain, and always will remain after such a process has gone as far as it can, certain vital problems in human life and human thought which cannot be dealt with in purely rational terms. For example, it does not seem likely that the problem of a future existence will be solved as most of the other problems of life are solved by empirical investigations. The mind seeks solutions of this problem by formulating beliefs which are superrational. There is for every individual a realm of experience which lies beyond the limits of ascertained facts. This extraempirical world is the world of purely personal religion. It is usually true that the individual mind reaching beyond personally known facts is not willing to depend on its own judgments for solutions of such momentous problems. Men are so constituted as a result of ages of social interdependence that social opinion is welcome in the solution even of personal problems. Modern man, therefore, finds himself more or less controlled by social conventions in spheres of thought which lie outside of rationalized thinking. One may be ever so skeptical about the existence of a localized heaven, but one's thought will always revert to the word and to the idea. It is safe to say that there is not a modern man or woman who is not influenced to some degree in his modes of thinking by the religious doctrines accepted by the community in regard to an after-life of bliss or distress.

Religion can be variously defined. It is in part everyday behavior. As such it is the root from which have grown many of the clearly differentiated ethical and governmental institutions of modern life. Again religion must be thought of as a body of coöperative efforts to solve the mysteries of life. As such it will persist so long as the experiences of men carry their thoughts beyond their powers of complete explanation.

Such a formula helps us to understand why in the dawn of civilization the religious type of thinking was more authoritative than it is in modern life. Natural phenomena were in that early day completely shrouded in mystery and the solutions of the problems which they presented were out of the reach of men more than they are to-day. Primitive man had only one formula which he could use in trying to explain natural facts. That was the formula borrowed from his own subjective world, the formula of personal volition. Whenever anything happened, he thought of it as the doing of some personality like himself. If the happening was injurious to him, he attributed it to a malevolent purpose on the part of the unknown personality. If it was beneficial, he was grateful to some helpful and favoring spirit.

The adoption of the personal formula for the explanation of natural phenomena led to a great variety of ceremonies which were aimed at propitiation of the unseen and unknown sources of sorrow or happiness. The ceremonies were of course difficult to direct because the personalities to be reached were unknown and their answers were in most instances wholly ambiguous. It was very natural under these circumstances that men should seek, as do modern men and women, the aid of social tradition in dealing with these obscure situations. If one is told in the case of disease that this or that remedy will be efficacious, it is not at all unlikely that one will try the remedy even though there is no personal reason for supposing it to be appropriate. So it was with primitive man. Disease was brought upon him by some remote and mysterious personality. He was helpless and in distress. He seized upon any suggestion which society offered him. Sometimes the suggestion was wholly fantastic. The effect was not always negation even in such cases. The ceremony sometimes furnished the basis for new courage or subjective composure and while the supposed remote personality was a myth, the effort to propitiate was helpful and even curative. There were other cases in which the suggestions of society, while seemingly fantastic, contained germs of genuine rationality. Some of the practices of the medicine men were directly aimed at the highly advantageous end of bringing the patient into a state of perspiration. Social tradition and ceremonial contributed in such a case not what they purported to contribute but something which served the end better than the originators knew.

There is in the religion of primitive peoples a kind of conformity to nature which corresponds closely to that phase of art which was the subject of discussion in the last chapter, where it was pointed out that human experience gradually conforms to the laws of nature because these laws are constantly guiding and checking activities. Religion when thought of in the light of that analogy is a series of social experiments in the formulation of the rules of conduct. When men do not know what to do, they try something. This something is often unnecessary and ineffective, but it is the human response to an emergency. If in the course of ages this process is repeated frequently enough and with the variations that are inevitable because of human restlessness, it is altogether probable that a ceremonial will be hit upon which has in it something that is useful. The useful ceremonial thus discovered will not be understood, but it will be perpetuated because social tradition will transmit it. Further experimentation will refine it and turn it into a social command.

It requires very little examination of primitive religions to show that they contain much that is in the sense just described both useful and true. The periods when religions were reduced to records such as one finds in China and India and among the Egyptians and Hebrews were from the point of view of human experimentation doubtless relatively late. Social practices had matured to the point where that which was useful and true preponderated by far over that which was artificial and arbitrary. The precepts of these religions survive, therefore, as expressions of the race's discovery of that which is just and right.

So long as religious injunctions rest on the basis of blind

experimentation, there is one abuse to which they are peculiarly susceptible. They can become, and have in the course of history often become, means of promotion of the interests of a single group within the social organism. The priestly class has always been a powerful class. Its position as custodian of religion gave it the power of extracting from the other classes in society that toll which knowledge and power always extract from ignorance and weakness. The priestly class, while it had truth and used it at times for the betterment of society, sometimes used it for selfish ends. Religion thus becomes an important factor in the political history of the world.

One thinks of the control exercised in Greek affairs by the oracle at Delphi. The cleft in the rock and the tripod at Delphi are probably reminiscent of the time when sacred places were guarded by primitive man as sources of fire, that greatest of all equipments of human life. Whatever the origin of the sacred place, it is quite certain that the pilgrimage thither of people from all parts of Greece soon put the priestly custodians of the shrine in possession of information which was not assembled at any other point in that little group of states. The priests had knowledge. That they used it as other human beings would, sometimes to the advantage of Greece, but always to the advantage of their friends, is not to be wondered at.

Again, one thinks of the crusades and the political consequences which flowed from these outbursts of religious zeal. Some of the consequences were doubtless accidental, but others were quite certainly the results of intrigue or political planning.

The use of religion to support and augment political power has come down into modern life in many forms. Our own generation has heard the echoes of the dogma of divine right of kings which sounds very strange in democratic ears but was so frequently repeated to the common people of the unhappy lands where it survived that even the defeated nations of to-day half believe it to be a dogma of truth.

The evolution which it has been the purpose of this chapter to outline has at every stage encountered the opposition of that group which has vested interest in the maintenance of a religion of mystery. It is not to be wondered at, therefore, that emphasis on superpersonal controls still persists in some countries in a very intense form.

In the meantime personal experience, divided between the adoption of ethical principles and adherence to religion, and often confronted with problems that seem impossible of solution by any known methods of rational explanation, exhibits a great variety of chaotic forms. William James, with his unbounded sympathy for everything human, has recorded in his volume on the *Varieties of Religious Experience* a curious collection of human mental struggles. One cannot read the book without wondering whether there ever was in the world a time when human minds were more adrift than to-day in regard to matters of belief. The explanation of the situation is to be found most certainly in the fact that the old formulas and the old fixed social standards of social worship and social belief have been superseded by a more comprehensive code of social practices and responsibilities. This broader code is, however, at many points less dogmatic than were the older religious formulas. The individual finds himself as a result adrift where he would have been subject to explicit guidance under the older system.

Our consideration of religion has brought us, as did our study of music and art, to the point where we must recognize the fact that social evolution does not in all instances compel social conformity. The individual is compelled to adopt many of society's institutions in order to live. In these days we must all become parts of the economic machinery of industry and exchange or we shall go hungry. We must use language and weights and measures. We must learn to be on time. In matters of religion, however, we are allowed a degree of freedom unknown in social units of an earlier day. We talk about tolerance in religion. We practice no tolerance in respect to the Arabic numerals. In short, we have brought forth in the course of human civilization a modern social solidarity and a modern individualism.

CHAPTER XIV

INDIVIDUAL EMOTIONS AND SOCIAL INSTITUTIONS

The last three chapters have shown that the institutions which are closely related to personal emotions have a history wholly different from that of the institutions which deal with the more impersonal adjustments of science, trade, and mechanics. The use of the word "impersonal," which is common in describing the science of mathematics and in considering the requirements of punctuality and grammatical regularity, shows that we do not think of individual desires and needs when we deal with the institutions of number and time and language. On the other hand we take individual experiences very much into account when we are thinking of religion, music, and drawing and painting, and we are therefore less likely to speak of these as impersonal.

It is important, however, for a complete understanding of civilization that we do not overlook the fact that even the impersonal institutions are very intimately related to emotional life. In fact, as it will be the aim of this chapter to make clear, the evolution of institutions has not merely resulted in the development of modes of individual behavior; it has also affected emotions to such an extent that we are entirely justified in saying that civilized man has an emotional equipment which is widely different from that of primitive man and the animals.

By way of illustration let one think of so impersonal an institution as money. It can be viewed, and often is viewed, wholly from the objective point of view. It then appears to be a device invented by society after long experimentation to facilitate exchange of labor and goods. It can, however, be viewed from the subjective side when it appears as the center of eager longings or intense anxiety.

Emotion is so immediate and vivid a part of human experience that it is little wonder that it has received more emphasis in the science of psychology than have the institutions which in our higher civilization are closely related to present-day desires. Indeed, the tendency of writers on social psychology has been to treat the emotion as the primary fact and the institution as the derived fact. Thus money has been described as an outgrowth of the love for gold or as a creation of the race intended to satisfy its native instinct of acquisitiveness.

This chapter will aim to prove that the types of personal emotions which are known to civilized men are products of an evolution in which emotions have taken a new direction. In the course of this evolution human adaptation to its physical and social environment has been going forward. The instruments and means of this adaptation are the institutions, some of which have been described in foregoing chapters. Each institution as it has become established has developed in all individuals who come under its influence a mode of behavior and an emotional attitude which conform to the institution. The new mode of behavior and the new emotional attitude could not have been perfected until the institution itself was created.

The effort of individuals to adapt themselves to institutional demands results in what may be properly described as a wholly new group of pleasures and displeasures. For example, if we think of the pleasures which come from reading literature, it is evident that we are dealing with an emotion which could not exist before language was evolved. Indeed, the individual must go through a long series of educational experiences before he can participate in any degree in the higher pleasures of reading. During the process of education, the developing individual cultivates certain expectations and ultimately nothing will satisfy him which does not meet these expectations. Even so elementary a demand as that which calls for correct grammatical structure must be met; but above and beyond this, what is read must have verisimilitude and unity and clearness. If the literary selection conforms to all the elementary demands and at the same time appeals to certain personal desires which are in keeping with the ambitions of the individual, there results an emotion which can be described in general terms as pleasurable but is in a class wholly distinct from the pleasures derived from the tastes and odors which give satisfaction to the instinctive yearnings for food.

Some writers have made the mistake at this point of saying that the pleasures of literature are identical with those that come from the senses and from the instinctive forms of behavior. The fallacy of identifying the higher and lower emotions is the fallacy of taking the emotion out of its organized setting. Certain elements of the nervous processes may be alike in the higher and the lower emotions, but the nervous system is responding in the one case to a stimulus which would not affect at all an untrained organism. No animal can derive pleasure from literature though the animals have all the nervous mechanisms necessary for the emotion of pleasure in the presence of agreeable sensations. The higher character of the human enjoyment in this case is that which results from a new relation into which the capacity for enjoyment has been brought by training.

What is true of satisfactions is true also of disappointments. Civilized life has created an infinite variety of new forms of distress. For example, the modern business man has learned to assume certain responsibilities which go to

make up that which we call the credit system.   If for any
reason there is the slightest difficulty in meeting his responsibilities, the business man is thrown into a panic.   His
organic processes of digestion often suffer and not infrequently excitement keeps his nervous system from its normal functions of sleep and rest.   Contrast with the trained
business man the shiftless individual who has not taken on
the ways of civilized industry and commerce.   The nervous system of the shiftless one is capable of distress and
responds when food is lacking or when bodily pain is present, but is utterly unaffected by inability to meet financial
obligations on time.   Can such a contrast be considered
without reaching the conclusion that the emotions of the
personality trained to accept responsibility are in fact
different from those of the untrained personality?   What
justification is there for overlooking the fact that the one is
aroused by one kind of a situation, the other only by simpler
situations?   The one is responsive to social institutions, the
other only to physical stimulations.

The relation of personal emotions to social institutions
will perhaps be more clearly understood if we review briefly
what individual psychology has to say about the nature of
the emotions.   It was William James who first gave to
science an acceptable account of the nature of emotions.
That account has been cleared of its ambiguities and made
more serviceable by investigations carried on during the
last thirty-five years, but in essence the modern view with
regard to the nature of the emotions is that contributed to
psychology by James.

This accepted view is that whenever the nervous system
of an individual is stimulated, there is set up a train of
excitations which issue in some form of action.   Either the
glands of the body respond or muscles change their tension or both series of reactions unite in a complex form of

behavior. These organic reactions to stimulation are the individual's efforts to achieve self-preservation in the presence of his environment. In the inner world of experience there is an emotion as the mental counterpart of the system of reaction.   To repeat James' statement :

If we fancy some strong emotion and then try to abstract from our consciousness of it all the feelings of its bodily symptoms, we find we have nothing left behind.[1]

Present-day psychologists go further than did James. Not only are emotions to be explained by motor processes, but there are no motor processes in the individual's life which are not paralleled by some kind of emotional experience.   Feelings of familiarity, of approbation, and of dissent accompany our various attitudes and responses to stimulations.   There is no sense impression without reaction and no reaction that is not reflected in the conscious emotional life of the individual.

With this general idea in mind, let us consider some of the examples with which the psychology of social institutions is concerned. Employers have found that laborers often become ineffective because they worry about old age. Put in institutional terms, the situation is this. The modern man sees that the economic organization of society is such that he can have food and shelter and comfort only when he obeys orders and appears each morning at the blowing of the whistle. This same man knows that the time is coming in his own old age when response to the whistle is going to be out of his personal power. This knowledge serves to arouse within him certain emotions which are paralleled by reactions. These reactions do not reinforce the particular activities which he is executing at the moment. Indeed,

---

[1] JAMES, WILLIAM — *The Principles of Psychology*, II, p. 451; Henry Holt & Co., 1890.

the present performances for which society is paying him and his private reactions to the idea of impending old age get sadly confused, and the work which ought to be going forward with whole-hearted devotion is interrupted. The idea of old age is thus sometimes enough to destroy individual efficiency.

To the individual who exhibits the phenomena described in the foregoing paragraph, the whole situation is present in consciousness as an agonizing emotion. The more he tries to work at to-day's task, the more unhappy he is because of the conflict between his job and his fears. Yet he knows that if he gives himself up to the distressing ideas and their contemplation, the social agencies which drive the wheels of industry will grip him. The inner world of the laborer becomes finally an intolerable chaos. The physician or the philanthropist who looks at this distracted man from the outside may describe him in cold scientific terms as a victim of hysteria and may classify his inner state as that of fear, but to the man himself the world is a universe of conflicting experiences.

Again, let us take another type of industrial situation which has of late come to be recognized as of the largest significance. In the old days when men worked, each with his own tools and each producing something which bore the mark of his personal craftsmanship, there was a glow of pride and self-satisfaction at the completion of each task which left the worker ready to take up with enthusiasm and devotion the next undertaking. When we describe this situation from the outside, we say that craftsmanship is possible only when the product carries the mark of the worker's skilled individuality. To the worker himself this situation is one warm with emotional coloring. The thing that leaves his hand is not merely an object ; it is much more ; it is a center of all the reactions of satisfaction which follow success.

Now comes the modern system of standardized coöperative manufacture. Enormous gains have been effected by the new system so far as mechanical precision and efficiency of construction are concerned, but let us look into the inner world of the worker's mind. We find there none of the satisfaction which comes from reactions of pride and ownership. The inner world is robbed of zest and enthusiasm. The individual seeking substitutes for the satisfactions which came in earlier days as a part of the craft invents new forms of what may be called institutionalized excitement. If one cannot be proud of one's work, one can be proud of one's clothes or of one's automobile or of one's social influence in a lodge. The inner world emptied of one kind of satisfaction begins to fill up with others. Or, if no form of satisfaction is readily found, there come a bitterness, a reaction of resentment, and a disposition to recoil against present conditions. The inner world of personal emotions is in either case a very real fact in the worker's life.

The descriptions which have been given of emotions aroused by the economic system could be paralleled in every sphere of social life and contact with social institutions. For example, in the sphere of social communication one tries to express ideas in forceful language and suffers from a lack of words. One listens to someone whose command of language seems to suffer no such limitations. Both experiences are more than mere facts of human speech. They are indeed phenomena for the lexicographer and for the student of philology, but to the individual involved they are sources of emotions — of irritations and of satisfactions.

Again, consider the innumerable examples which turn up in the world of æsthetics and religion. One passes a church built in some cheap and gaudy design, the evident blunder of an ignorant contractor who posed as an architect. The external fact can be described in a thousand ways. We may say that the church violates all the traditions of ecclesiastical construction and is inappropriate in form and decoration to the purpose for which it is to be used. Or turning from such an external fact, we may speak in terms of inner reaction and say that our sensibilities trained by contact with structures suited to the feelings of devotion are violated by the hideous thing which runs counter to all the cultivated expectations and stirs up all the resentment which can possibly be bestowed on an object lacking in proportion and calm and quiet.

Much recent psychology has been content to treat such emotional excitements as manifestations of instincts. It would be equally appropriate for the biological sciences to withdraw from the study of life on the ground that chemistry is acquainted with all of the elements which enter into the composition of living bodies. The fear of old age may have in it elements similar to those which animals experience in the presence of an enemy, but the fear of old age is part of a complex experience in which economic demands and harrowing imaginations and thoughts of injustice must be included before an adequate scientific explanation can be given of what takes place in the suffering individual's mind and body. Psychology must deal with the total situation if it is to be true to the facts. It cannot stop with an account, however valid, of the beginnings of individual emotional life; it must give an account of the stages by which these beginnings have been superseded by higher complexes of emotion which in turn are aroused by causes that would never have been effective in arousing instinctive reactions.

When enthusiasts for instinct psychology have seen the inadequacy of an appeal to the lowest levels of reaction they have sometimes introduced the concept of conditioned reflexes. This concept is supposed to explain acquired reactions and the higher emotions by referring to the fact that any form of instinctive behavior of which the animal is capable may be attached by training to a stimulus which was originally wholly unrelated to the instinct. For example, a reflex or instinctive response which originally was aroused by a blow may through training be aroused by the sound of a bell. All that is necessary is that the bell shall be sounded for a certain number of times at the same instant that the blow is struck and the reaction called out. Conditioned reactions are thus thought of as natural instinctive reactions which in the course of life are transferred and made parts of systems of experience to which they were originally quite foreign.

Even if one accepts without qualification the formula of conditioned reactions as satisfactory for the explanation of the fears and other emotions of adult life there still remains the important fact that much of this transferring of reactions has been accomplished through the operation of definite causes which are themselves products of mental effort. The transfer of fear to the idea of old age requires the consideration not only of fear and of the idea of old age, but also of the economic system which induces the transfer. The economic system as we have seen is the product of a social evolution which cannot be explained without an appeal to the facts of human intelligence and human coöperation.

Perhaps it will be better to avoid such elaborate arguments as the foregoing and meet the advocates of instinct psychology on their own ground. Let us therefore turn to a brief consideration of the physiology of fear and a study of the conditions which appear when fear manifests itself.

One of the simplest cases of fear is that which appears when an infant or an animal hears a loud, strange sound. Under these circumstances the incoming stimulus enters the ear, passes through the central nervous system, and goes out along the motor nerve fibers. The outgoing stimulation

is directed to what may be called a general preparation.
Since the sound is unfamiliar this preparation is possible
only in a very indefinite way; the order sent to the active
organs of the body from the nervous system calls all the
resources of the body into play. The glands begin to work
and the muscles tighten up all around. The action of the
glands throws adrenalin into the blood, thus putting the
body in a better chemical condition to act; sugar is called
out from the body's reserve and carried by the circulatory
system to the muscles so that they may be prepared to
resist fatigue. The blood stream is set into more vigorous
motion. The greatest possible supply of blood is taken to
the central nervous system so that there may be a keenness
and readiness of response when the object heralded by the
sound arrives. Another large supply of blood is carried to
the muscles so as to coöperate in the support of vigorous
action. In short, the sound leads to a preparation of the
whole inner organism for strenuous action. While all this
preparation for action is going on, there is a quicker flow of
inner experiences known only to the mind, which has its seat
in the excited nervous system. This inner experience will
take on various colorings as the process goes on. If the body
responds well to the summons to prepare, and if action begins
when the strange sound comes nearer, the emotional experience will be one of exultation in the readiness for action.
There will be a thrill of response. If, on the other hand, the
preparatory reactions within the organism conflict with one
another, if one set of contracting muscles drives the body
forward and another pulls the body back, if the secretions
of the glands are excessive or the circulation of the blood too
rapid, an internal condition of chaos may result. If, as the
sound continues, the opportunity for effective action does not
appear, and if the preparation issues in no definite response
but continues in a general way and increases the conflicting

oscillations between forward movement and retreat, the conscious experience of the individual may become one of violent agitation and distress.

Come back now to the man who has an idea of old age. This, too, is a warning. It came into the worker's nervous system, not as a simple sound, premonitory of possible danger, but as an exciting stimulus for which there is no familiar response, and in this respect it is like the unrecognized sound, and, furthermore, like the sound, it calls for preparation. So the muscles become tense, the adrenalin pours into the blood, and the blood surges to the brain and muscles. All is ready for the next step. Note in passing that this physiological preparation for old age is not unlikely to have broken the thread that was in the weaver's hand as he plied the industry of modern life, or it may have led to the dropping of the wrench with which he was about to tighten the bolt that his trade had intrusted to him. Whatever the consequences in the world of routine, the idea of old age runs its inner physiological course because human nature is so constructed that a warning leads to preparatory tension. What happens next? Is the preparation a source of exultation as it was in primitive life? Does the thrill of action issue in some exhilarating hand-to-hand encounter? Does the thrill of action lead to flight? The pathetic fact is that there are in modern conventionalized life no hand-to-hand encounters, no escapes through swift running. The worker sits before his machine full of preparation. His muscles grow more and more tense. Adrenalin flows out of his glands in sickening excess. Blood is supplied to the brain and only excites a more vivid idea of the horrors of old age. The inner world in such a condition as this is certainly not filled with the thrill of action; it is desolate with the tension of fear.

We must pause for a moment to comment once more on

the fact that much current psychology speaks of fear as a primary emotion. Indeed at times one gets from the literature the impression that fear is thought of as a cause in itself. Men are supposed to be driven hither and thither by this strange thing. All this is the fallacious teaching of a psychology which was devised by an individual who was limited to observation of his own inner experience. From the point of view of inner experience, fear when it comes is the only fact visible on the horizon. But we were not made by nature to go skulking through a world of fearsome darkness. The fact is that fear is one of those secondary necessities which follow on the evolution of a highly sensitive and highly effective organism. So long as the organism performs its primary functions, its sensitivity and its readiness for response are distinctly advantageous. The delicate mechanism can, however, encounter situations which are not those to test its efficiency but rather those to test its endurance. Fear is the trial of a delicate mechanism.

We are told by the alienists that fear is one of the increasing dangers of civilization. We find people everywhere interested in religious cults which offer relief from secret fears. We find, when we become intimately acquainted with those about us, that strange fears are harbored in most lives, curious fears for which anyone except the frightened individual has great difficulty in developing any sympathy, persistent fears for which there is no adequate explanation in the objective world.

There are two outstanding facts in modern life which contribute much to an explanation of the prevalence of fear. First we lead a less strenuous life than did any generation that ever lived. The luxuries of a modern mechanical civilization have put us so far beyond the primitive needs which kept men busy in earlier days that we can hardly find enough real channels for the discharge of our well-nourished muscles and nerve cells. We are, as a result, constantly going through preparatory stages of action which are never consummated. We have what must be called fears of imagination; that is, unnecessary muscular contractions and glandular secretions which begin in response to ideas but from the nature of the case can never be effective forms of behavior because the situations for which they were intended never arise.

A second fact no less important than the first is that the individual is daily becoming less and less able to cope by personal reactions with the forces which man's inventive genius has released in the world. The day was when production and distribution of the things which are needed for life and comfort were very direct and open to observation. Men saw the winter's supply of food and knew where it came from and felt the delight which was inspired by confidence that provision had been made for a long future. Now all that is changed. The winter's food supply is somewhere out of sight and out of the individual's control. Society has created a world of superindividual life, but that does not help the individual nervous system. When the question arises what our family is to do if the economic system in the midst of which we live does not bring us the winter's food, there often seems to be nothing to do but let the blood surge through the brain and the muscles tighten up.

Even more, society has decreed that our private fears shall not be expressed. This decree is in the interests of general comfort. We live in such compact groups that if everybody gave violent expression to all his emotions, the draft on collective sympathy would be intolerable. In order that the world's work may go on, therefore, society has told each individual to train himself to keep the tightening of his muscles as much as possible to himself. The result is that in our effort to avoid sharing fears we suffer from a surplus of strictly private reaction.

Does not this description of fear in its modern setting make it evident that the function of emotion and its significance for individual life have been wholly changed by the transfer of man from the forest into the factory? Fear in the forest is part of a general pattern of life. It is part of the organized scheme of self-protection of a being who lives by hand-to-hand encounters and flight. Fear in the factory is part of a totally different pattern. It is aroused by new causes; it runs a new and ineffective course; it leads to new consequences; it is a type of psychological fact different from primitive fear.

There are other emotions which, like fear, have been much emphasized in recent literature. We may take an extract from a very interesting book, which is somewhat above the level of a great deal of the modern sociology, but is nevertheless guilty in the most flagrant degree of the fallacy of regarding social phenomena as secondary, and instincts and emotions as primary. The following lengthy quotation is typical of the whole book which carries the title *Personality and Social Adjustment.*

The pugnacious instinct, with its corresponding emotion, anger, is another member of the ego hierarchy. When self-assertion is seriously hampered, anger or fear originates. Anger is the aggressive reaction to attacks upon self-interest; fear is the contrary reaction connected with self-preservation. Anger leads one to assail the offender; fear impels retreat. The angry man tries to fight; the frightened person attempts to get away from the impending danger. Both fear and anger are violent reactions, each being one of the strongest emotional experiences known to human experience. In rage, the entire personality is captive to the emotion that has resulted from the reduction of self-feeling. The evolutionary value of rage has of course been great, since in primitive times it has secured the survival of those who have been most forcefully driven by this emotion to the attack. Thus anger in the earlier history of men had a greater significance than at present as a factor of social survival. Its significance is still great and its importance both in personal and group behavior is largely open to overemphasis.

Anger has had such biological meaning that the organism has been adjusted to the emotion so as to produce under its influence the maximum strength of the body. The muscles become tense. The jaw sets. The body advances. The teeth show themselves after the manner of the lower animals. The blood is affected chemically by adrenalin, the product of the adrenal gland, in a way that tends to prevent the realization of fatigue. It is thought also that the adrenalin aids the coagulation of the blood and thereby reduces the risk of hæmorrhage when the individual becomes wounded. In other words, anger prepares the body for the fighting function.

Watson tells us that anger in its earliest childhood expression is related to situations that hamper the infant's movements. For example, the holding of the child's head produces in him at once the physical expressions of rage. The child starts crying, the body stiffens, the arms and legs correlate in striking movements, the breath is held until the face of the child reddens. From birth, almost any baby can be thrown into a rage by holding its arms tightly to its sides. Anyone who has hampered a young child in any of its body movements can testify to the ease with which anger can be produced.

Although anger produces in the body its maximum fighting strength, it nevertheless frequently so clouds judgment that in the contests characteristic of modern life, fierce anger may act as a handicap in a struggle. The prize fighter, for example, who loses his temper is likely to suffer defeat as a consequence of his impulsive, imprudent actions. This explains the purpose of those who in an athletic contest attempt to stir up anger in their opponents. Anger in spite of its energizing quality interferes with skill and the self-control necessary for successful competition. This illustrates the decreasing value of anger in modern life.

The risk of temper is so generally recognized that parents usually attempt from the beginning to train children not to give way to anger. No instinct receives more social coercion; no instinct is more frowned upon by parents and teachers than is pugnacity. The child is forced very early to attempt the control of anger. Morality, religion, law, public opinion, continue the repression which began in the home. Society at every point puts its stamp of disapproval upon exhibitions of anger in the ordinary associations of life. We cover up as far as possible any outward evidence of our anger unless we feel sure that it will be shared by our associates or unless we know it will be recognized as so devoid of personal attitude as to be considered righteous indignation. We impose upon ourselves penance after the manner of O. Henry's husband, who always after indulging in a family row gave to his wife something eagerly coveted by her. Therefore, he was purposely enraged by his wife that she might enjoy the proceeds of her matrimonial strategy. Those of tender conscience fight even the faintest suggestion of anger and perhaps by the process of repression create complexes that find eventually some circuitous method of expressing the long-pent-up emotion.

It is certainly one of the constant strains of modern life that so many situations irritate and lead naturally to the emotion of anger while social opinion is at the same time restricting its expression. The body machinery is put in preparation for the old-time primitive attack, and the individual, well-trained by years of social discipline, hardly lifts an eye-lid.[1]

The descriptive account given by the author of the foregoing pages is admirable, but when this sort of thing is offered as an explanation of social adjustments, it becomes positively misleading. Furthermore, the formula of repression, without any statement of how or why repression is to be accomplished, does not furnish society with a positive program. It may, indeed, be true that parents warn children against being angry, and prize-fighters try to keep their tempers, but this is only the last paragraph of a long story. What society has in reality accomplished in the long

[1] GROVES, ERNEST R. — *Personality and Social Adjustment,* pp. 102–104; Longmans, Green & Co., 1923.

ages is the substitution for the method of settling disputes through personal combat another method, the method of intelligent social discussion, the method of clear and precise adjustment of values through the use of adequate standards, the method of collective judgment as distinguished from outbursts of personal preference. Even in prize fighting, the reason the contestant keeps his temper is because it has been found much easier and safer to parry an opponent's blows by calmly and intelligently watching his eyes and preparing for attack in the direction in which he looks, than to give him the advantage which comes from a blind and undirected waste of energy in all directions.

The secret of social adjustment is the development of new and indirect methods of dealing with situations. These new methods are the embodiments of the long wisdom of the ages and are, therefore, superior to anything which can be suddenly devised by an individual and to anything which can be transmitted through the relatively simple processes of physical heredity. It is only when social adjustments are distinctly superior to instinctive adjustments that the former will supersede the latter. As a matter of fact, social adjustment has proved itself to be infinitely superior to instinct in providing mastery over nature and in giving men, as contrasted with most animals, the advantages of co-operation, but the individual organism has to go through a long course of training before it behaves as it should in view of these facts.

What does one do when one tries to overcome anger? Does not the intelligent course in such a case lie in the direction of a mastery of a new mode of behavior which leads one to use some of the devices of civilization rather than teeth and fists?

An especially striking example of the civilized method of dealing with situations which formerly produced anger is to be seen in the modern treatment of criminals. Formerly anyone who trampled on the rights of others was dealt with in summary fashion. It became the duty in primitive society of one who had suffered injury to take vengeance on the criminal. Later, society took vengeance through its agents. To-day, society deals with the criminal through constituted courts of law where judges do not get angry. Modern society undertakes by measures of an educational and reformatory type to correct the unsocial tendencies of the criminal. Anger and vengeance have been replaced by social devices which are more promising of effective results.

When anger appears in civilized society, it is a symptom of inability to deal with the situation by any of the better and more effective methods. The angry man is usually the man who is impotent. The nervous excitement which is stirred up by the situation that makes one angry is not carried off into motor channels of effective response and, as in the case of fear, the violent emotion is to be explained by internal tensions and forms of glandular action which are preparatory but ineffective. The antidote for anger is to begin doing something which will correct the situation.

When anger persists in civilized life, it is often directed toward situations which are unknown in primitive life. One gets angry in modern society when one is accused of being a liar. One gets angry when one hears of an injustice where the strong have taken advantage of the weak. In these cases the subject of anger is wholly different from the subjects to which the original reactions of anger were applied by nature. One cannot properly remove the imputation of falsehood by exercising physical vengeance on the accuser. The natural brute impulse has become dislocated because man lives in a world where ethical standards are dominant. The way to deal with this accusation is not to fight but to prove the truth of what one has said. Anger is not effective from any point of view in such a case. So far as it appears at all, it shows that nervous and muscular reactions have been initiated which do not fit the demands of the present situation.

It is certainly not in keeping with the facts to assert that anger has been the impelling force which has driven human society to organize courts of justice and policing agencies. Anger is not a force; it is a symptom of a condition. It is the subjective side of a certain physiological preparation for action. It is a secondary fact, the primary fact being an organized tendency to react. This organized tendency to react may be simple as in the case of animals; it may be directed by the immediate physical environment as it usually is in animals; or it may be of the modified type which has been cultivated by civilized man who is surrounded by social institutions. The most highly organized reactions evolved in response to civilized surroundings will have certain preparatory stages which may result in emotions like anger or fear. The truly civilized emotions are, however, not those which accompany incipient behavior or ineffective effort, but the emotions of exultation at the successes of skill and emotions of delight which come from observing the well-coördinated operations of harmonious society. That anger persists in modern life should not blind us to the fact that accompanying every one of the higher forms of civilized behavior there is a higher form of civilized emotion.

Another example which justifies criticism of the instinct-emotion theory of society may be taken from McDougall, who started the fashion of looking for causes of social evolution in individual instincts and emotions. McDougall can be convicted out of his own writings, as will be readily seen by the careful reader of the following extract from his *Social Psychology*.

After giving the most detailed account of the various human instincts McDougall is speculating late in his book on the way in which the earliest forms of organized human society came into being. He assumes the existence of what he calls the primal law — the command of a patriarch who rules over a polygamous family which is subject to his will. McDougall assumes that at maturity the young males have been banished because of the patriarch's jealousy. These banished males are constantly trying by combat to replace the patriarch. But the youths must proceed with caution.

For offence against the " primal law " meant death to the offender, unless he proved himself more than a match for the patriarch. Hence the ruthless pugnacity of the patriarch must have constantly weeded out the more reckless of his male progeny, those least capable of restraining their sexual impulse under the threat of his anger. Fear, the great inhibitor, must have played a great part in inducing observance of the " primal law " ; and it might be suggested that the principal effect of the enforcement of this law must have been to increase by selection the power of this restraining instinct. But those males who failed to engage in combat would never succeed in transmitting their too timorous natures to a later generation ; for by combat alone could the headship of a family be obtained. Hence this ruthless selection among the young males must have led to the development of prudence, rather than to the mere strengthening of the instinct of fear.

Now, prudent control of an impulse implies a much higher type of mental organisation, a much greater degree of mental integration, than is implied by the mere inhibition of an impulse through fear. No doubt the instinct of fear plays a part in such prudent control, but it implies also a considerable degree of development of self-consciousness and of the self-regarding sentiment, a capacity for deliberation and the weighing of motives in the light of self-consciousness. If an individual has such capacities, a moderate strength of the fear-impulse will suffice to restrain the sex-impulse more effectively than a very strong fear-impulse operating in a less-developed mind. The operation of the " primal law " will, therefore, have tended to secure that the successful rival of the patriarch should have strong instincts of sex and of pugnacity, and a but moderately strong fear-instinct, combined with the more developed mental organisation that permits of deliberation and of control of the stronger impulses through the organised coöperation of the weaker impulses. That is to say, it was a condition which secured for the family community a succession of patriarchs, each of whom was superior to his rivals, not merely in power of combat, but also and chiefly in power of far-sighted control of his impulses. Each such patriarch, becoming the father of the succeeding generation, will then have transmitted to it in some degree his exceptional power of self-control. In this way the "primal law," enforced by the fiercest passions of primitive man, may have prepared human nature for the observance of laws less brutally and ruthlessly enforced, may, in short, have played a great part in developing in humanity that power of self-control and law-abidingness which was the essential condition of the progress of social organisation.

If we consider human societies at a later stage of their development, we shall see that the pugnacious instinct has played a similar part there also. And in this case we are not compelled to rely only on speculative hypotheses, but can find inductive support for our inference in a comparative study of existing savage peoples.

When in any region social organisation had progressed so far that the mortal combat of individuals was replaced by the mortal combat of tribes, villages, or groups of any kind, success in combat and survival and propagation must have been favored by, and have depended upon, not only the vigor and ferocity of individual fighters, but also, and to an even greater degree, upon the capacity of individuals for united action, upon good comradeship, upon personal trustworthiness, and upon the capacity of individuals to subordinate their impulsive tendencies and egoistic promptings to the ends of the group and to the commands of the accepted leader. Hence, wherever such mortal conflict of groups prevailed for many generations, it must have developed in the surviving groups just those social and moral qualities of individuals which are the essential conditions of all effective coöperation and of the higher forms of social organisation. For success in war implies definite organisation, the recognition of a leader, and faithful observance of his commands; and the obedience given to the war-chief implies a far higher level of morality than is implied by the mere observance of the "primal law" or of any other personal prohibition under the threat of punishment. A leader whose followers were bound to him by fear of punishment only would have no chance of success against a band of which the members were bound together and to their chief by a true conscientiousness arising from a more developed self-consciousness, from the identification of the self with the society, and from a sensitive regard on the part of each member for the opinion of his fellows.

Such conflict of groups could not fail to operate effectively in developing the moral nature of man; those communities in which this higher morality was developed would triumph over and exterminate those which had not attained it in equal degree. And the more the pugnacious instinct impelled primitive societies to warfare, the more rapidly and effectively must the fundamental social attributes of men have been developed in the societies which survived the ordeal.

It is not easy to analyse these moral qualities and to say exactly what elements of the mental constitution were involved in this evolution. In part the advance must have consisted in a further improvement of the kind we have supposed to be effected by the operation of the "primal law," namely, a richer self-consciousness, and increased capacity for control of the stronger primary impulses by the coöperation of impulses springing from dispositions organised about the idea of the self. It may also have involved a relative increase of strength of the more specifically social tendencies, namely, the gregarious instinct, the instincts of self-assertion and subjection, and the primitive sympathetic tendency; the increase of strength of these tendencies in the members of any social group would render them capable of being more strongly swayed by regard for the opinions and feelings of their fellows, and so would strengthen the influence of the public opinion of the group upon each member of it.[1]

[1] McDougall, William — *Social Psychology*, pp. 285–288. Methuen & Co., 1908.

It seems very extraordinary that McDougall, after recognizing how inadequate primal law is as an explanation of the moral code, should fall back on other instincts or primal laws such as he mentions in the last paragraph quoted, namely, "the gregarious instinct, the instincts of self-assertion and subjection, and the primitive sympathetic tendency." Why not give up this obsession for finding the whole of society in the primary modes of individual behavior and recognize once for all that civilization consists in the cultivation of prudence and coöperation and that society has created certain institutions such as economic wealth and government as devices for promoting the cultivation of prudence and social harmony and has insisted that men be not controlled by any of the primal laws?

McDougall has supplied the descriptive words which are necessary for the statement of this view. The young warriors when attempting to overcome the patriarch cultivate self-control. Surely this is something new as contrasted with pugnacity. They cultivate prudence, and one might go on to say they develop a desire to establish justice and organize society so that there shall be a recognition of equity and mutual forbearance. In short, they substitute institutional control for instinct.

The same lesson can be derived from a reconsideration of the illustration, introduced in earlier paragraphs, of the worker frightened by the thought of old age. This man is very little benefited by any of the forms of behavior supplied by his natural bodily reactions. It is much more social and much more appropriate for him to be induced to take out old-age insurance. The idea will then issue not in an instinctive form of behavior but in a highly organized train of institutionalized acts. On the way to such a complete solution business houses have found it advantageous to set up schemes of saving and bonuses for long-time faithful service. These cannot be described as instinctive forms of protective reaction. They must be described by saying that coöperative wisdom has shown that the idea of old age can be made to express itself advantageously only when society provides social solutions for situations which are created by social organization.

Strong emotions arise only where there is protracted tension. Tension implies a process of adjustment during which the individual is striving to adapt himself to his environment. Strong emotion therefore means that there is for the time being some failure of the individual to adjust his relations with his surroundings. The natural effort of the excited individual is always in a direction which will terminate the excitement. Looked at from the point of view of the inner subjective world, excitement and the effort to extricate oneself from the exciting situation are the all-important and primary facts. Looked at from the point of view of the science which aims to explain the individual and his behavior, the emotion is a very secondary fact. The primary facts are the environmental condition which created the demand for a response on the part of the individual and the responses which the individual cultivates in meeting the condition.

It is not surprising that psychology has magnified the importance of emotions. Psychology naturally begins with the world as seen from the introspective point of view. It will be a long step in the direction of the scientific explanation of human nature when the introspective evaluation of emotion is superseded by a recognition of the fact that the psychological environment outside the individual is quite as important in guiding human action as are the internal tendencies which were born with the individual.

CHAPTER XV

SCIENCE AS A DEVICE FOR THE PROMOTION OF ADAPTATION

A discussion of the place of science among human institutions must begin by combating the prevalent notion that science is something quite apart from social conventions. The student of physics or chemistry is likely to be somewhat extravagant in his assertions of his independence of human nature. He is likely to think of society as something which is perhaps interesting and fairly consistent in its operations but certainly not capable of affecting the scientific definition of the natural forces which he catalogues and measures.

To the antisocial attitude of many of the students of science can be opposed certain impressive historical facts. Science is very recent. Why is this? The answer is that until modern times men had no methods of making and recording exact measurements. It was necessary as a human preliminary to scientific measures that men should for long ages quarrel in simple barter and in primitive commerce and build with crude instruments in order that they might evolve weights and measures. Until this long training of men through unscientific transactions could produce a new mental attitude — the attitude of interest in exact evaluations — there could be no science.

Not only so, but science is impossible without ready means of making and preserving records. The evolution of language to the point where discriminating expressions could be selected and descriptions could be formulated with accuracy was a condition antecedent to the development of modern science. The physicist of to-day owes much to even the most highly speculative imaginings of the ancients, because from that source came the discriminating use of words. Words also must be recorded and records must be made accessible. The most enthusiastic advocate of natural science will recognize, if his attention can be captured for a little time, that modern science is dependent for its rapid rise and spread on the art of printing, which makes possible such records as are found in scientific journals. He may be unwilling to follow this admission to its logical limits, but the printing of a scientific journal is nothing more nor less than a social achievement.

These historical facts are, however, comparatively superficial though not unimportant. The fundamental fact is that science is a method of thinking which the race has evolved through a long history of comparison and criticism of social experience. When the first men experienced a thunderstorm or gathered around a fire, their minds were filled with modes of thinking which could in no measure support the structure of modern science. Primitive men were individualistic in their every thought and attitude. They projected themselves into every movement which they saw in nature. Their attention was fastened on items which touched merely their own personal comfort. They were, like children, unable to distinguish between what they saw and what they felt.

Starting from an utterly unscientific view of the world, men have blundered through long ages in the effort to evolve a view of the world different from that which was possible to primitive man. One of the chief motives for this progress has been the desire to arrive at social agreements. Men did not become scientific at first because of a desire to be better artisans. They started on the road toward science through the desire to be better story-tellers. It is mythology, not artisanship, which is the first ancestor of science. The great body of ignorant speculation in which men indulged when they explained to one another and to their children where the solid earth came from, where the sun goes at night, why the moon changes its shape, is the source of science. Science could not begin until men commenced to ask the kinds of critical questions which naturally arose out of these speculations, and science could not express its truths until men gained experience in formulating in language trains of more or less coherent ideas.

This is not the place to attempt a history of science nor yet an exposition of the logic of science. It is appropriate, however, to extend the foregoing references to history by pointing out that all of the present-day categories which serve science are drawn from human modes of thought rather than from the world of things. When the scientist uses such a word as "force," he is consciously employing an abstract idea which he has thought out in his effort to develop a clear method of considering a body of widely differing concrete facts which he groups together.

One of the masters of modern scientific method has expressed this idea very clearly in the following paragraph :

Our discussion of these spacial conceptions will the better have enabled the reader to appreciate the nature of scientific conceptions in general. Geometrical surface, atom, ether, exist only in the human mind, and they are "shorthand" methods of distinguishing, classifying, and resuming phases of sense-impression. They do not exist in or beyond the world of sense-impressions, but are the pure product of our reasoning faculty.[1]

The fact that science is a body of comparisons dependent on modes of thinking can be brought out by commenting once more on methods of measurement. The process of

[1] PEARSON, KARL — *The Grammar of Science*, p. 206;   London, Adam and Charles Black, 1911.

scientific measurement consists in evaluating a given phenomenon in terms of a standard which human thinking has established and refined. Space facts, for example, are determined by careful comparison with the yard or meter. At some later time and at some other place, another phenomenon is subjected to a similar comparison with the standard. Through two comparisons of phenomena with a conventional standard, it is possible for the mind to bring together in thought objects that in reality are far apart. By reference to a common scientific standard a mountain in Europe can be compared with a mountain in Asia or North America.

Even after measurement has been completed, the process of comparison usually requires the aid of mathematical formulas. Number, as we have seen, and, still more, algebraic symbols are devices which the mind has worked out. All higher mathematics is a refined product of social coöperative thinking. Every quantitative comparison is, therefore, a logical and psychological fact, not a fact of objective nature.

Human evolution has gradually been making progress in the direction of scientific thinking because it has been found that such thinking greatly facilitates living. It is needless to offer evidences of this fact because our age is so fully convinced of the practical value of science that it is prepared to give to it the highest place in public esteem.

We are, however, interested in pointing out some of the obstacles which science encounters in its progress and some of the purposes which it serves as a social institution.

Among the most serious obstacles encountered by science in the course of human history are those which arise out of the opposition between personal, limited views of the world and the broader views which come through coöperative observation. Take the commonplace illustration found in one of the conclusions of science which is universally accepted in civilized society, namely, the conclusion that the earth is spherical. This runs counter to ordinary experience. To the individual looking out on a landscape, the appearances are all in favor of the conclusion that the earth is flat. If science is to modify this personal view, the individual must be taught to give up his personal ways of thinking based on what his eyes see, and adopt the conclusions of social experience. Men have sailed around the world. That must suffice for the rest of mankind, even though most of them have never been away from the level surroundings of their homes.

We hardly realize how fundamental a change has come into thinking along with the conviction that the world is spherical. We have a kind of modern scientific credulity which almost makes us neglectful of our own observations. We are told that light and heat are forms of vibration, that solid bodies are porous, that the stars are some of them huge beyond comparison with our sun. We do not hesitate to accept all these statements and hundreds of others besides. The medieval world burned men at the stake for offering the public mind such contradictions to established modes of thinking. Primitive man even to-day is incredulous when he is told truths which run counter to his direct observations.

We and our ancestors before us have been willing to accept the results of coöperative thinking most readily in those spheres where our personal interests are least involved. Most of us are complacent to be scientific about the stars, but we soon reach the limits of credulity when it comes to personal matters. Let our doctors tell us something about our interior mechanisms, and we begin to assert our independence; are we not in receipt of direct reports from these quarters? It is for such reasons as these that science began and flourished first with reference to things remote and detached from our personal lives. Even the most scientific man among us has his lapses when it comes to dealing with personal interests. We are still human, even though modern science has made great progress in the direction of developing a broader view of nature than can be compassed by any individual's observation.

Science may be defined as the recorded experience of the race refined by criticism and experimentation. Science is superindividual. Science is capable of bringing to the aid of a given generation not only the collective experience of all of its members but also the exact and carefully formulated experience of other generations. Science serves to guide conduct very much more advantageously than can the most mature experience of an adult. Such statements with regard to science must be qualified by the admission that there is still much imperfection in our collective knowledge. Science is still in the making, and science still has to reckon with the fact that the conduct of civilized men does not always keep pace with their most advanced thinking.

The reason for the lag in conduct is to be found in the fact that a principle discovered by science must be assimilated and must be transformed into a motor process before it can become a guide of life. Science may teach that it is undesirable for one to live in the midst of uncleanliness, but it is not until much effort has been expended in drilling into one's habits of action the practices of neatness that the scientific principle becomes a true guide to life. Science may teach that light is refracted in passing from a denser medium to a rarer medium, but it requires a great deal of practice to learn to locate an object seen under water.

Science and its applications have become so far separated that in many cases society has delegated to one group of individuals the task of discovering principles and recording them and to another group of individuals the task of applying these principles. This type of social differentiation of agencies can go on because science is not a mode of mere individual thinking; it is a form of coöperative thinking. For the same reasons delays and difficulties encountered in turning science into conduct are not fatal. They are compensated for by the fact that science is permanent in its records and general enough in its character to effect in the long run a great many situations which were not thought of at the time scientific principles were formulated.

Another difficulty in the way of both the development and the application of science is that the modes of discovery and the methods of formulating principles in different spheres of scientific thinking are so different that while attention is concentrated in one direction it is likely to be withdrawn from other directions. The botanist looks at plants, but just in the degree in which he does so he looks away from the stars. Specialization in science is the result of the limitation of human modes of thinking. Each science has its particular methods and each scientist becomes expert in these particular methods.

The pooling of the results of the different sciences is becoming because of specialization an ever increasing difficulty. The world has reached the stage where no single mind can follow the various sciences with anything like a balanced recognition of the teachings of all of them. It is becoming necessary to develop institutions in which groups of workers in different fields shall deliberately cultivate methods of uniting their findings in usable formulas which shall embody the results of many different lines of investigation. A laboratory supported by a manufacturing plant is one example of such an organized effort to combine many sciences in productive ways. A federal department of agriculture or a federal bureau of standards is another. A group of specialists in medicine organized into a hospital staff is still another.

The psychological effect on human thinking of this manifold development of science is not merely to be sought in the
modes of thought and applications resulting from scientific
study.   There is a general effect which may be called a growing confidence in science as a mode of dealing with the world.
Our generation has come to the conclusion that the best
way to guide conduct is to think carefully and critically
before taking any practical steps.   In other words, we have
learned by long experience that the most direct road to success and comfort in life is through conformity to the findings
of exact thinking.   So completely is our age persuaded of
this that it bestows on abstract scientific research some of
its richest resources.

The science of the present has achieved its most conspicuous successes in the spheres where relations are least complex.
In the sphere of man's relations with physical and chemical
forces, science is accepted without serious misgivings by all
civilized men as the guide in individual and social adjustments.   In the world of biological relations guidance is less
certain.   Here the vital interests of human beings are so
much more directly involved that general social experience
cannot always get itself established in the face of individual
prejudices.   The line of consideration suggested by this
discussion is complete when it is stated that science has up
to the present been least fully developed in respect to human
nature and human relations.   There is practically no un-
disputed principle of social science.   The need of more energy of critical thinking and investigation in this sphere is
evident from the present lack of agreement even on fundamentals.

The student of civilization is led by following such an argument as the foregoing to make the plea that more stress be laid
in modern life on a careful critical study of the best methods
of adjusting interhuman relations.   It is in the sphere of

human interactions that the major unsolved problems of modern life are to be found. No one can contemplate the present state of European civilization without being convinced of the truth of this assertion. We have seen the most advanced knowledge of physical science marshaled in the service of a violently destructive effort of man to overpower man. We have seen the complete unwillingness of nations to conform to some of the most fundamental principles which have been evolved out of human economic experience because national animosities and fear dominate thought and action. The plea which is made by the student of the psychology of civilization that the race devote itself to a study of human relations is no philanthropic preachment. It is a plea that men be true in the treatment of human problems to the conclusion which has been amply established in the sphere of the natural sciences. If it is true that the safest guide to conduct is critically refined experience, why not go about solving the problems of human relationship by a study of human nature and human institutions as intensive as that carried on with reference to physical phenomena?

There is one inhibition to the fullest development of the social sciences which grows out of the perfection of the natural sciences. The highly developed sciences which are concerned with physical facts have so captured the imaginations of men and so gained the profound respect of everyone that their formulas dominate all thinking. The law of analogy controls human thinking to a very marked degree; there is a strong tendency, therefore, to explain all the facts of human life on the analogy of physical phenomena or on the analogy of biological principles. There has been frequent occasion in earlier chapters to combat this tendency. It has been pointed out again and again that the biological sciences have been accepted in many quarters as safe guides in explaining human society. No sooner did the biologists find that animals and plants evolve into more complex forms through wholly unconscious variations and natural selection than many students of society fell into the fallacy of asserting that human life is also nothing but a succession of unconscious variations and naturally selected survivals. So far have some writers gone that they assert that social institutions are to be explained without reference of any kind to conscious processes.

This book has been throughout an argument against such superficial thinking in mere analogies. It has been an effort to set up a psychological rather than a biological explanation of human conduct and human thinking. Language, number, the practical arts, trade exchange, æsthetical endeavor, and religion are not biological facts. To attempt to bring them down to that level is to prostitute the high to the infinitely low. The explanation of human society cannot be found in the life of the herd; nor can the explanation of the division of labor be found in a beehive. The explanation of human society must be sought in the institutional ways of promoting success which have been developed by the highest of the animals through long ages of coöperative effort.

Not only so, but the further development of social institutions requires just as much precise thinking as has been required for the development of physical science and for the mastery of nature. It is time for society to reach a higher and a self-conscious stage with regard to its own institutions and to bestow on them the same kind of careful and impersonal research that it has bestowed on physical phenomena.

CHAPTER XVI

GOVERNMENT AND JUSTICE

One method which has been adopted of bringing individuals into conformity with social conventions has been governmental compulsion. There are occasions when it seems futile to wait for the operation of methods of persuasion. There are individuals who seem at times to be so out of sympathy with the efforts of the group to live in productive harmony that the only feasible method of protecting the group is through the exercise of violence in the interests of unity.

The group is usually strong enough when it unites against the individual to have its way. Sometimes the group is not a unit. Then the individual may for the time being defy the group or even disrupt it permanently.

Again, the individual may evade the group by carrying on unconventional practices in such a way as to escape observation. The group is, for this reason, compelled to appoint agents whose duty it is to see that there shall be no evasion of its conventions.

Finally, the group often has difficulty in formulating with definiteness what it really wants individuals to do. In such cases there must be found a way to clarify group judgment and to make pronouncements which shall be accepted as guides of conduct.

A vast number of experiments have been tried in the course of human history in the formulation and enforcement of group demands. We are apparently not yet at the end of such experiments.   Any review of the situation at this point can make no claim to completeness.   It is desirable, how-ever, that some reference be made in any discussion of social institutions to the experiments in forceable control which have been tried in the past, in order that the reader's thinking may be drawn to a recognition of the fact that government is a psychological device for directing human practices.   Gov-ernmental control is a method wholly different from science and historically much older and more prevalent.

As a first step in this discussion, reference may be made to a study which was completed some years ago of the gov-ernments of primitive tribes.   Three British students of human institutions made a canvass of the literature relating to primitive practices and brought together in tabular form and in textual description an account of the stages of evolu-tion through which primitive group control has passed. Chapter II of the work referred to supplied the title of the present chapter and will be drawn upon for a series of state-ments contrasting primitive governmental control with the higher forms of control known to civilized society.

The first problem to be discussed in considering govern-ment is the size of the group which is subject to a single system of authority.   The earliest groups were small. The findings of Hobhouse and his collaborators are as fol-lows :

The simpler societies, particularly those of hunters and gather-ers and the lower agriculturists and pastoralists, for the most part live in small communities, varying in number of inhabitants from perhaps a score to two or three hundred.   Information on the ques-tion of numbers is unfortunately too often vague and uncertain to admit of the construction of any table on this point.   But among the lower gatherers we generally hear of quite small groups, 2 or 3 to 5 or 6 families in the usual sense of that term, making one or perhaps two "enlarged families" of brothers or possibly cousins with their wives, children and grandchildren. It may be re-marked that if we suppose an old man and his wife, two sons and their wives with 3 or 4 growing children apiece to be living together, we get a group of 13 people. Two such households would form a group of 26, which is as large as many of the groups of jungle tribes seem to be. Two pairs of such groups would be 52, which seems to be about the average of an Australian local group, and in many cases, though we are unfortunately not able to say in how many, the little society appears in fact to be constituted by people thus nearly related, the elder males being brothers or cousins. But often, es-pecially as we go a little further up the scale, we hear of small villages or bands, and sometimes of numbers such as two hundred or more, and often we learn nothing definite about the relation-ships or affinities connecting their members.[1]

The limitations of small communities become evident on a moment's consideration. The variety of skills at the command of a small group is always very small. The strength of such a group in defending itself against an out-side foe or against the internal depredations of one or more offensive members is small. The power to collect and master any large body of material resources is seriously limited. The advantages of small numbers are those of direct con-tact. Surveillance of all the members of the community requires no special agencies because everyone can observe directly the doings of all. Discrimination between for-eigners and members of the community is instant and cer-tain. Sympathy inside the group is usually strong because interests are immediately recognized as common.

The tendency of social groups to expand is a result of the discovery that large groups and strong groups are better adapted to survival than are limited communities. The large group, in order to persist, must, however, be able to evolve

[1] HOBHOUSE, L. T., WHEELER, G. C., and GINSBERG, M. — *The Material Culture and Social Institutions of the Simpler Peoples*, pp. 46–47; London, Chapman and Hall, 1915.

devices for communication through greater distances, devices for distribution of labor and goods, and devices for compensation of talent and protection of both life and property.

In primitive society we find the expansion of the group going on through the union of small family communities into a larger tribal community. The agencies of government are then divided into local and remoter agencies. Hobhouse and his associates describe this condition as follows :

As far as concerns government, the main result of these considerations is that we must distinguish between smaller and larger groups. If we speak of a chief or a council, we must know whether it is the chief or council of a local group or of a tribe. But we must remark further that a tribe may be divided, not so much into locally distinct groups as into totems or clans, that pervade its whole area but yet have a semi-independent organization of their own. To use the most general expression possible, therefore, we have distinguished primary and secondary social groups. The primary group is the smallest organization above the simple family which has a recognized unity and a measure of self-government. The secondary group is an aggregate of primaries. The primary group may be an enlarged family; it may be a clan recognizing common descent or a totemic band; or it may be a local band. Moreover, these divisions of a tribe may coexist, and there may be more than one group which might deserve the name of primary. In such cases we give the name of primary to the group which exercises most of the functions of government. Often we shall, in fact, find that there is something analogous to government fairly well developed in the primary group, while there is little or nothing of the sort beyond it.[1]

In such tribal and group consolidations there always emerged one man or a small council to whom matters were

---

[1] HOBHOUSE, L. T., *et al.*, — *op. cit.*, p. 48.

referred for decision. In other words, there was set up very early a center from which pronouncements were issued representing the judgments of the whole group. The method of selecting the leader and council was at first of a type which may be called natural. Heredity operated to perpetuate the power of a strong man in his son, or leadership in war which was accorded to the individual because of personal strength or courage resulted in leadership in all phases of group life.

As with the individual leader so with the council; it was at first selected because of the natural prestige of its members. Often it consisted of the older members of the group, sometimes of the warriors or hunters only. Its influence was also dictated by the accidents of social need. In some instances it had only slight voice in the control of the group; at other times its decisions were binding.

The fact which stands out most clearly is that with the progress of social evolution the functions of government and of its responsible agencies are more and more clearly defined. If we think of the modern nation, we recognize the progressive tendency to locate governmental functions with precision and to give them definite limits of influence.

The problem of finding leaders continues to be, even in the most highly organized communities, one of the crucial problems of government. The demand in civilized society is not for a leader of physical strength; and, of late, evidence has accumulated rapidly to show that modern states are not satisfied to believe in heredity as a basis for acceptance of a leader. Popular choice has again and again proved to be unintelligent in its selections and, even if it were much more certain than it is to operate without the hazards of unfounded prejudice, there is always the difficulty that the supply of leaders must from the nature of the case be small.

Our generation in this country is committed to the method of selecting its governmental leaders by ballot. The day is probably distant when this method can be raised to a higher level by the collection of anything like scientific information about candidates.

The purpose of such governmental machinery as is evolved is to adjust relations within the group and between groups. The conception which modern society has of the desirability of properly controlling these relations is the conception expressed in the word " justice." Relations are to be set in order, and whatever is done is to be done in such a way that all parties to the relation shall be able to carry on their subsequent activities with the greatest possible advantage. There must be rules which are applicable again and again to like situations and suitable for adoption by all the members of the group as safe guides of conduct.

The evolution of justice begins with personal revenge. At first the desire to avoid vengeance at the hands of those who are injured is the only safeguard against infractions against the comfort or lives of others. The second step is taken when primitive society comes, as it does very early, to the help of the avenger with the somewhat loose and irregular support of public opinion, or in some cases with direct aid. Not infrequently the avenger gains, even in primitive groups, the support of the chief, but even in such a case the actual administration of punishment is at first left to the individual.

After personal revenge comes public justice. There is some evidence that the first public justice concerns itself with protection of the interests which are recognized as social. From this point on there are gradually drawn under public control all of the relations that are involved in coöperative life. The paragraphs from Hobhouse and his collaborators on this matter are as follows :

To begin with, the public authority, be it what it may, may concern itself only with offenses held to injure the whole community, *e.g.*, ceremonial offenses, breaches of the tribal marriage laws, witchcraft, and especially murder by witchcraft, indiscipline, treason, cowardice, violation of the rules of the hunt. These we class as "Tribal or Sacral offenses," and we find in fact a large number of instances in which such offenses are punished by some public effort and no others. Thus among the Bellacoola, a Salish group, we find that for transgressing the laws of the Kusiut ceremony, *e.g.*, by performing a dance to which a man has no right or making a mistake in dancing, the penalty is death, adjudged by the assembled chiefs. The execution is by a shaman, who bewitches or poisons the offender, but if the offender recovers he is not molested further, and a relative may, if willing, be substituted. There is no account here of the treatment of other offenses, but of the Salish, Kwakiutl, Nootka, Tsimshian, Thlinkeet, and Haida peoples, Niblack (Smithsonian Reports, p. 253, 1888) says: "In cases such as witchcraft or offenses of medicine men, sentence of death or of fine is adjudged by the leading men of the village after trial. In most instances, however, the law of blood revenge, an eye for an eye, leaves little need for other than family councils, as they are purely totemic offenses and are arranged by the injured gens." These are clear cases of the distinction between sacral offenses deemed to concern the tribe, and private matters. More doubtful instances are those from the Makh-el-chel, a Californian tribe among whom, according to Powers (p. 214), we are told that a woman could be put to death by the chief for marriage or adultery with a white man. So again among the Nishinan, a very low Californian tribe according to the same authority (pp. 318, 320), kidnapping was punished by the community, but the leading case is that of a chief who sold a woman to the Spaniards. Probably both these instances are to be regarded as acts of quasi-treason to the community. Among the Seri, again, there was a kind of ostracism which might culminate in outlawry for associating with aliens, deformity, incurable indolence, disease, mental aberration, decrepitude, and a certain breach of the marriage law. Of these, indolence was an offense against the clan, because it had to support each of its members; and the marriage regulation was that a bride should for a year be at the disposal of the bridegroom's clan fellows. If he exercised his own rights during that time, he offended them collectively. All these, therefore, we should class upon the whole as of the nature of public offenses. Sometimes again, breaches of order in the hunt might be punished by a special Hunt police, as among the Omaha, while among many Australian tribes, it is well-known, breach of the marriage rules was the most definite occasion for the intervention of the collective force of the group. Next, the community may intervene irregularly or in special cases. It may avenge the death of a chief or popular man. It may expel or kill a man who has killed two or three others in cold blood or who has made himself generally unpopular. This sort of public justice falls far short of any regular rule assigning definite punishment to a specific offense. It is more like lynch law, or the exceptional act of a civilised government in troubled times. We class such cases as acts of "Occasional" public justice.

Next a public authority may deal with some cases of private wrong and not others, *e.g.*, with homicide, and not theft, as in some Australian groups; or with theft and not homicide, as in some South American instances. These come under our heading "Public justice in some private offenses."

Again, the system we find may be one in which private and public elements are intermingled. The injured party may, for instance, get the chief or some officer to help him, to find the stolen goods, or to arrest and confine the murderer of his brother. But he initiates the proceedings. He decides whether he will forgive or accept compensation or exact life for life, and he executes the sentence. Possibly there is even a regular trial, but sentence is left to the accuser to execute, and if he cannot enforce it there is no further means of redress. Again, it may be wrong for him to exercise revenge until he has obtained a judgment in his favour which states what the revenge ought to be. Or it may be that he can avenge himself on the spot, but if time has elapsed he ought to go to a court. In all these cases there is a blending of opposite principles. We class them as cases in which private justice is assisted or controlled, or both.[1]

It requires no citation of examples to show that modern society is engaged in trying to discover adequate methods of administration of justice. Every court of law is an expression of the demand for justice and most modern legislation is intended to serve as a clear definition of rights which shall make unnecessary the intervention of courts of law.

The impressive fact revealed by the experience of men with justice in both ancient and modern times is that it can never be made automatic. Justice always gets its definition in detail from the social environment. The justice of earlier days is not the justice of modern times. The justice of the army is wholly different in its details from the justice of the factory. Justice is a mode of arranging relations and is, therefore, a changing equilibrium.

There is one broad general principle which has been evolved out of all of the concrete efforts to establish justice, namely, the principle that group interests and, in general, group judgments are superior to individual interests and judgments. Individual standards usually have too narrow a basis. Group experiences are broad and embody the results of much past experimentation.

There is an expression frequently heard in courts of law which brings out clearly the importance of group experience in establishing justice. That expression is "common law." Whatever has become common law after trial by social groups is likely to be useful in guiding conduct in the direction in which it should move in order to produce the most fortunate adaptations. Common law reaches back into the life of primitive tribes and brings down to the communities of later stages of civilization that body of expe-

[1] Hobhouse, L. T., *et al.*, — *op. cit.*, pp. 54–57.

rience which no individual could secure within the period of a single lifetime.

There is one striking example of the way in which under pressure a code of law closely resembling common law was rapidly evolved. This example is so instructive because of its revelation of the methods of group activity that it may be described somewhat fully. The description is borrowed from a leaflet published during the war by the United States Food Administration and the United States Bureau of Education. It was prepared by George P. Costigan, Jr., professor of law, Northwestern University :

To trace a law to its remotest origins is an impossible task. The practices of a civilized community have gradually been developed from earliest times. When a community enacts a law, it is merely expressing in a formal way a principle which has long been in operation. This process usually goes on gradually and one loses sight of the fact that law originates in practical adjustment. There is one interesting historical example, however, of a system of laws now in operation in this country which was put together on so large a scale and at so exact a date that it exhibits very clearly the way in which laws originate. The so-called American mining law, which was enacted by Congress in 1866 and in 1872 in substantially the form which it has to-day, was derived directly from certain rules and practices set up in 1848 to 1851 by the people who went to California to mine gold. There was at that time no established system of laws which controlled the mining of the precious metals. The miners adopted rules which afterwards became laws with little or no modification. . . .

It was several months after the actual discovery of gold in California before the rush of prospectors and adventurers began. From the very first, however, those who came for gold insisted that they were entitled to take it regardless of whether the United States owned it and, after California became a State, regardless of whether the State of California or the United States owned the right to the minerals as sovereign successor of Mexico. Though they were technically trespassers upon the public domain, they insisted that they had a right to be there and to take the minerals found by them. In June and July, 1848, Col. Mason made a trip through the California gold fields and at that time, because he had not enough troops under him to do anything else, decided to yield perforce to the doctrine of free mining. On August 17, 1848, he reported upon his trip to the Adjutant General of the United States Army as follows:

"The most moderate estimate I could obtain from men acquainted with the subject was that upward of 4,000 men were working in the gold district, of whom more than half were Indians, and that from $30,000 to $50,000 worth of gold, if not more, was daily obtained. The entire gold district, with very few exceptions of grants made some years ago by the American authorities, is on land belonging to the United States. It was a matter of serious reflection with me how I could secure to the Government certain rents or fees for the privilege of procuring this gold; but, upon considering the large extent of country, the character of the people engaged and the small scattered force at my command, I resolved not to interfere but permit all to work freely, unless broils and crimes should call for interference."

The 4,000 men working in the gold field in June and July, 1848, rapidly increased in number until there were several hundred thousand miners and others dependent on mining. Those who rushed into the gold field were not, as some people think, lawless adventurers, but in the main, law-loving and law-enforcing. Even when half were Indians, as was the case when Col. Mason made his trip to the field in June and July, 1848, they were law-abiding. In his report of that trip he stated:

"I was surprised to learn that crime of any kind was very infrequent and that no thefts or robberies had been committed in the gold district. All live in tents, in brush houses, or in the open air, and men have frequently about their persons thousands of dollars' worth of the gold; and it was a matter of surprise that so peaceful and quiet a state of things should continue to exist. Conflicting claims to particular spots of ground may cause collisions, but they will be rare, as the extent of country is so great, and the gold so abundant, that for the present there is room and enough for all.''

The ideal condition thus pictured did not last, however, and early the miners found it necessary, in the absence of Federal and later of Federal or State regulations, to provide rules for the location and retention of mining claims and even for the punishment of crimes. They early adopted the very effective system of miners' regulations enacted at meetings of miners in self-constituted mining districts and early recognized and enforced through the district organization various customs which grew up in the districts. These regulations and these enforced customs, so far as they pertained to mining, were so reasonable and so fair to all as to call forth the highest praise from all who consider them.

Of these miners' rules and regulations, and the relation which the Act of Congress of 1866 bore to them, Mr. Justice Field, in his summing up of a case, said:

"The discovery of gold in California was followed, as is well known, by an immense immigration into the State, which increased its population within three or four years from a few thousand to several hundred thousand. The lands in which the precious metals were found belonged to the United States and were unsurveyed and not opened by law to occupation and settlement. Little was known of them further than that they were situated in the Sierra Nevada Mountains. Into these mountains the immigrants, in vast numbers, penetrated, occupying the ravines, gulches, and canyons and probing the earth in all directions for the precious metals. Wherever they went they carried with them that love of order and system and of fair dealing which are the prominent characteristics of our people. In every district which they occupied they framed certain rules for their government by which the extent of ground they could severally hold for mining was designated and their right to such ground secured and enforced and contests between them either avoided or determined. These rules bore a marked similarity, varying in the several districts only according to the extent and character of the mines; distinct provisions being made for different kinds of mining, such as placer mining, quartz mining, and mining in drifts or tunnels. They all recognized discovery, followed by appropriation, as the foundation of the possessor's title, and development by working, as the condition of its retention, and they were so framed as to secure to all comers, within practicable limits, absolute equality of right and privilege in working the mines. Nothing but such equality would have been tolerated by the miners, who were emphatically the lawmakers as respects mining upon the public lands in the State. The first appropriator was everywhere held to have, within certain well-defined limits, a better right than others to the claims taken up, and in all controversies, except as against the Government, he was regarded as the original owner from whom title was to be traced."[1]

The history of American mining laws gives a very vivid account of the way in which law in general is developed. As one writer has put the matter:

"This adventurous class of our people met, as their kinsmen and ancestors have always met, every emergency, with good sense, promptitude, and fairness, and from their actions resulted a set of usages and regulations known as the Miners' Common Law, or the Miners' Law of Right, which were inspired by such a keen sense of practical justice that they are found, upon analysis, to contain the best elements of the most carefully formed mining codes of the older world, and the best elements of the code finally enacted by Federal legislation."

The reason why these rules and regulations were so successful is found in the fact thus stated by the same writer: "The government of the miners was in form a pure democracy, in which all were voters, lawmakers, and triers of causes by right."[2]

This matter has been presented at length because it illustrates more fully than do any of our present-day methods of enacting statutes the character of law as an outgrowth and

[1] *Lessons in Community and National Life.* Series A, pp. 145–149; United States Government Printing Office, 1918.
[2] *Ibid.*, p. 152.

expression of the effort to adjust individuals to one another and to the group.

Enough has perhaps been said to reveal the reason for including a discussion of government in a volume on psychology. It remains to point out one general and highly significant psychological change which has been wrought in individuals through the evolution of government and justice. The individual has learned to respect government and to desire it. He has become law-abiding, which means that he has given up the natural tendency to follow his personal impulses and has adopted as his own the wisdom of the group.

The fact is that the will of the group has become so influential in guiding individual behavior that even when social judgment expresses itself, not in statutes, but in that much vaguer form known as public opinion, it operates powerfully to limit and direct the activities of citizens. Public opinion is a half-formulated statute. It is often blundering in its pronouncements, but it is on the road to refinement and ultimate adoption.

It is appropriate at the close of this chapter to contrast government as an institution with science as an institution. Government is the earlier and more forceful form of control. The ideal condition to which we may look forward is that in which science and government will coalesce and all statutes will be based on the kind of critical analysis of experience which is characteristic of science. In that distant day the scientific knowledge about human nature and its interrelations will be as highly perfected as is the physics of to-day and group judgments will invariably point to the most satisfactory modes of adaptation.

CHAPTER XVII

THE UNIQUE CHARACTER OF HUMAN EVOLUTION

Each of the chapters of this book has been made up of two parts, one a description of social institutions, the other a discussion of the mental processes related to the institutions described.

The descriptive parts have not aimed to cover all that goes to make up civilization. The important institutions of marriage, the family, the church, social clubs, and public opinion and many others have not been included. It is not the function of psychology to give an exhaustive description of all these. That is the province of the various social sciences. For the purposes of a treatise of the type here attempted it is legitimate to select certain type cases. These have been chosen with a view to emphasizing certain significant contrasts and only in such number as seemed necessary to supply an empirical basis for the study of the way in which the human mind works when it works in groups.

The essential outcome of the psychological analyses which have accompanied the descriptions of institutions can be expressed in the following general statements. Man has perfected in the course of his evolution certain methods of social coöperation which have completely transformed individual behavior and individual experience. The inner life of a human being is not merely the inner life of an animal somewhat enlarged in scale ; the constant use of words, the resort to tools, and respect for justice have produced so fundamental a change in the character of consciousness that man and the animals must be described as essentially different.

The conclusion of our study thus stated in broad terms will undoubtedly be met by certain objections. It will be pointed out that there is a great deal that is common to the life of animals and that of man. Both have sensory experiences; both exhibit habits of reaction; the higher animals adjust themselves to the world in which they live by the use of what is called intelligence. Science has made so large a contribution to the understanding of life by showing that there is continuity in animal evolution and by making it clear that the higher forms of animal life are derived in a natural sequence from the lower forms that any statement which does not reiterate the doctrine of continuity invites rejection.

In answer to anyone who is bent on attaching human life and human civilization to animal life in order to protect his thinking from the shock of recognizing discontinuity, it is proper to make the statement that there is at least one other point in the history of the world at which science has to face the fact that evolution produced a radical and qualitative change. That is the point at which protoplasm appears. The chemical elements of the primeval world underwent no increase in number and no change in character so far as we know through their union in that unique and complex form which we call living tissue, but at the moment that living tissue put the chemical elements together in a new way the history of the world was changed. At that moment the world started in a new direction. The new direction can be scientifically described only by recognizing that organization brought into being something which cannot be understood by enumerating its elements, something which can be understood only by reference to the new modes of action characteristic of protoplasm and to the new influence which protoplasm exercises on other forms of reality.

The apparent discontinuity which has to be faced by science in its discussions of life is not a disturbing fact. Life is a continuation at a higher level of the processes of combination which at lower levels produce inorganic compounds. The appearance of life is not a breach in nature but a transition to a new level of organization.

Once science draws attention to the fact that a description of organization is quite as important in the explanation of phenomena as is a description of the elements which enter into organization, it is easy to make a case for the statement that the whole process of animal evolution has been one of producing at stage after stage new and more complex forms of adaptation. Let us consider intelligence. The essence of intelligence is that animals, especially those of the higher forms of organization, evolve nervous organs and modes of life by the use of which accumulated experience becomes the basis of conduct. The animal which learns through experience where to find food and how to avoid danger is recognized as of a higher type than is the animal which persists without deviation in a few original modes of behavior. The ability to profit by experience depends on clearly recognizable physical conditions. The nervous system of an intelligent animal is always larger than the nervous system of an unintelligent animal. In other words, in order that a higher mode of behavior may arise nature had to evolve a complex organ and to this extent had to increase the complexity of the whole inner organization of the animal. Here, as in dealing with the appearance of life, science has to recognize the fact that evolution brings into being new forms of organization and new modes of behavior.

An appeal to the analogies supplied by the appearance of life and of intelligence may be ineffective in persuading those who have been drilled in the formulas of individual psychology to think of social consciousness and social institutions as products of a higher form of organization or as realities worthy of full scientific recognition. A given human being is so concrete and tangible a fact in the world, his nervous system and his hand are so accessible to the scientist, and his behavior is so readily capable of measurement that one feels oneself to be on solid ground when one formulates explanations of human nature by saying that social groups in the large are made up of aggregations of these individuals. From the point of view of individual psychology, language and money and tools and the other social institutions are merely expressions of individual intelligence or products of human reactions to external reality.

There are two inadequacies in such an easy individual psychology. In the first place, it takes no adequate account of the effects of coöperation. What the individual contributes to language is infinitely little. What the individual contributes to government is so small a part of the history of human effort to build up nations that we find ourselves lost when we attempt to explain society as an assemblage of individuals. Human society is a unique fact in a world which has no other system of intelligent social coöperation. Society has absorbed all the intelligence and skill of the individuals of many generations and has evolved in its institutions just as tangible a body of accumulated wisdom as the individual possesses in his nervous system. To think of society as a mere abstraction is to forget the accumulated wealth of the world in literature, in economic systems, and in art.

Individual psychology is, in the second place, wholly inadequate in its explanation of a mature human being. Individual psychology has a formula for the explanation of the mature animal. The animal starts life with certain structures: sensory, central, and muscular. In the course of its life it receives sundry impressions and makes responses,

thus producing tracts through its nervous system and producing internal states which make up what we call its consciousness. The animal remains throughout this process an
individual determined in its traits and in its character almost
wholly by inheritance and determined in its intelligence by
individual experience.

Such a formula does not adequately explain the mature
human being. The mature human being has, like the animal, inherited and acquired tracts through the brain. Like
the animal, but at a somewhat higher level of complexity,
the mature human being stores up experiences derived from
sensory impressions and from his efforts to meet these sensory impressions. But the unique fact in human life is that
a method has been evolved which makes it possible to take
over into the individual's nervous system a vast body of
experience which has been accumulated through racial
experience and is too complex to be transmitted through
physical inheritance. The same ear that detects the sound
of approaching danger or makes one aware of a companion
brings into the brain of man the spoken word which society
has loaded with a freightage of gradually accumulated wisdom.
The word is not to be responded to by a direct act of grasping or rejecting; it is taken into one's inner life and there
used to enlarge that inner life. The mode of behavior which
is involved is very indirect and complex. The whole process
is a means of extending individual experience so that it
reaches back of the present and makes the individual master of impressions which the race received long ago. Even
more, the word suggests to the individual certain reactions
which are not dictated by his native desires. The acceptance of a social idea by the individual means that a
process of transformation is in progress. So important is
the racial experience which is deposited within the individual
that it becomes a dominant fact. Purely individual expe-

riences and modes of reacting to impressions sink to a level of inferior importance. The individual becomes an embodiment of social tendencies. The individual nervous system is in this way taken over by society and the modes of behavior exhibited by the individual become those which are determined by society's needs and modes of operation quite as much as by natural personal traits.

There are no phrases too strong for a description of the transformation which society makes in the human individual. There are times when the individual's natural modes of reaction and personal traits seem important. Within one's private consciousness one tends to accept the assumption that society does not dictate what shall go forward; one interprets introspective experience to mean that one could at will be independent of all outside dictation. If science is allowed to take a full account of the facts, it will be found that even in the moments of the most egoistic independence one is putting experiences together in the vernacular which one learned from one's parents. One uses the forms of criticism of one's own logic which have been acquired through long social experimentation on the part of one's race.

The transformations which take place in individual nature as a result of listening to words and using them are perhaps more general and more important than are any of the other enlargements in experience which result from social influence, but something of the same type follows the introduction of the individual to the use of tools or money or the less tangible institutions of governmental control.

History and romance are full of incidents illustrating the fact that men are parts of society, not merely mature animals.

Walter Page, the American diplomat, writing to President Wilson his impressions of a royal dinner given by the King of England to the King of Denmark, says:

This whole royal game is most interesting.   Lloyd George and
H. H. Asquith and John Morley were there, all in white knee
breeches of silk, and swords and most gaudy coats — these that
are the radicals of the Kingdom, in literature and in action.   Vet-
erans of Indian and South African wars stood on either side of
every door and of every stairway, dressed as Sir Walter Raleigh
dressed, like so many statues, never blinking an eye.

*   *   *   *   *   *   *   *

Whether it's the court, or the honours and the orders and all
the social and imperial spoils, that keep the illusion up, or whether
it is the Old World inability to change anything, you can't ever
quite decide.   In Defoe's time they put pots of herbs on the desks
of every court in London to keep the plague off.   The pots of
herbs are yet put on every desk in every court room in London.

*   *   *   *   *   *   *   *

Do they keep all these outworn things because they are incapable of changing anything, or do these outworn burdens keep
them from becoming able to change anything?   I daresay it works
both ways.   Every venerable ruin, every outworn custom, makes
the King more secure;   and the King gives veneration to every
ruin and keeps respect for every outworn custom.
Praise God for the Atlantic Ocean!   It is the geographical
foundation of our liberties.   Yet, as I've often written, there are
men here, real men, ruling men, mighty men, and a vigorous stock.[1]

An example of a wholly different type may be borrowed
from H. G. Wells :

The primitive civilizations were, we may say, "communities of
obedience"; obedience to god-kings or kings under gods was their
cement; the nomadic tendency on the other hand has always been
toward a different type of association which we shall here call a
"community of will." In a wandering, fighting community the
individual must be at once self-reliant and disciplined.   The

---

[1] HENDRICK, BURTON J. — *The Life and Letters of Walter H. Page*, I, pp.
167–170; Doubleday, Page & Co., 1922.

chiefs of such communities must be chiefs who are followed, not masters who compel.[1]

In both of these quotations human nature is described as reacting upon itself. Because men are what they are, they devise pageantry and submit themselves to leaders. Can anyone seriously consider such facts and yet think of the native tendencies of human nature as the most important items in a scientific explanation of man's experience and behavior?

To one who becomes absorbed in the study of the relations of the individual to society it seems very curious that the scientific formulas which have been used in attempting to account for human life should so often have been drawn from the sciences which deal with animal life. When language is described as a form of reaction rather than as a device for socializing the individual, when money is left out of the textbooks in psychology even though it is one of the most potent influences in shaping men's lives, when art is explained as a result of surplus energy, it is evident that there remains a large field for the study of a higher type of life.

Of the importance of carrying science to the point where it shall develop adequate explanations of society, it is hardly necessary to write at length. The mastery of the physical world has gone far, thanks to the accumulated experience of the race, but the mastery of man's relations to his fellows is a matter of the future. The social sciences with their energy for exploration have revealed a vast treasure of information with regard to the way in which institutions have grown and the way in which men have adjusted themselves to the conditions which surround them. It is time that the

---

[1] WELLS, H. G. — *The Outline of History*, II, p. 143; The Macmillan Company, 1920.

social sciences take the lead and refuse to be dominated by the sciences which derive their principles of explanation from a study of bees and ants and anthropoid apes.

The great leader in the establishment of the type of thinking which has made biology as influential as it is saw that his doctrine of the origin of the species did not adequately explain man. It was this insight which led Darwin to supplement what he had said about the lower animal forms by a later volume on the *Descent of Man;* but his *Descent of Man* has furnished no foundation for the social sciences. The reason is obvious. Darwin did not take into account the fundamental facts about society. The *Descent of Man* differs from the *Origin of Species* in that the latter is a carefully formulated discussion of crucial facts and experimental evidence while the former is a hasty and slight expression of a restless feeling on the part of its author in regard to matters which he saw to be of cardinal importance, but which he had not studied.

There is in contemporary thought a very striking manifestation of the clash between common sense and the biological sciences when the latter attempt to treat human experience as of the same type as animal experience. The common man has heard of late some of the statements of the biologist which seem to him to identify him with the lower forms of life. He resents these statements. He knows that he has religion, language, art, tools, and government and that the lower animals are without all of these. He thinks of himself in terms of a long history which is the history of a progressing civilization and he knows that animals are not moving along that road. He therefore refuses to accept the theory of the biologist and is prepared to resort to force if necessary to maintain his own dignity.

It is not the intent of these paragraphs to declare in favor of the common man and against the general doctrine of evolution. On the contrary every chapter of this book goes to show that evolution is in progress to-day. It is equally not the intention of the writer of these pages to neglect the opportunity to warn science that it cannot derive from the study of lower forms of life formulas which will serve to explain man and his complex life and consciousness.

CHAPTER XVIII

EDUCATION AS SOCIALIZATION OF THE INDIVIDUAL

Modern society has reached the stage in its evolution when it aggressively imposes its institutions on the individual. It has gone so far as to set up special agencies in its schools in order to insure the transformation of every child, so far as possible, into a being able and willing to conform to the social pattern of action and thought. Not only so, but in many of its other institutional organizations society expends a great deal of energy in the aggressive promotion of social practices. We use the general term " education " to describe these facts. Government is in this sense in large measure a device for educating citizens; social clubs and religious bodies are educational agencies. Wherever individuals are introduced to social institutions and encouraged in cultivating social traits education is going on.

There was a time in the history of the race when education was in large measure incidental. Society of the primitive type gave the child an opportunity to profit by the experience of the group; it offered him certain tools and certain types of information, but it left very largely to the option of each person the choice of accepting or rejecting these proffers.

Incidental education gave place to a regular program of training when the group began to realize that the behavior of one of its members affected vitally the welfare of the tribe. The individual who killed game during the closed season, the individual who encroached on the hunting grounds of a neighboring tribe and induced reprisals, the individual who refused to share in the responsibility of protecting the members and property of his own group had to be taken in hand in some fashion and trained to conform to group practices. The most economical way of insuring conformity was not to wait for an infraction of social custom and a consequent period of more or less general suffering, but to forestall difficulty by giving practice in the accepted mode of action and by making conformity as desirable as possible through ceremonials and rewards.

We find, accordingly, that even primitive tribes do not rely entirely on incidental imitation but have systems of education. These early systems deal with those matters which are of most vital concern to the tribe and the lessons are couched in terms of governmental and religious sanctions.

There are many interesting facts about primitive educational systems. Since men and women were subject to very different social laws, boys and girls were given their instruction separately. Since the crucial period in the relation of the boy or girl to the life of the tribe is the period when childhood ends and the responsibilities of adult life are assumed, educational ceremonials were largely centered about the age of puberty. Since the tribe attempted to control the individual only in the most urgent matters, the penalties for breach of social custom were violent and summary.

With the growth in complexity of social life there came a corresponding development of the system of teaching. There has always been, however, a margin of what has been called, in an earlier paragraph, incidental education.

Until very recently the schools have not thought it their duty to train in the ordinary occupations or in the activities of home life. The steady progress of recent years in the direction of the inclusion of even these types of social adaptation gives evidence of the tendency of society to socialize pupils in every line. Formerly schools, even in highly civilized countries, limited themselves to those forms of training which the home was not prepared to give.

The first schools of medieval Europe were those which gave instruction in law and theology and in the literary arts which were necessary for these professional studies. Furthermore, these schools were for the upper classes, not for the artisan and peasant classes.

When at a later period schools for the common people were organized, they also taught the subjects which were thought of as distinct from home life; they taught religion and reading and arithmetic.

All of these statements can be summed up in one general formula. Schools are society's agency for training pupils in the social arts. They always attack their problem at the point where general social life is least likely to be effective in giving training.

This general statement opens the way for the understanding of certain characteristics of all schools. Let us consider several of these characteristics as they appear in the schools of our own time.

First the core and center of the school curriculum is language. In the American school reading is the form of language which is most stressed. It is an impressive fact that many educational theorists have attempted to reduce the amount of attention given to language because they observe that the devotion of the school to language has carried education so far away from the individual's practical life that teaching sometimes becomes purely verbal and formal. It is an equally impressive fact that the theories of these educational reformers have never been successful in transferring emphasis from language to other subjects.

Rousseau opened his book on education by drastically condemning all social contacts. It is books and the practices of social groups that ruin the individual's character. So Rousseau advocated taking children away from people and letting them grow up in contact with nature. No sooner did Rousseau provide for the removal of his boy from society than he repudiated his own theory by taking society along in the person of a wise tutor who supplied all the accumulated wisdom of the race and gave the learner all that is best in human experience and practice.

As it was with Rousseau so has it been with more recent reformers. Dewey advocated at one time that reading should be taught only incidentally. Pupils were to learn how to live by practicing the simple arts and discussing with one another and their teachers what they observed. Reading was to be picked up incidentally as a method of getting vicarious experience when the child found that he could not solve some difficulty without the aid of books.

Stanley Hall, impressed by the delight which pupils experience in playing in sand piles, would postpone books to the later years of childhood. He would have pupils live their own lives unassailed by the demands of a society which will, he says, all too soon cramp the personal freedom of the child and curb his spontaneous and uncritical imaginations.

There are other leaders who like those mentioned have attempted to overthrow language as the core and center of the modern course of study. They have all failed to accomplish the reform at which they aimed. The reason for their failure is easy to understand when one recognizes the school as society's agency for socializing the pupil. There is one institution which all the members of a human community must master; that institution is language. Training in its use begins before the child goes out from the home. The school carries on the education which begins in the home and introduces the child to the complicated forms of language which are involved in writing and reading. To be sure, there is danger of excessive devotion to language in the school. Pupils may be made so skillful in the use of words that they will never overtake the school training by any real contacts with the experiences which are referred to by the words which their teachers make them pronounce. It is doubtless this danger that has led reformers to be critical of school practices. But their criticisms and suggestions have never succeeded in changing the practices of schools. Language is too necessary in all social relations to be neglected, whatever dangers may attach to its emphasis in teaching.

The devotion of schools to language teaching has been carried to great lengths. It is a tradition of the learned class that to be truly intellectual one must have a knowledge of languages other than one's vernacular. There are to-day a great many members of the teaching profession who think of the extensions of personal experience which come through the mastery of more than one language as the most liberalizing influences in life. There are others who find in the vernacular an adequate medium for the transmission of all the ideas possessed by the race. The dispute between these two parties is sometimes referred to as though it were a dispute about the fundamental importance of language as a social institution. The dispute is in reality one regarding the best method of meeting for the individual the difficulty which arises out of the fact that up to this time in the history of the race, national groups have persisted in refusing to unite with other national groups in a unification of all mankind. The separate groups have developed diverse languages and other distinguishing social institutions and have through these been kept apart and often brought into antagonism. How far education can cope with this situation and how far it is the duty of the schools to attempt to give all pupils a first-hand knowledge of languages and institutions other than those of their own nation are problems which the schools have by no means solved to the satisfaction of pupils or teachers.

A second general fact regarding education which becomes clear in the light of our study of social institutions is that the schools must teach methods of exact thinking. This they will have to do by introducing pupils to number, measurement, and punctuality. It has further come to be a well-known fact among teachers that compliance with this demand that pupils be trained in exact thinking is no easy task. There is no subject in the curriculum of the elementary school in which failure is so common as it is in arithmetic, and mathematics in the high school bars the road to intellectual progress more frequently than do all other subjects combined.

The difficulty of teaching arithmetic is readily understood in the light of our study. Number is a highly abstract instrument of thought. It was perfected, as we have seen, not by the common methods of reacting to the objects of the environment, but through the genius of a remote people. The number system in its perfection may be compared with an intricate mechanism constructed by a group of mechanical experts. The number system and the mechanical contrivance are to be thought of as turned over from the hands of the experts who made them to manipulators who are in most cases utterly without expert training or insight. Even when the inexpert operators escape wreckage because of the perfection of the mechanism, they are sure to find sooner or later that their control of the delicate creation is limited.

There was a period in American education when teachers of arithmetic did not expect most pupils to understand mathematics. They spent the short time at the disposal of themselves and their pupils in drilling the learners in a few simple methods of solving the most common problems. For the last few decades there has been a disposition to think of drill as formal and stultifying to the individual and to give more of the time of the school to discussions of mathematical principles. The result of the present methods of teaching has been wholesale failure.

There is a further and even more disastrous consequence of the failure of the modern school in the teaching of number. The general notion of the value of weights and measures has been either omitted from the teachings of the school or so covered up and obscured because of the confusion of number with all forms of precise thinking that pupils have failed to understand what is meant by precision. The schools have taught weights and measures as though they were tables of numbers and have let pupils go out into life without the slightest appreciation of the great social significance of these devices for regulating human relations and controlling action.

The discussion of arithmetic can be summed up in a single statement. The school concerns itself with number because it is one of the highly developed social arts, but it has not discovered the method of successfully transmitting to pupils this complex social institution.

A third line of discussion which is suggested by our study has to do with the broad scope of modern education. As was pointed out in an earlier paragraph, primitive education was meager in the number and range of activities with which it aimed to deal. As civilization has advanced, the store of racial experiences has accumulated to the point where the problem of selecting those lines of training which are worthy of general cultivation has become grave. The school has not adopted any clear-cut policy in this matter. In our own country, especially in the upper levels of education, schools have included almost every subject that can be suggested. They have thrown responsibility largely on the individual for reducing the complex of possibilities to a working program of personal education. The elective system is a frank recognition of the fact that the range of social experience is so vast that a given individual will have to be content to limit himself to a small share of the whole. In the meantime it is true now as it has always been that the only way to be successful in a community is to acquire command of its fundamental institutions. An inevitable competition has consequently arisen between general education and special education.

It is not the purpose of this chapter to attempt to enumerate all of the problems which confront the modern school. Much less is it the purpose to propose solutions of these problems. The sole purpose of this discussion is to make clear by concrete illustrations the fact that education is a socializing process. No consideration of individual traits however comprehensive can explain what goes on during the educational process. That process is one of transforming individuals so that they will conform to social institutions. Individual psychology must be supplemented by a study of the psychology of social institutions if one is to reach a truly scientific understanding of education.

INDEX

Abacus, 95

Adams, John Quincy, 130, 131, 132, 133, 134, 137, 140, 141, 143

Adjectives, comparison of, 200

Aldus, Manutius, 175

Alphabet, 160; and drawing, 247

Anger, 288; civilized substitutes for, 292

Anglo-Saxon letters, 175

Animal consciousness, 9

Animal evolution, 324

Application distinct from science, 304

Arabic numerals, 98; importation of, 94

Architectural forms, 240

Arithmetic, 338

Arndt, Wilhelm Ferdinand, 169, 171, 172, 174, 175

Art: ecclesiastical, 250; and emotions, 219; graphic, 239; of music, 218; national standards in, 239

Artisan, 18; consciousness of, 13

Attention: bifocal, 8; and cerebrum, 10; multifocal, 34; unifocal, 7

Banker as specialist, 54

Barker, E., 74

Barter, 33, 35

Bastable, Charles F., 36, 37

Behavior, higher types of, 325

Bells, 222

Bill of exchange, 53

Biological evolution, 331

Biological sciences, 306

Bonding, 54

Brearley, Harry C., 123

Bricks, making of, 20

Bronze, 26; age, 5

Browning, 251

Calendar, 112

Carat, 44

Carlile, William W., 39, 40, 41

Case forms, 203

Cerebrum: and intelligence, 10; as organ of variation, 65

Chaldean numbers, 87

Chaldean weights and measures, 129

Children, experiences of, in exact thinking, 155

Child's invention of words, 195

Chinese: graphic art of, 250; musical sounds of, 224; stagnant civilization of, 179; writing of, 163

Christmas, 265

Church music, 233

Civilization: and fear, 286; and institutions, 217

Civilized emotions, 278

Civilized traits, 1

Clocks: mechanical, 121; primitive, 118

Coinage, 45

Coins, 34; children's understanding of, 248; confidence in, 47; as symbols, 49

Collective words, 201

Common beliefs, 214

Common law, 317

Communication: through institutions, 17; and national solidarity, 214